POSTCARD HISTORY SERIES

Bowling Green

IN VINTAGE POSTCARDS

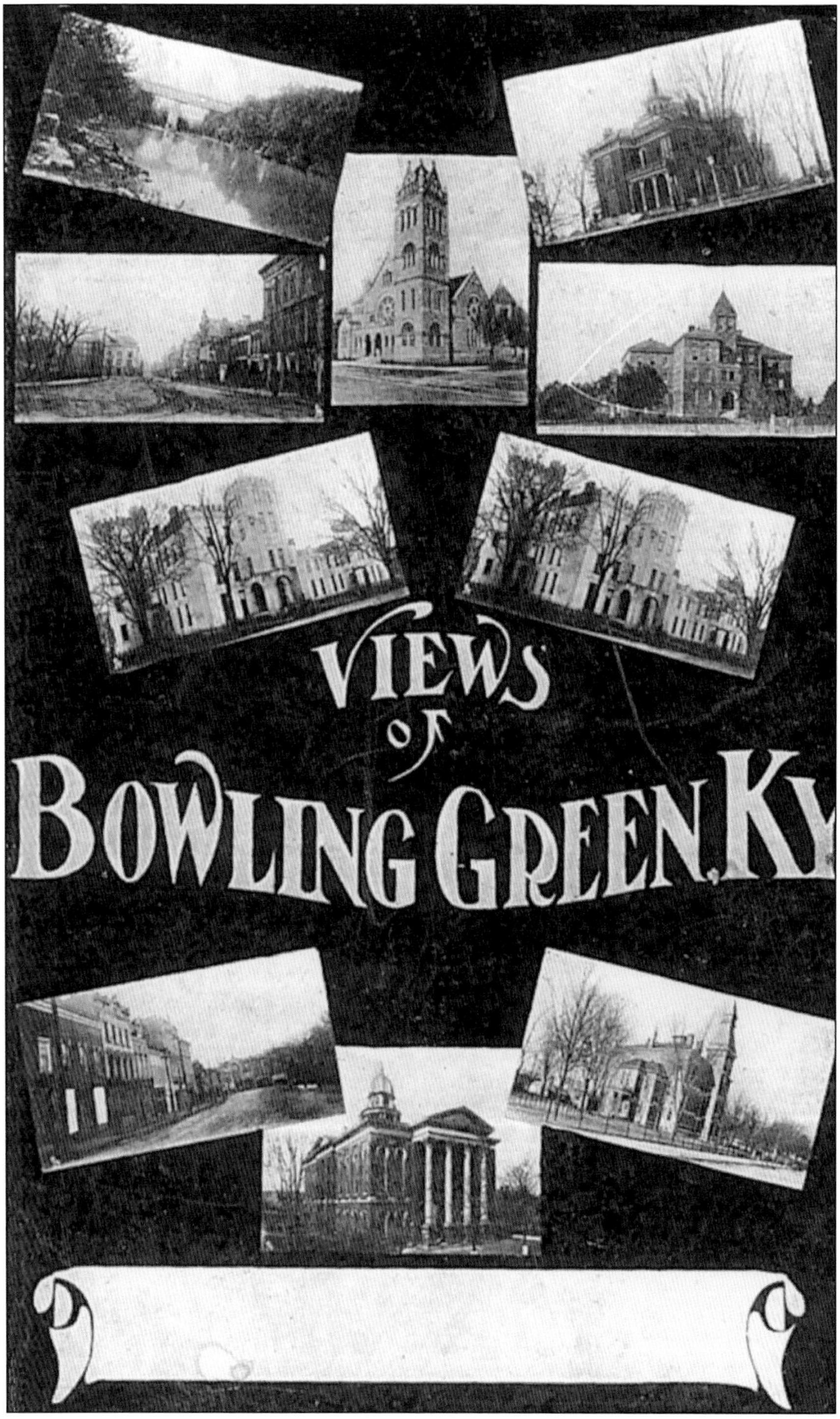

BOWLING GREEN VIEWS. This wonderful *c.* 1905 postcard is a composite of ten other postcards, each one featured in this book. Interestingly, the postcard's proofreader overlooked the duplicated images of the Business University, which appear above the word "Views."

POSTCARD HISTORY SERIES

Bowling Green

IN VINTAGE POSTCARDS

Jonathan Jeffrey

ARCADIA PUBLISHING

ISBN 978-0-7385-1464-2

Published by Arcadia Publishing
Charleston, South Carolina

Printed in the United States of America

Library of Congress Catalog Card Number: 2002107724

For all general information contact Arcadia Publishing at:
Telephone 843-853-2070
Fax 843-853-0044
E-mail sales@arcadiapublishing.com
For customer service and orders:
Toll-Free 1-888-313-2665

Visit us on the Internet at www.arcadiapublishing.com

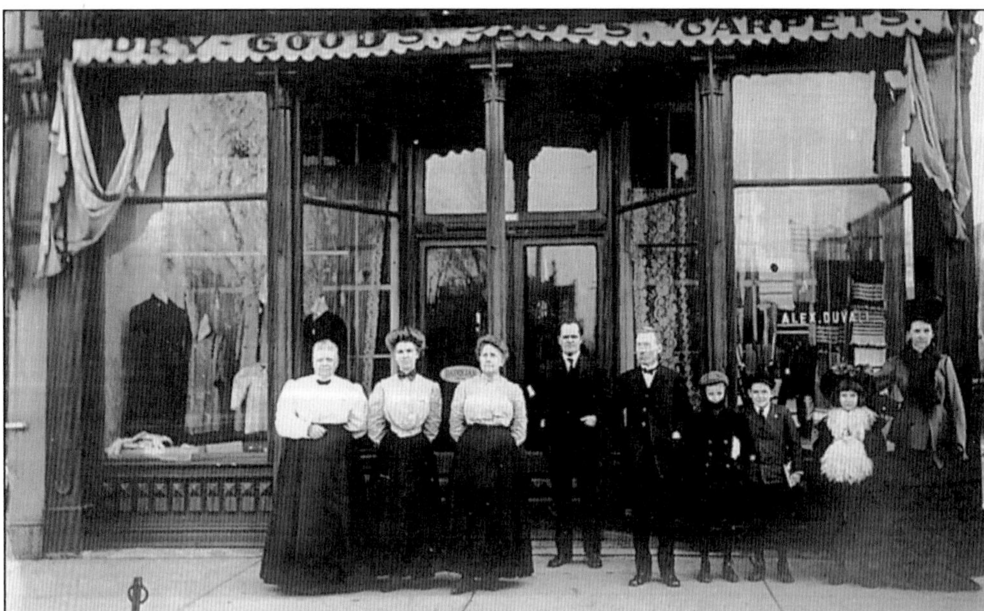

Alex Duvall Store. Located in the Ogden Building at 448 Main Street, Duvall's was a dry goods store that operated from July 1893 to 1911, when it moved to 411 Park Row. This 1908 postcard indicated that the three women out front were clerks. Mr. Duvall is the older, distinguished-looking fellow, and "the others were just people that were passing at the time." Duvall closed his Park Row Store in December 1920.

Contents

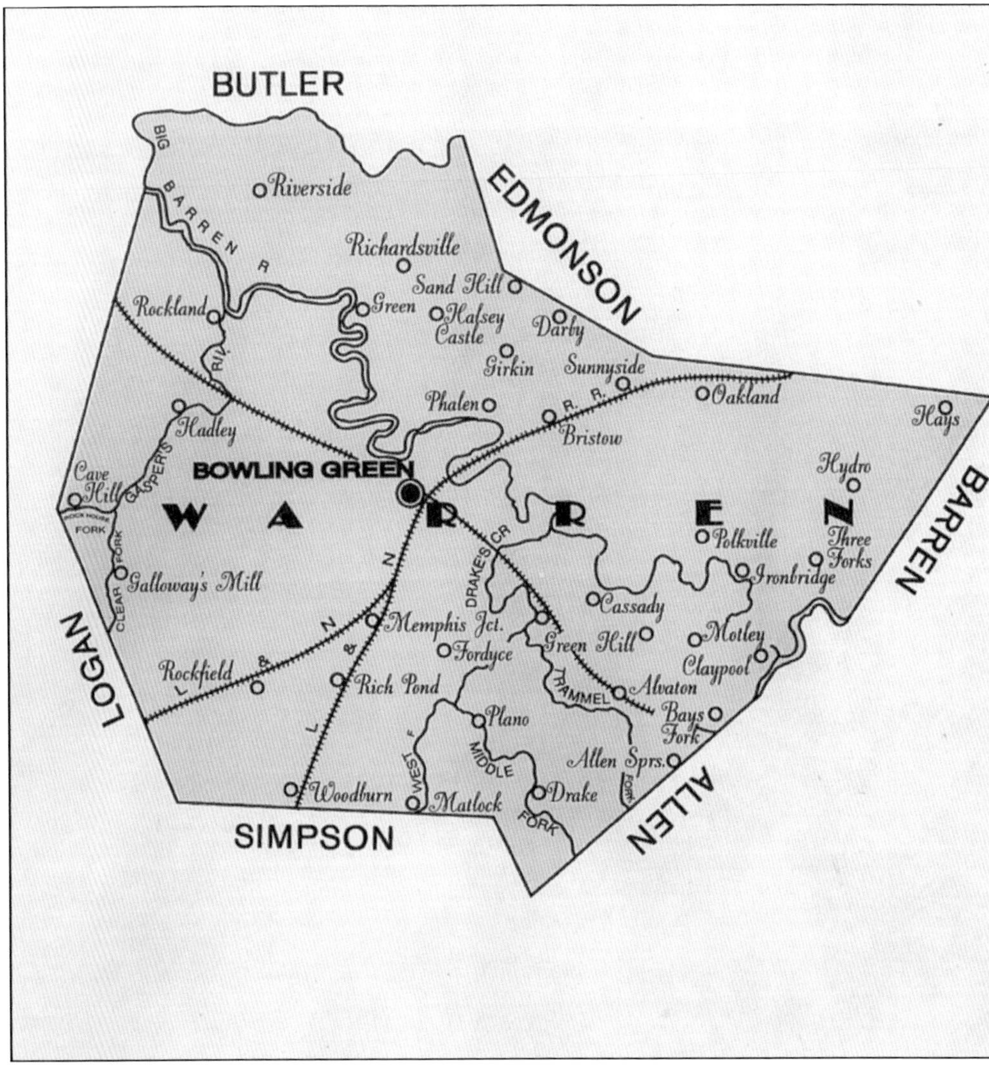

MAP OF WARREN COUNTY. This map of Warren County comes from the *Eleventh Biennial Report of the Bureau of Agriculture*, 1894. The mapmaker's only faux pas was not including the county's second largest town, Smiths Grove. (Courtesy Kentucky Library, WKU.)

INTRODUCTION

Nostalgia is quite marketable today. Antique and collectible stores pepper even the smallest communities; "Antiques Road Show" and "Treasures in Your Attic" are Public Broadcasting Service (PBS) hits; and E-Bay has mushroomed the collectibles market. The word nostalgia has a Greek origin that actually means "to cause pain." Often when we remember the past, we pine for simpler times without e-mail, personal digital assistants, computers, fax machines, cell phones, and automobiles that actually talk. The purpose of this book is to cause that pleasant pain of remembering the past through the medium of postcards. Bowling Green, which now boasts a population over 50,000, has a proud past, a good portion of which has been documented in postcards.

Postcards are a little over 100 years old. Most historians seem to concur that the Columbian Exposition of 1893 held in Chicago popularized the postcard concept. The United States government printed cards that cost a penny to post; private vendors sold souvenir cards at the same event, but they cost 2¢ to post. The cards were chromolithographs and black and white printed scenes—chiefly buildings—from the great fair. Postal service authorities first issued the term "post card," later "postcard," for use on printed cards in 1901.

Postcards were inexpensive ways to send quick notes accompanied by a pleasant tourist scene, drawing, or cartoon. By 1900 many towns issued cards of prominent locations and sites within their borders. Although we cannot date Bowling Green's first postcard, we can say with some certainty that the first card for the community was probably of Fountain Square Park and was most likely done around 1900. Shortly afterwards several panoramic views of the community taken from different vantage points were issued. Samples of these have been included in this publication. Soon thereafter, several local mercantile stores began to send negatives to printing companies in Germany to publish cards of high quality for the local market. The most prominent of this genre were a series of cards printed for drugstore owner George A. Scherer. Other prominent businesses issuing postcards included T.J. Smith, William Cobb, F.B. Fleenor, and B.H. Dalton.

Photographers of postcard scenes are rarely credited on cards. One important, local exception was Edgar Cayce who lived in Bowling Green from 1902 to 1907. There are almost two dozen Bowling Green postcards attributed to this fine photographer, and undoubtedly there are others. Cayce went on to become one of the world's best documented clairvoyants. He was already involved in performing medical readings while he was here in Bowling Green. His studio here burned twice. Although fires were not uncommon in the time period, one wonders if perhaps he was not welcome here. While here, Cayce left quite a photographic legacy, including a number of ethereal portraits and a whole body of work for the Cherry Brothers and their Southern Normal School and Bowling Green Business College. A private collector also has a number of cards with inscriptions indicating that Cayce's wife Gertrude was an avid postcard collector.

The author combed through only two collections to find the cards you find in this publication. From these two collections, he chose 236 from well over 1,000 possibilities. It should be noted that many of these cards are of the same building or site, i.e. there are at least 10 images of State Street Methodist Church. Numerous examples surfaced for Bowling Green's major attractions, including Fountain Square Park, Beech Bend Park, Lost River Cave, and Western Kentucky University. Still, the author was surprised at the non-existent cards of significant local attractions, including the Opera House interior or exterior, the 1920s waterworks, the Younglove Drugstore, the Gasper River, the interior of the courthouse, Fruit of the Loom, the county's iron bridges, and the Masonic Lodge to name a few. Warren County postcards outside of Bowling Green are scarce, and the author included as many as possible.

This publication includes approximately 20 real-photo postcards, which were photographs taken by individuals with a postcard format printed on the back. This service was offered by local photographers and film developers after 1901. These images were not usually mass produced or sold, so they represent the most unique postcards in both collections used for this publication. People are usually the major focus of real-photo postcards, so they add a personal dimension lacking in many cards.

The author would like to acknowledge the Kentucky Library at Western Kentucky University and Laura and Ray Buckberry for making their collections available for this publication. Although the Kentucky Library has an important local postcard collection, the Buckberrys have surpassed it in volume.

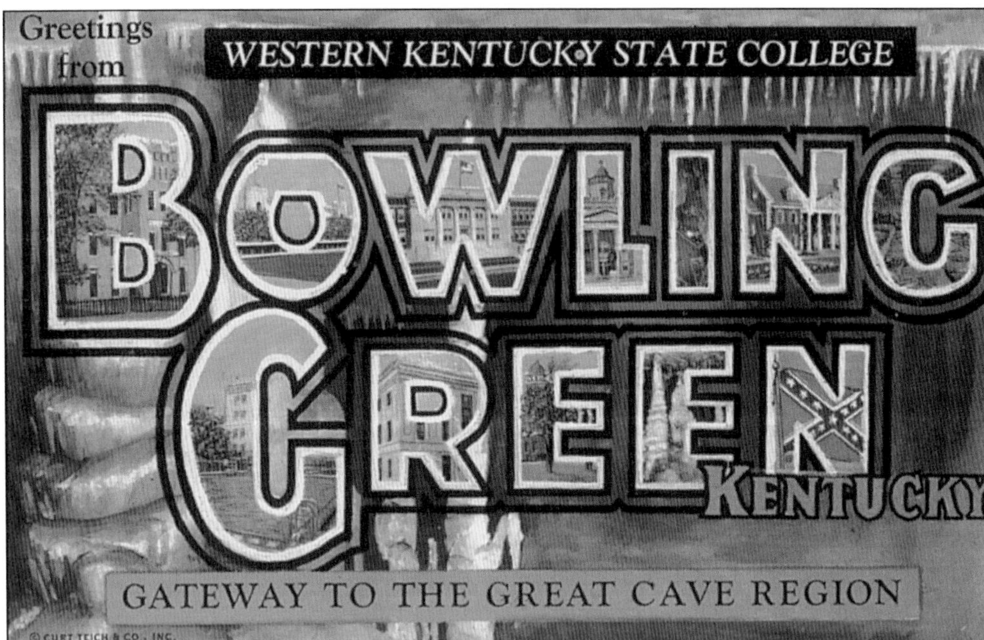

Novelty Card. Each letter in this "Greetings" postcard represented a Bowling Green area entity or attraction: B-Business University, O-Stadium; W-High School; L-Cherry Hall; I-Mammoth Cave; N-Kentucky Building; G-Tobacco auction; G-WKU pool; R-Post Office; E-Courthouse; E-Great Onyx Cave; N-Confederate Capitol of Kentucky. The card captured two of the Bowling Green area's greatest attractions: WKU and Mammoth Cave.

One

Downtown and Environs

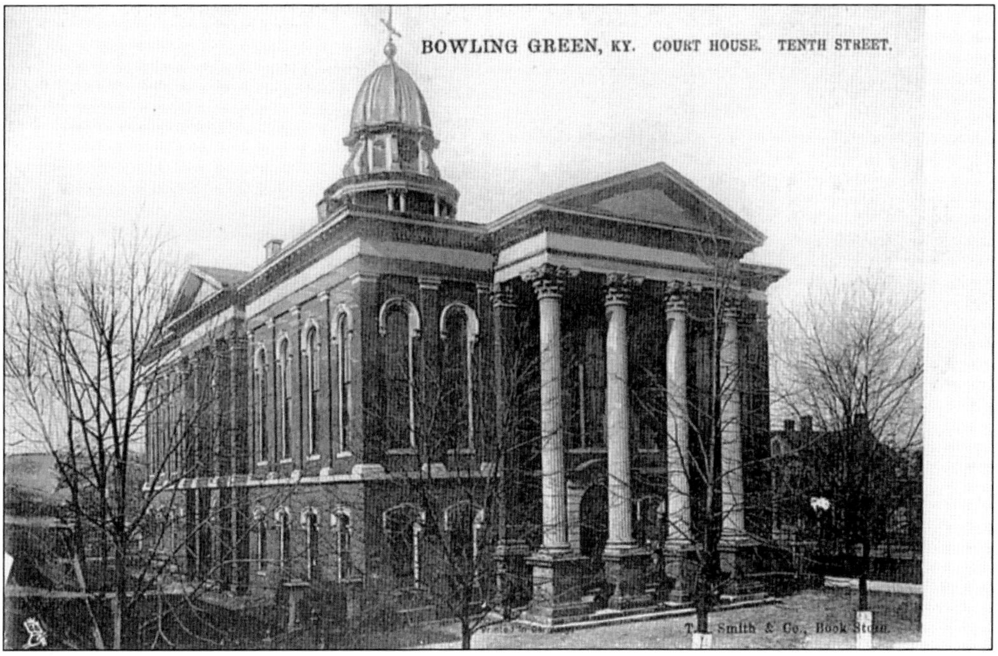

The Warren County Courthouse. D.J. Williams designed the third Warren County Courthouse in 1867, and it was completed in 1869. The Italianate structure boasts a Classical pedimented portico supported by magnificent fluted columns topped with massive Corinthian capitals, all carved from Bowling Green limestone. The architect masterfully crowned his creation with a lovely neo-baroque cupola, which has been rebuilt twice. The building's interior was completely remodeled in the mid-1950s, but little change has been made to the exterior.

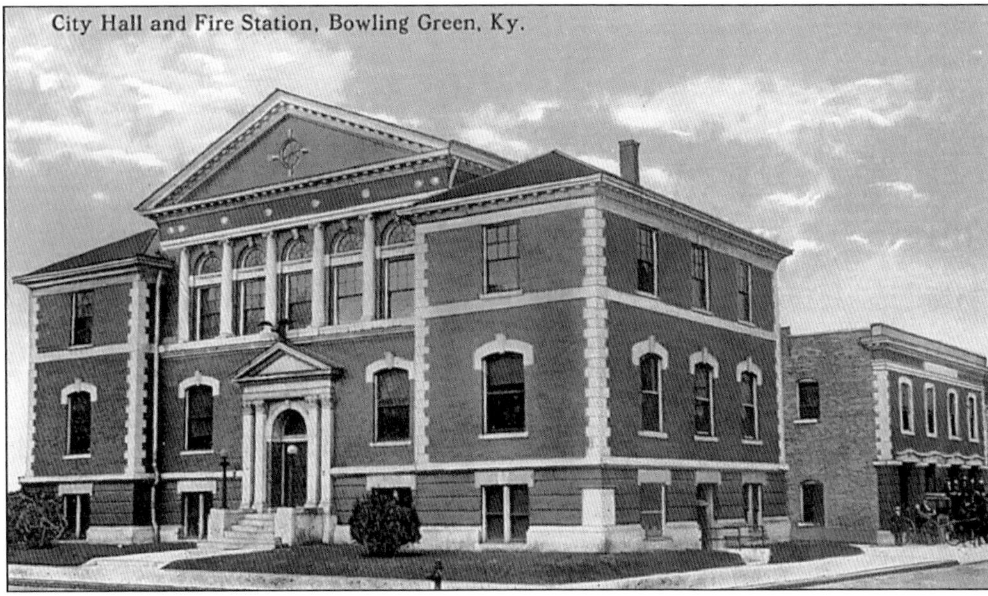

City Hall. City offices moved from the old McCormack Building to this lovely new structure in 1907. Mayor George T. Wilson and the city council hired Louisville architect Brinton B. Davis to design this Classical Revival structure. The centered entrance is flanked by a pair of limestone pilasters and capped with a pedimented portico on which a bronze eagle is perched. The building was extensively renovated in 1986.

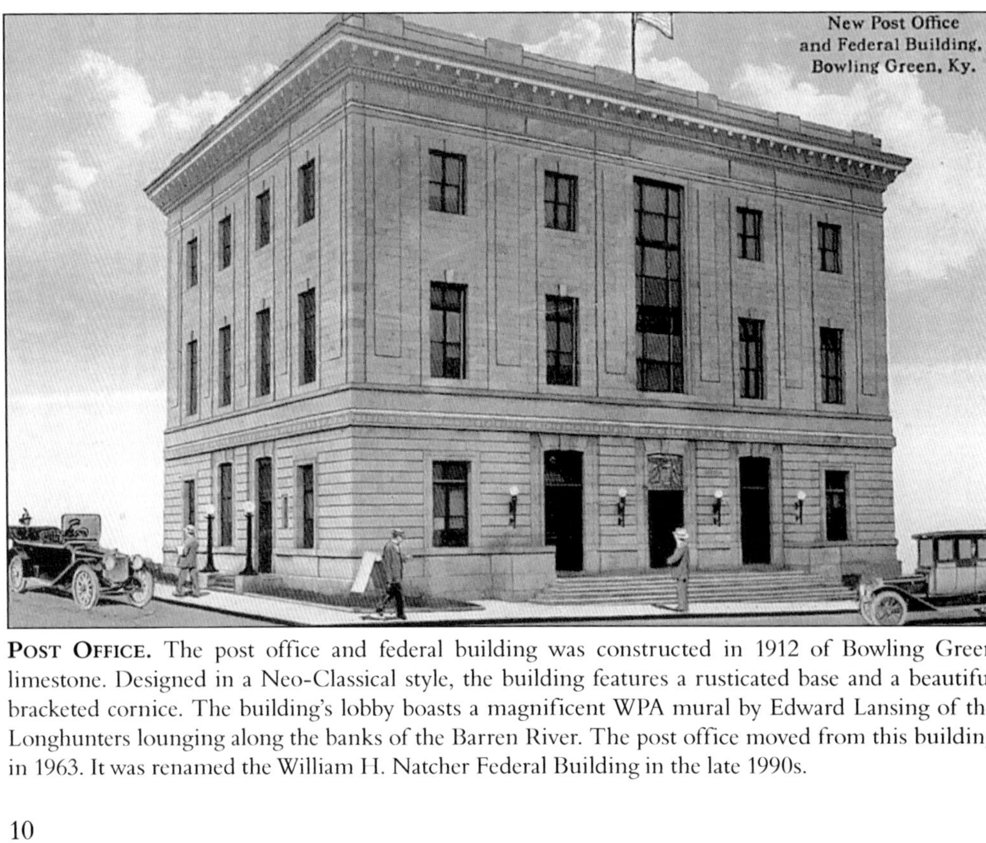

Post Office. The post office and federal building was constructed in 1912 of Bowling Green limestone. Designed in a Neo-Classical style, the building features a rusticated base and a beautiful bracketed cornice. The building's lobby boasts a magnificent WPA mural by Edward Lansing of the Longhunters lounging along the banks of the Barren River. The post office moved from this building in 1963. It was renamed the William H. Natcher Federal Building in the late 1990s.

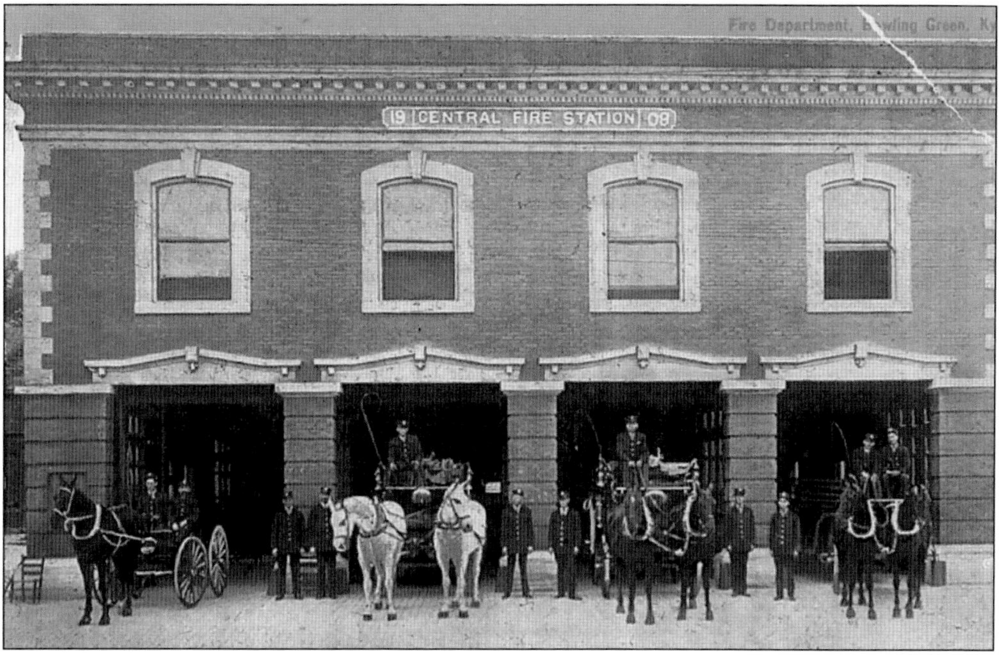

CENTRAL FIRE STATION. Bowling Green's paid fire department was organized in 1898. It had several locations before the completion of the Central Fire Station behind City Hall in 1908. Because Brinton B. Davis designed both buildings, they had a degree of architectural sympathy rarely enjoyed in municipal structures, including matching limestone widow surrounds and quoins and the same bracketed cornice.

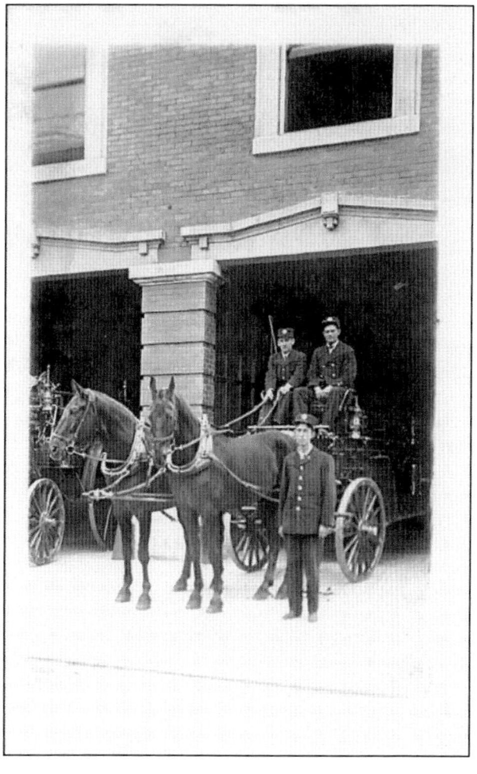

FIREMEN. This postcard is dated 1912 and the men are dressed in uniform, possibly preparing for a parade. Jessie Oliver, the man standing, is the only person identified. The fire department purchased their first motorized engine in 1914, but horses were not eliminated from the force until 1918 when the old wagons were mounted on commercial truck bodies.

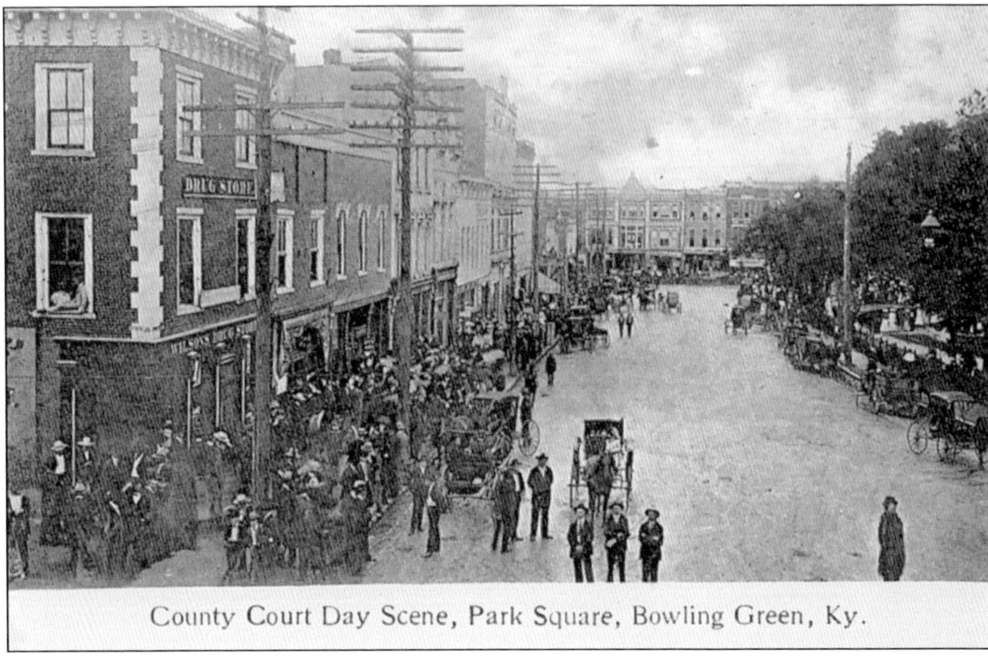

COURT DAY. People from all across the county came to Bowling Green when court was in session. They might be involved in a lawsuit or simply wanted to sell produce or livestock from their farms. Here you can see the throngs at the corner of State Street and Park Row. The prominent building on the corner on the left margin is the old Green River Hotel. This later became the site of Woolworth's.

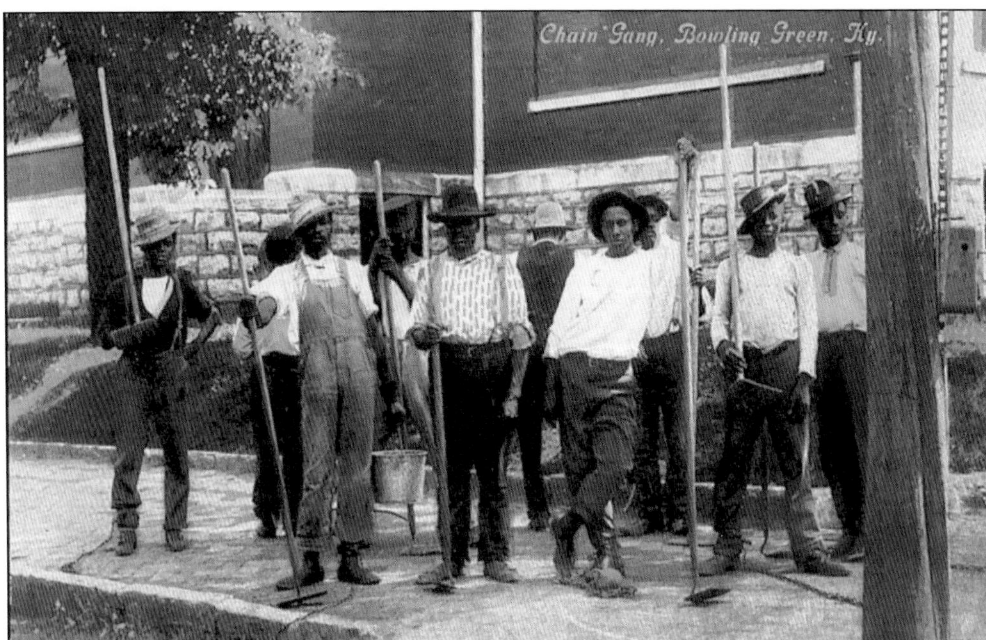

CHAIN GANG. The city and county allowed inmates to participate in work details, but they were chained. Here a group of prisoners, with hoes in hand, are helping maintain a lawn, *c.* 1910. This is one of the rarest postcard views from Bowling Green.

ODD FELLOWS BUILDING. Located at 427 Park Row, this building was designed by J.G. Zwicker of Nashville for local industrialist I.B. Wilford in 1892. It housed the Odd Fellows Aeolian Lodge for over 100 years on the second floor. The building is constructed of Bowling Green limestone and features lovely fenestration and elegant ornamentation. The second floor lodge once boasted a 45-light fixture, which came from the Opera House.

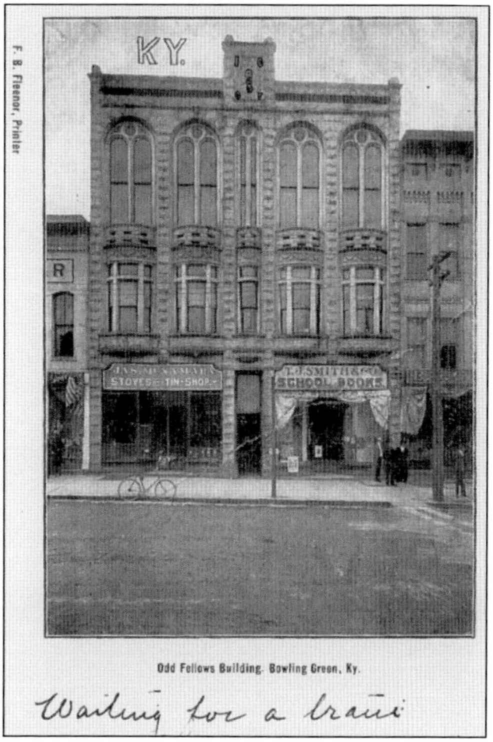

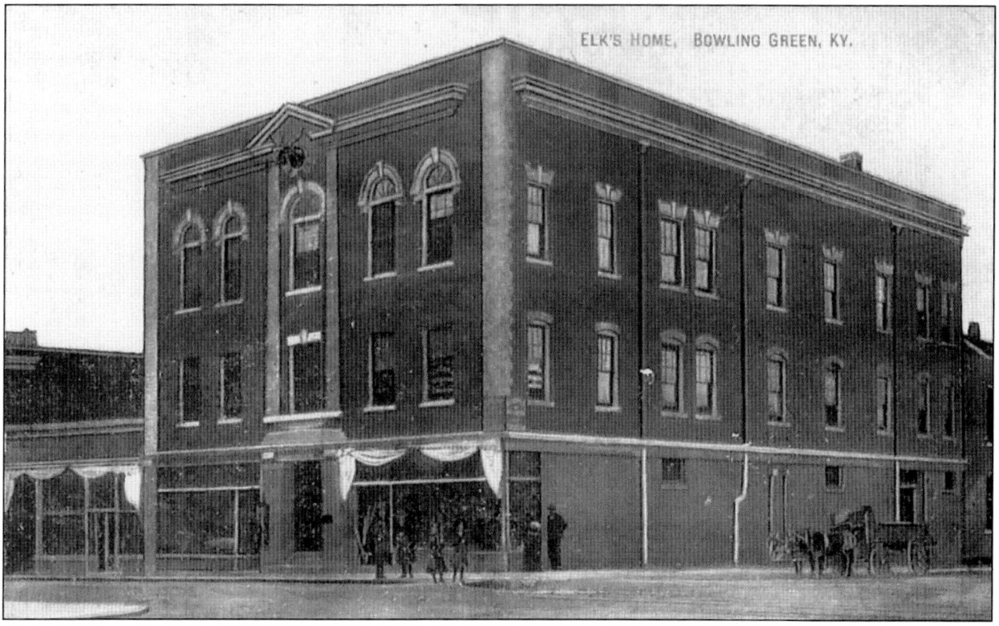

THE ELKS LODGE. This impressive structure was built for Elks Lodge no. 320, which organized here in 1895. Located at the corner of Main and College Streets, the building featured masonry construction with limestone detailing. The structure housed two storefronts on the ground level and professional offices on the second floor. The lodge itself on the third floor featured a meeting room, dining room, kitchen, reading room, and bar. A fire destroyed the building on January 29, 1978.

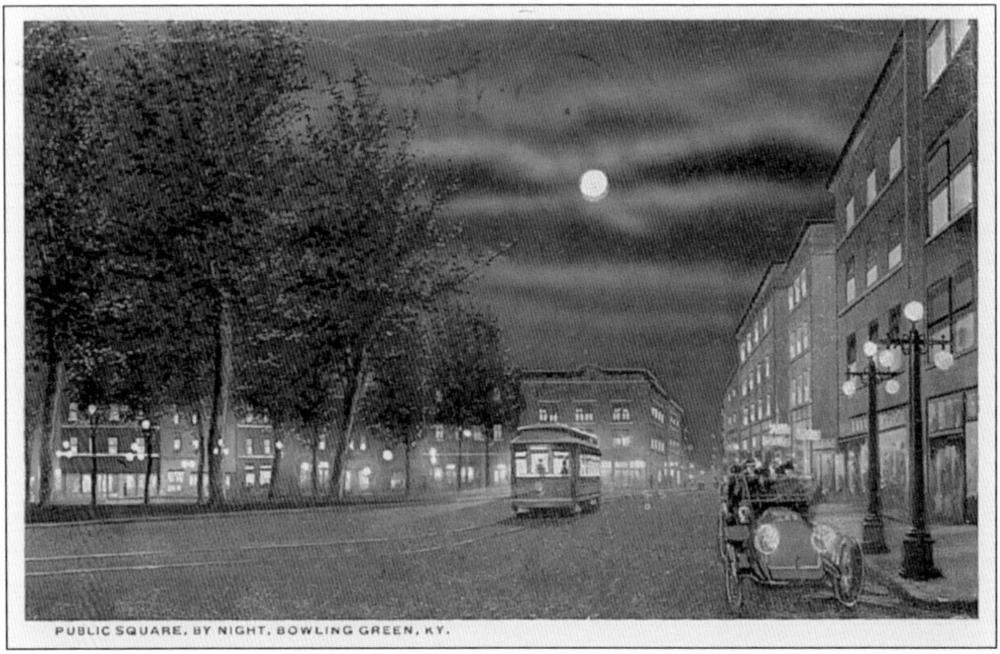

STREETCARS. This postcard shows one of Bowling Green's streetcars on Main Street in the evening. The Park City Railway began hauling passengers by streetcar in July 1889, when the cars were pulled by mules. By 1908, the company had seven and one-half miles of track, nine motor cars, and seven trailers; fare was 10¢. The service passed through several hands before it closed in 1921.

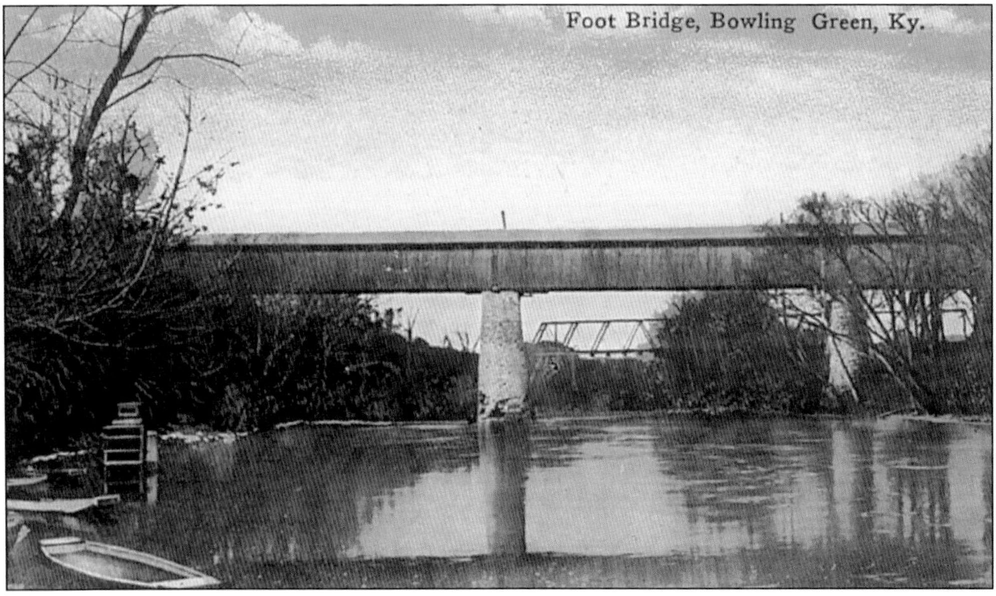

FOOT BRIDGE. This bridge crossed the Barren River at the location of the present College Street bridge. Although called a foot bridge, it accommodated vehicular traffic as well. A group of "night riders" burned the bridge on February 12, 1915, in protest of County Judge H.H. Denhardt's strong, anti-bootlegging policy. The present College Street bridge, part of the Riverfront Park, utilizes portions of the foot bridge's stone piers.

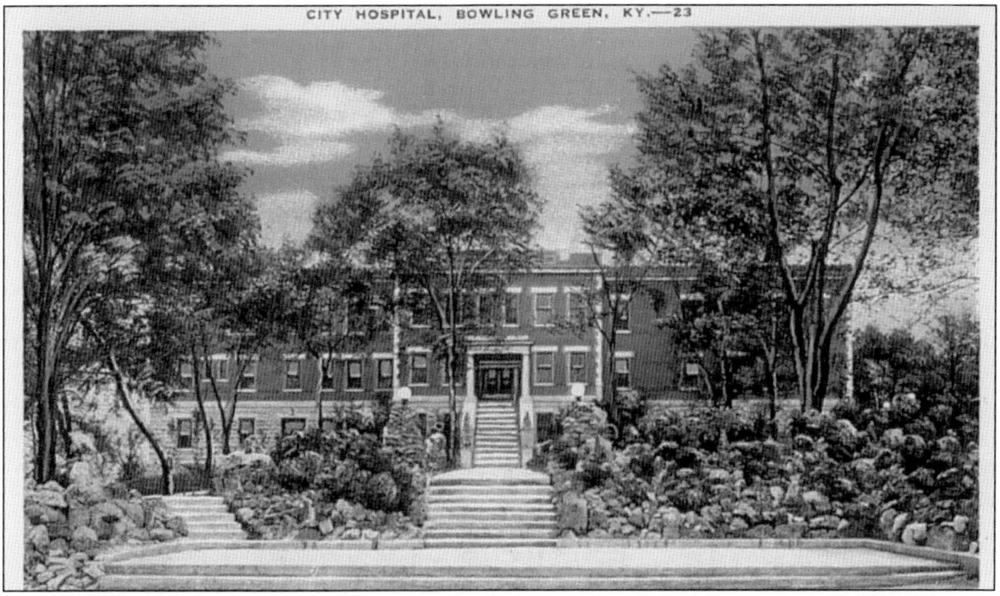

City-County Hospital. R.E. Turbeville designed this medical facility in 1925. It occupied one of the city's highest points and boasted commanding views of the surrounding countryside. The extensive rock gardens around the building were donated by landscape architect Richard Gloede of Evanston, Illinois, whose son received loving care at the hospital before his untimely death. The building now houses administrative offices for the Medical Center and a substance abuse facility.

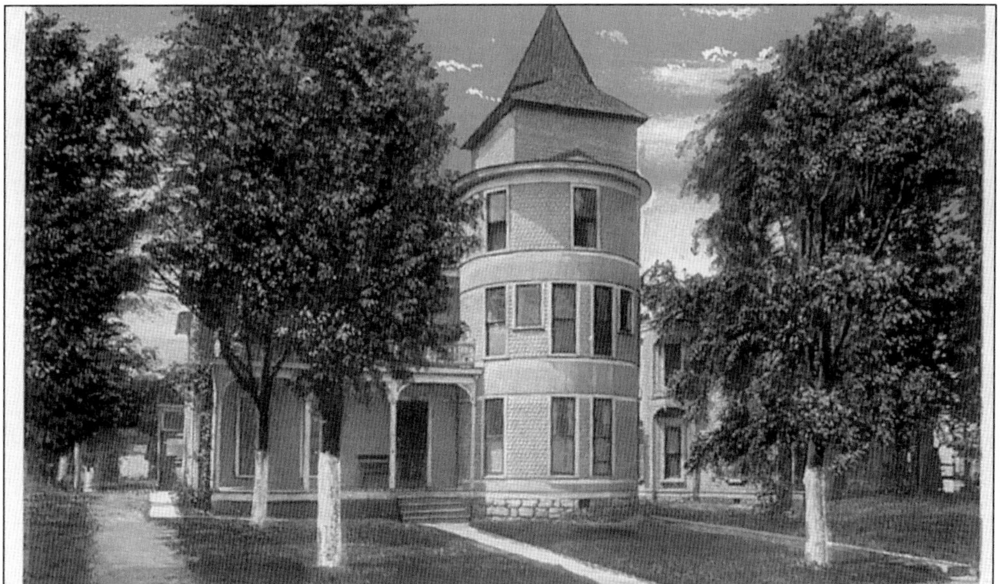

St. Joseph's Hospital. Through the years, Bowling Green has been home to several private "hospitals" or "nursing homes." A group of cooperative physicians opened St. Joseph's in September 1908 at 633 Twelfth Street. Although privately owned, all members of the Warren County Medical Society could practice there. The facility featured a modern operating room, x-ray and "electrical" room, an inhalatorium, and an attractive solarium for recuperating patients.

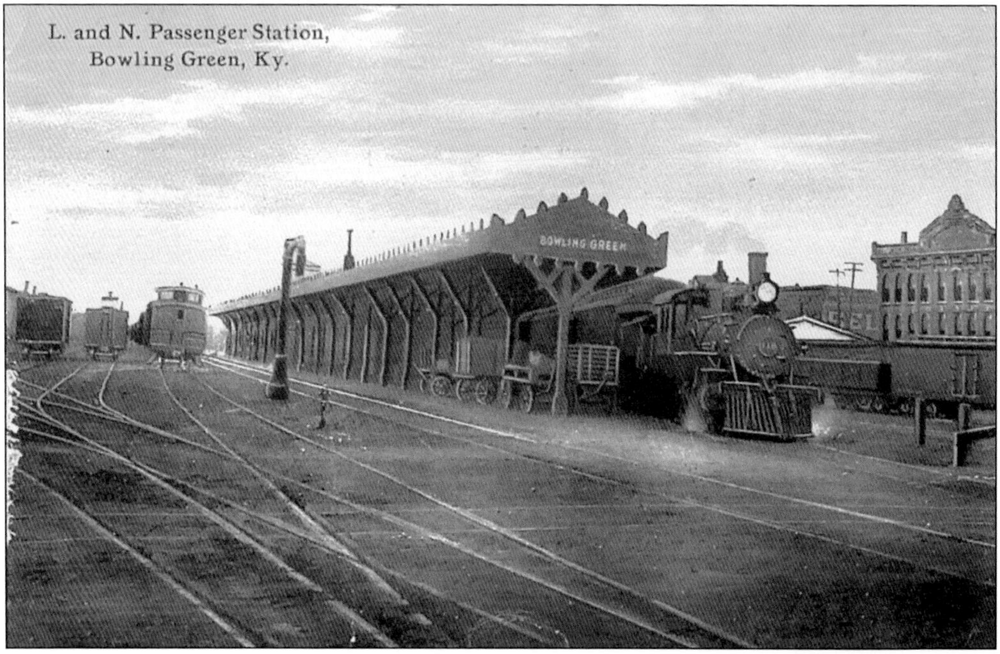

OLD L&N DEPOT. The second L&N depot was constructed shortly after the Civil War. Although heralded as "beautiful" in the 1870s, the frame depot had become unsightly by the turn of the century. It lacked sanitary toilet facilities, and passengers had to pay for a cup of water. One of the chief complaints about the old depot was the number of tracks passengers had to cross in order to enter the building. The depot was a long cigar-shaped building sited between numerous sets of tracks. This entry and egress problem led to a number of accidents involving pedestrians, wagons, and buggies. Beginning in 1900, Bowling Green citizens waged a 24-year battle with the L&N to replace the aging and "decrepit" frame building.

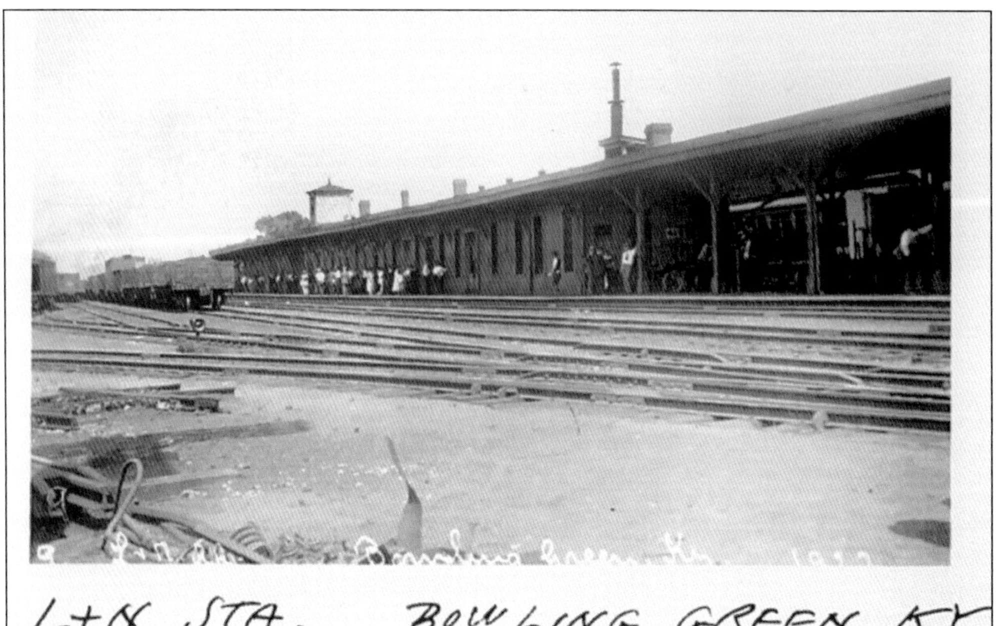

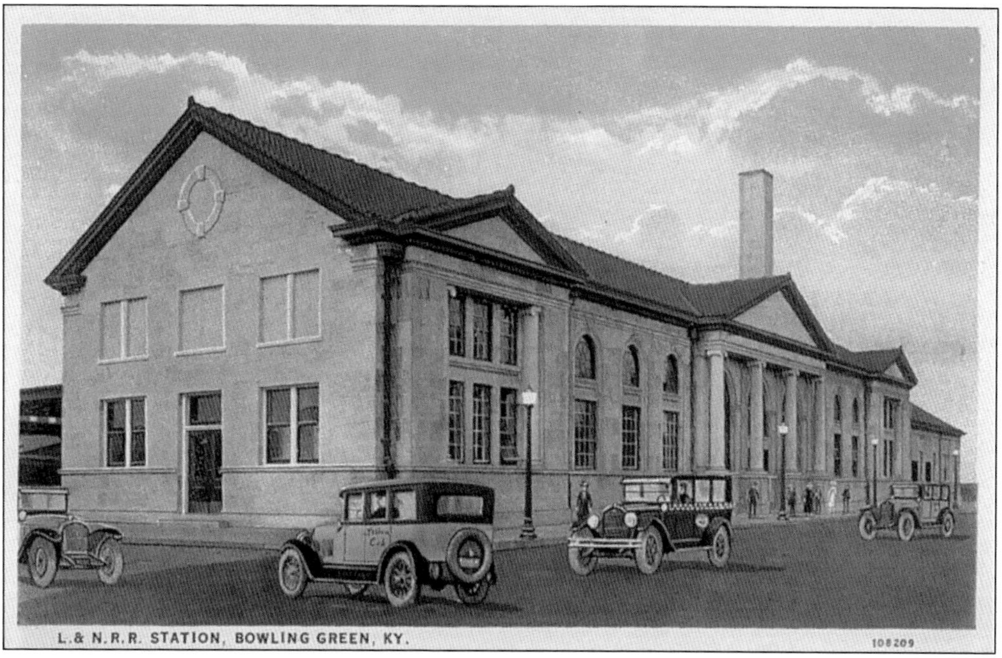

New L&N Depot. Bowling Green's efforts to get a new passenger station finally reached fruition in October 1925, when the L&N dedicated this gorgeous limestone facility. The building was clad with four-inch slabs of striated Bowling Green limestone. Continuously used until 1979, the building closed shortly after the last passenger train, the *Floridian*, left the station that year. After going through private hands, the building was saved by a group of concerned citizens. It now hosts Kentucky's first digital library. The taxis in front of the building are interesting, because a court case involving two competing cab companies at the depot actually led to a Supreme Court decision in 1927. The bottom card is dated 1956 and shows the train shed with some of the large four-wheel carts used in handling freight in sight.

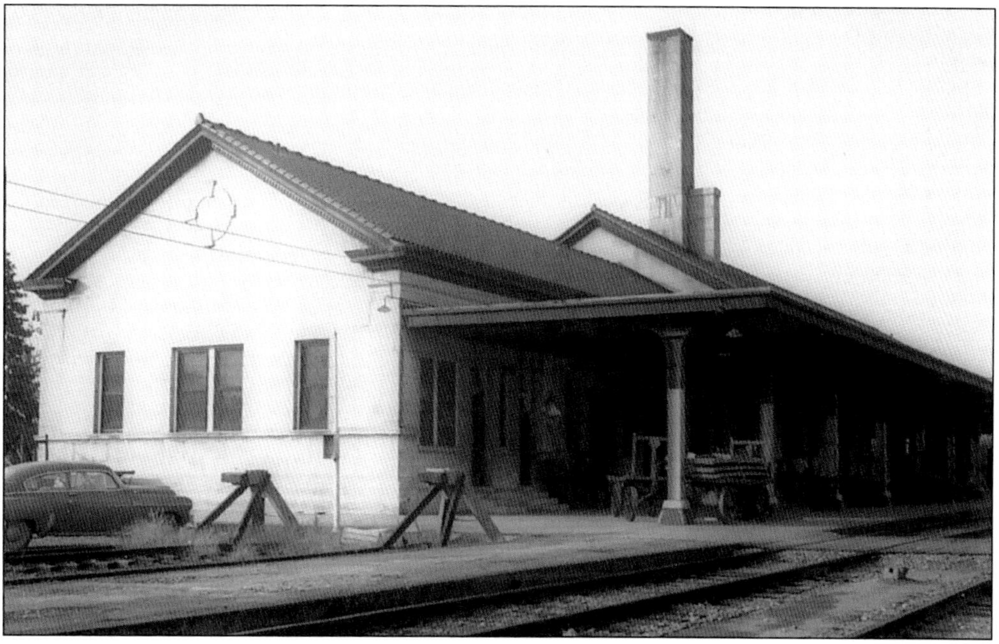

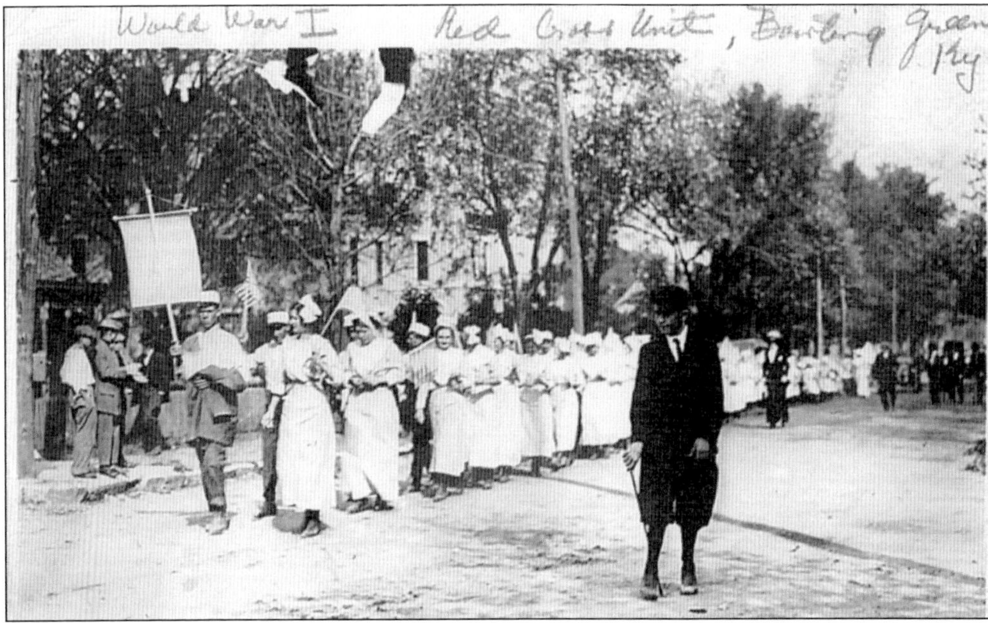

World War I Red Cross Parade. Bowling Green patriotically supported the approximately 1,000 Warren County citizens who served in the military during World War I. Parades were used to bolster support for the county's four Red Cross units and for the sale of liberty bonds. Red Cross members greeted soldiers passing through the city by rail, knitted garments and socks according to prescribed patterns, prepared bandages, salvaged leather and metals, and assisted during the devastating 1918 influenza epidemic.

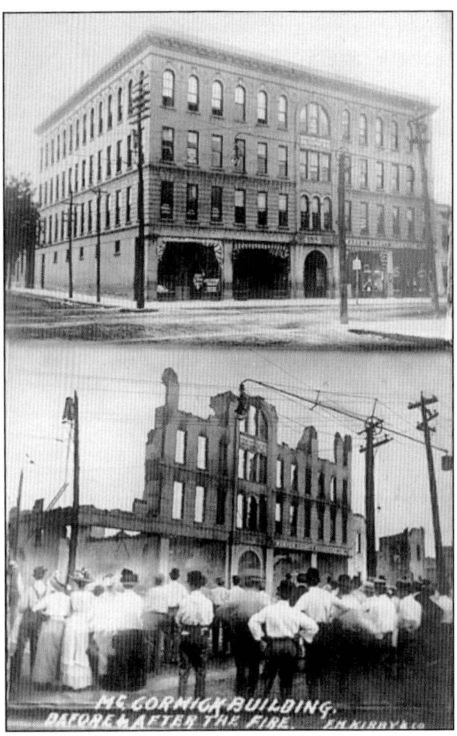

McCormack Building Fire. One of the largest conflagrations in Bowling Green history destroyed this prominent building at the corner of State and Tenth Streets on July 5, 1911. The 40,000-square-foot building erected in 1898 housed a large portion of the Bowling Green Business University, a grocery, a hardware store, a bowling alley, and professional offices. Much of the building's exterior stone and brick was salvaged and a three-story structure of similar design was constructed from it.

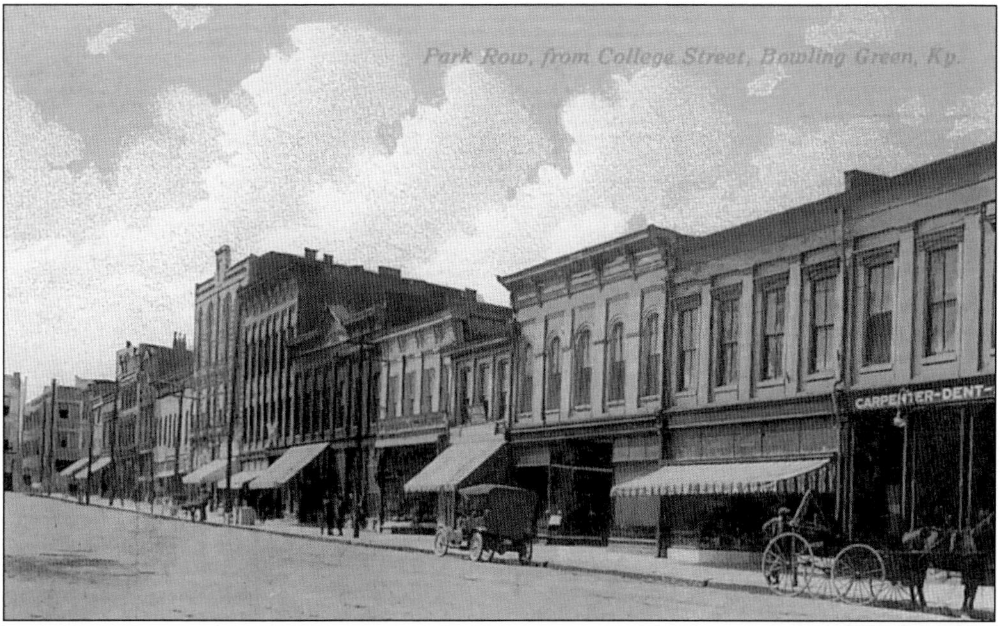

PARK ROW. The building on the right margin, for many years housed one of the largest drugstores in the area, the Carpenter-Dent-Sublett concern, and the Greer Furniture Store. It and the adjoining Charles Store building were destroyed by fire in June 1992. Park Row is sometimes referred to as Frozen Row, because ice and snow took more time to melt here than on the other sides of the square.

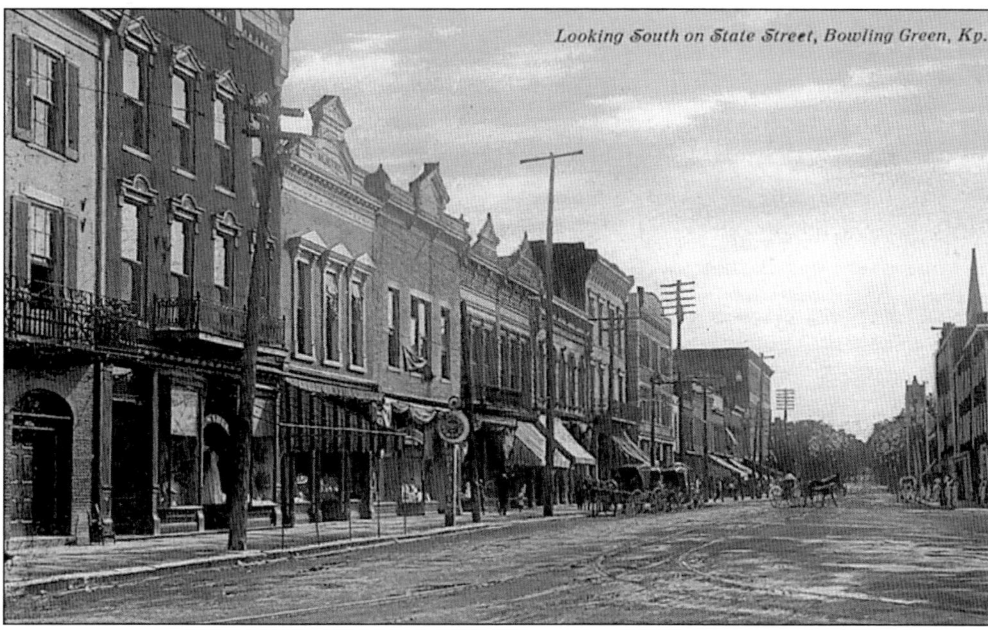

STATE STREET. What an impressive view of the State Street side of Fountain Square! All the elaborate cornices and the beautiful wrought-iron balconies are gone. Halfway down the block is the old town clock. At the very left margin is the original arched entrance to the Quigley-Younglove Building. During a 1937 remodeling, that entrance was removed and is now located at the old Cooksey home at 1318 Chestnut Street.

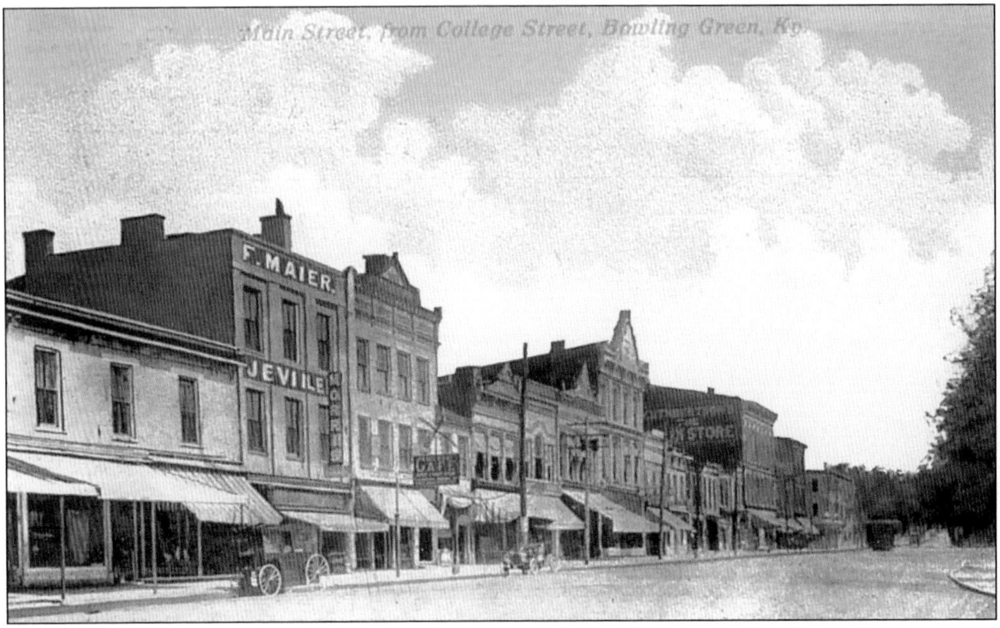

Main Street. Several significant changes have occurred on Main Street since this postcard was printed. The first building on the left margin is the old Rochester Hotel, which was razed in 1921 and replaced with the Pushin Building. Further down the street, three smaller buildings were removed in 1938 to make room for the Capitol Theater. In 1935, a building at 434 Main was replaced with the Johnson Building.

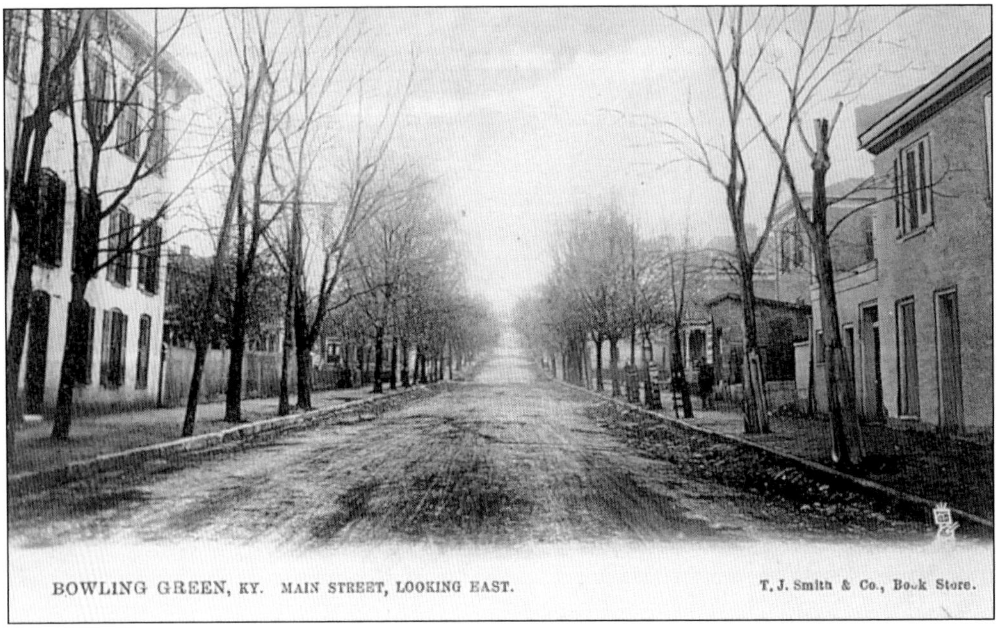

Main Street. This wide tree-lined avenue is made of packed dirt and leads up Reservoir Hill. City streets were sprinkled and oiled frequently to keep dust down. The building on the left is the old Morehead House Hotel, razed in 1917 to make room for the Helm Hotel. The structure on the right is the Quigley-Younglove building, erected in 1837 and still standing.

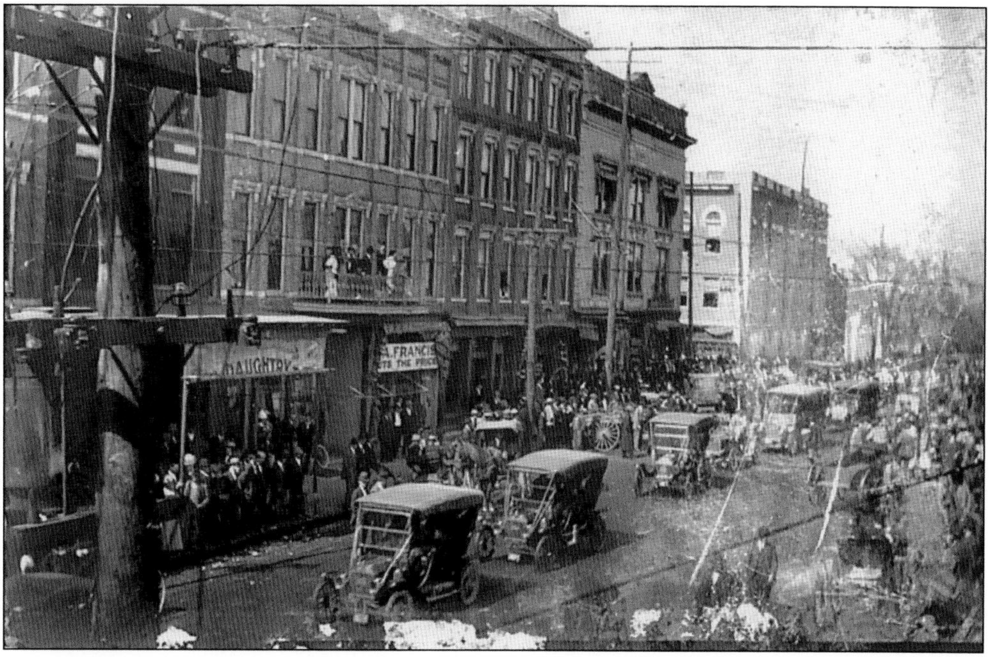

AUTO PARADE. Horseless carriages invaded Bowling Green during a Glidden Auto parade that came through town in 1914. Starting at the bottom left, the buildings in the 900 block of College Street are the Daughtery, Ackerman, and Watkins buildings, the Opera House, and the Elks Lodge. Bowling Green had two telephone exchanges at the time, which helps explain the profusion of wiring you see.

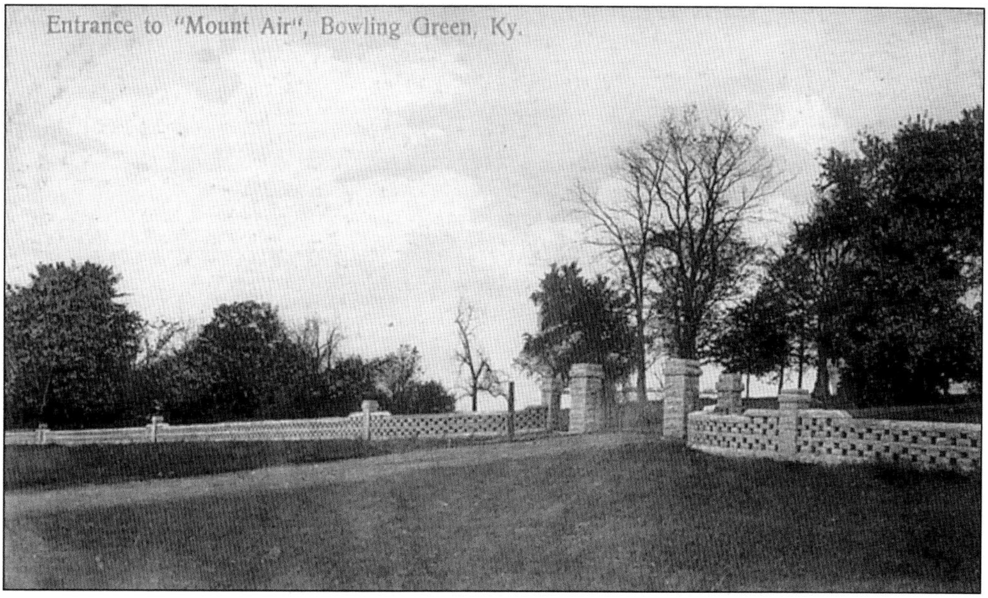

ENTRANCE TO MOUNT AIR. This serpentine fence and gate belonged to one of Warren County's most prominent farms. Perhaps the most famous owner of the property, which is sometimes referred to as "Mount Ayr," was Warner Lewis Underwood. The farm, located off Cemetery Road, was substantially decimated during the Civil War by troops from both sides. The fence was probably erected with stone from the Sweeney quarry off the Morgantown Road.

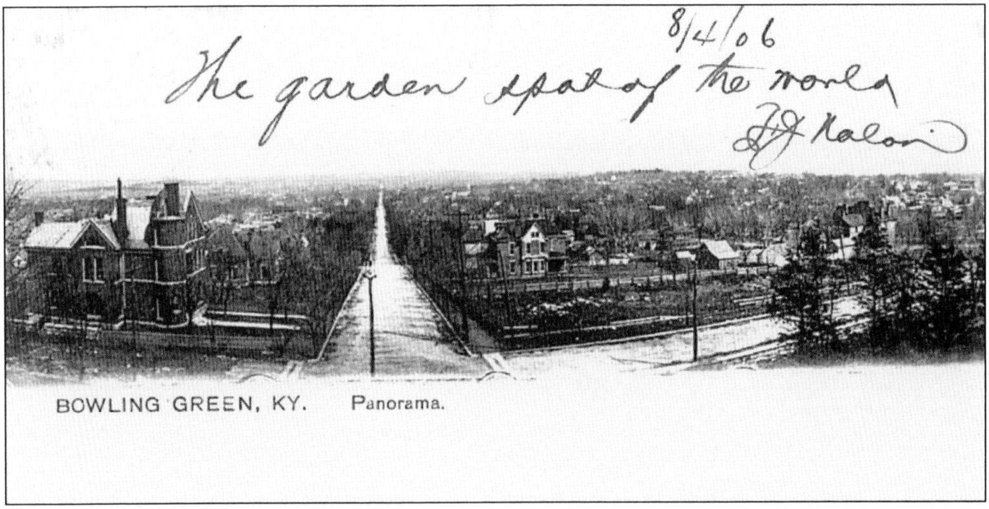

Panoramic View from Potter College. This postcard was taken from atop Vinegar Hill, which in 1906 was the location of Potter College. The thin photo is not uncommon, as you were required to write your message on the front of the card with the back reserved exclusively for the recipient's address. The sender deemed Bowling Green "the garden spot of the world."

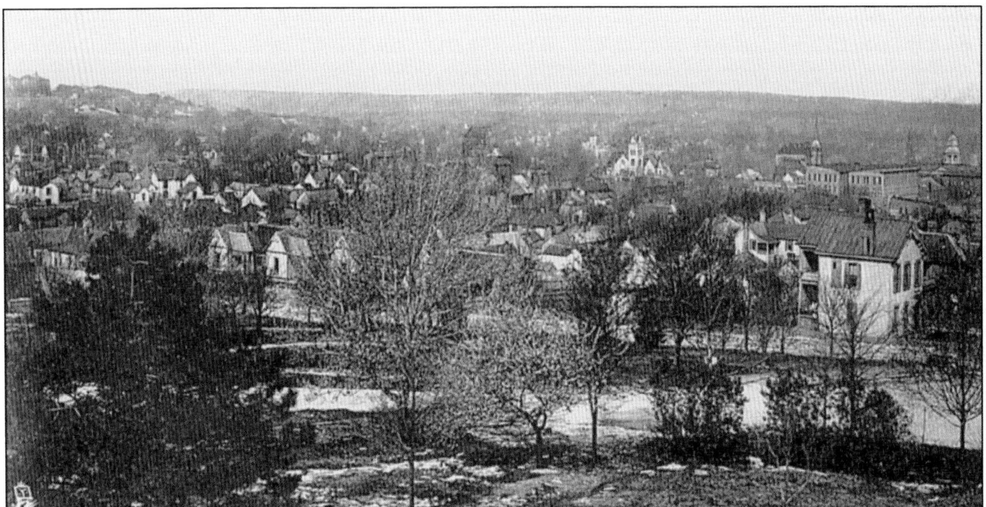

Panoramic View from Reservoir Hill. Panoramic postcards were almost always taken from a hilltop to include the widest scope possible. Here, the photographer stood on the western side of Reservoir Hill to take this view in 1905. The prominent house near the right margin is the old Natcher home at the corner of Main and High Streets. Further back on the right margin, you can spot the courthouse cupola.

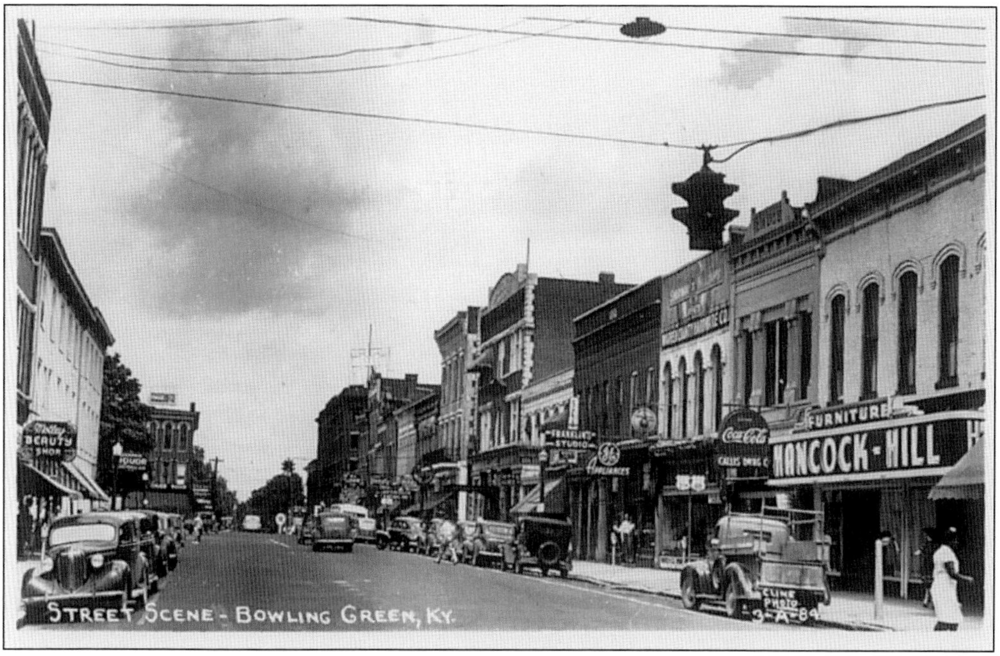

STATE STREET. Few postcards document the business section of Bowling Green beyond Fountain Square Park. This view shows the extension of the commercial district up State Street from the square. This is a valuable card for local researchers because almost every building on the left and right of the 1000 block of State Street is now gone. Notice the two-light (red and green) traffic signal.

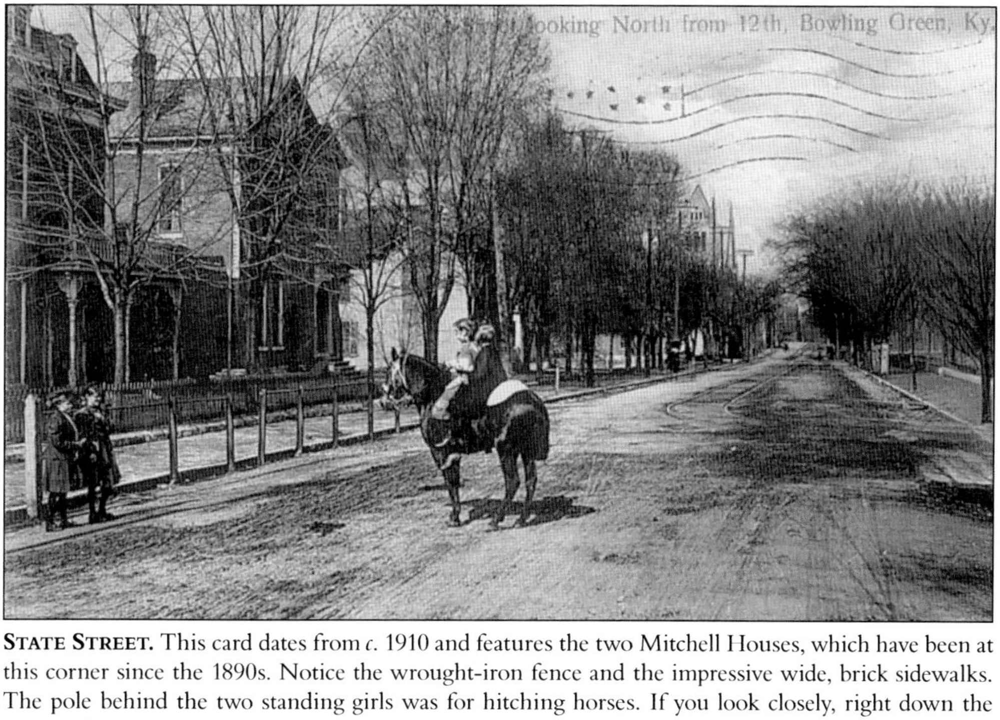

STATE STREET. This card dates from *c.* 1910 and features the two Mitchell Houses, which have been at this corner since the 1890s. Notice the wrought-iron fence and the impressive wide, brick sidewalks. The pole behind the two standing girls was for hitching horses. If you look closely, right down the center of State Street is part of the old streetcar track.

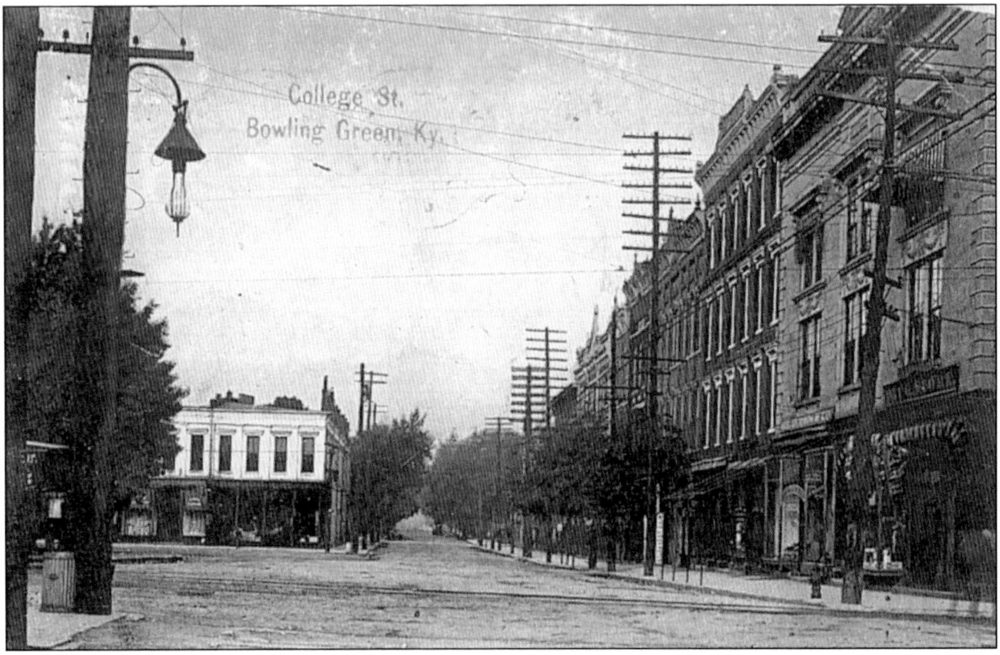

COLLEGE STREET. The College Street side of Fountain Square contained the massive Bowling Green Opera House, or Odeon Hall, at the corner of College and Main Streets. The Opera House contained store fronts on the first floor with the theater on the second floor and its balcony occupying a portion of the third floor. The sender of this card declares Bowling Green "a right pretty town."

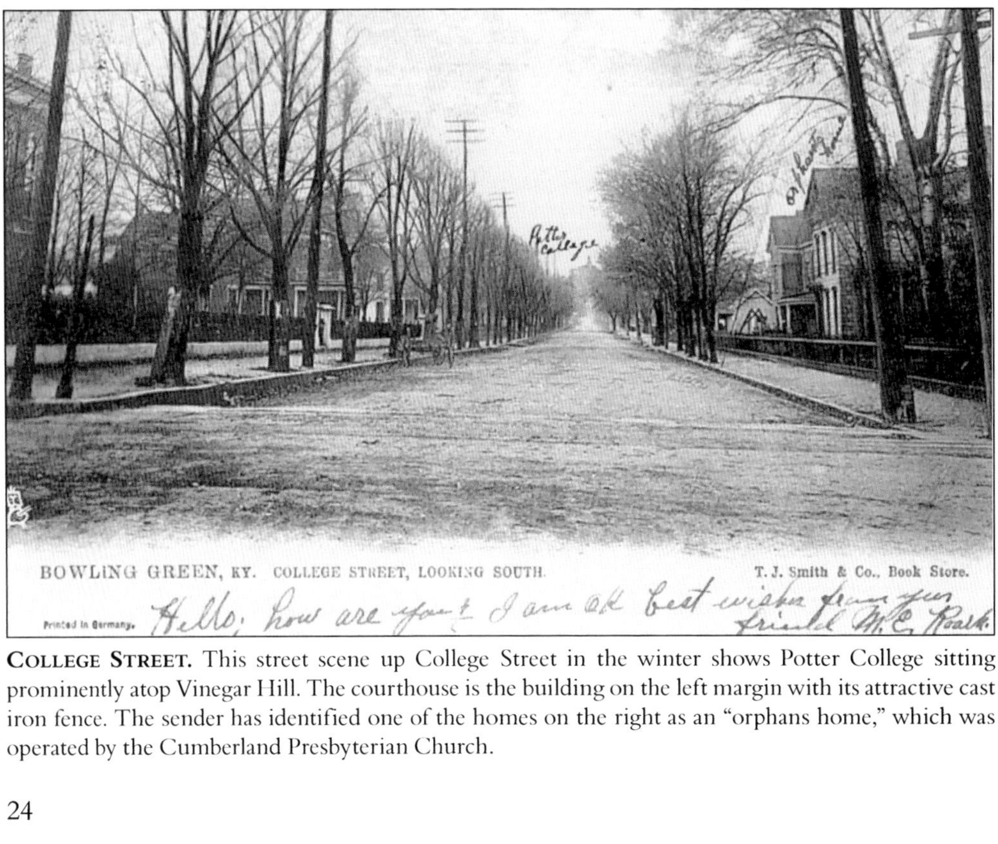

COLLEGE STREET. This street scene up College Street in the winter shows Potter College sitting prominently atop Vinegar Hill. The courthouse is the building on the left margin with its attractive cast iron fence. The sender has identified one of the homes on the right as an "orphans home," which was operated by the Cumberland Presbyterian Church.

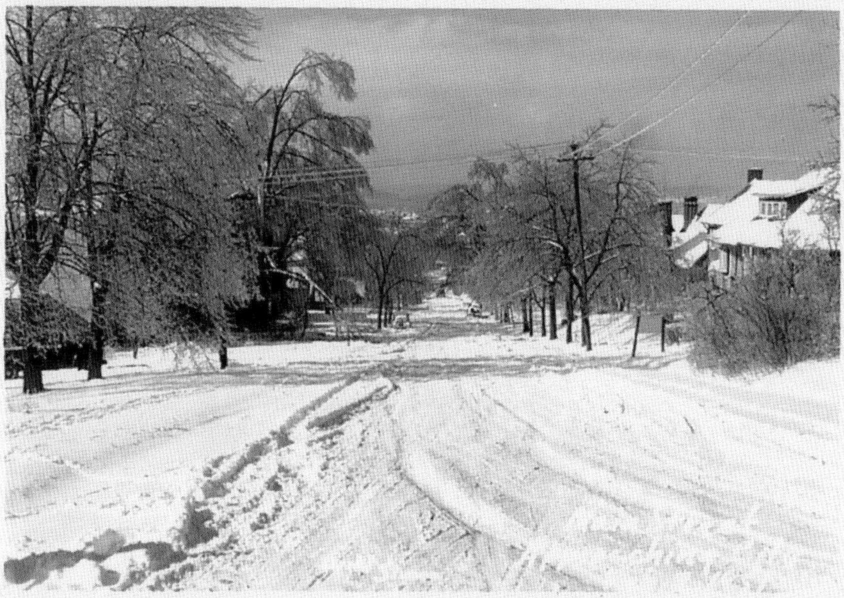

WINTER WONDERLAND. These real photo postcards were taken on one of the coldest days in Bowling Green history, February 2, 1951. The newspaper reported that a record low had been recorded the night before of 20 degrees below zero, which "eclipsed by three degrees the previous record minimum set on February 3, 1899." Cold temperatures perpetuated the nine inches of sleet and snow for several weeks. Repair crews for local utilities and communication companies were kept busy working on downed and snapped power lines. The paper noted that the trees in Fountain Square Park "sparkled in a nightmarish kind of brilliance."

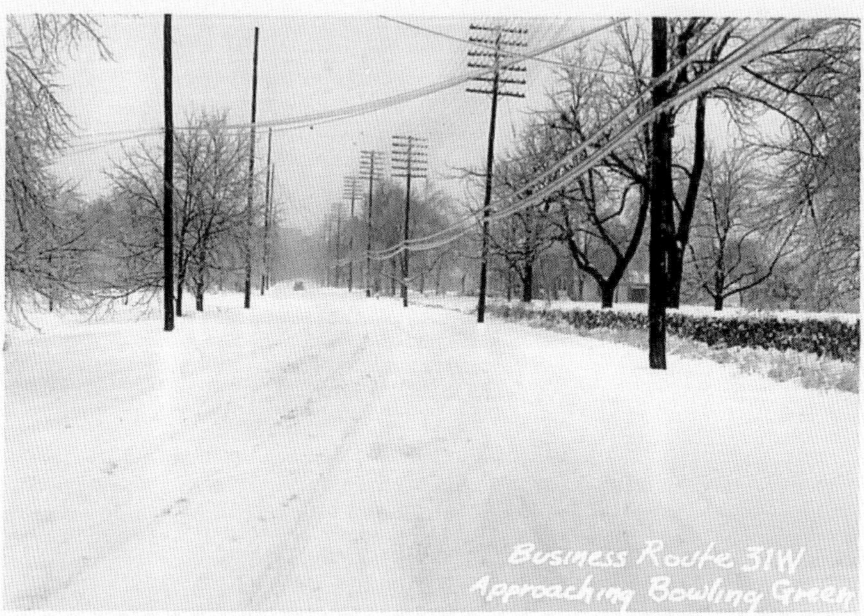

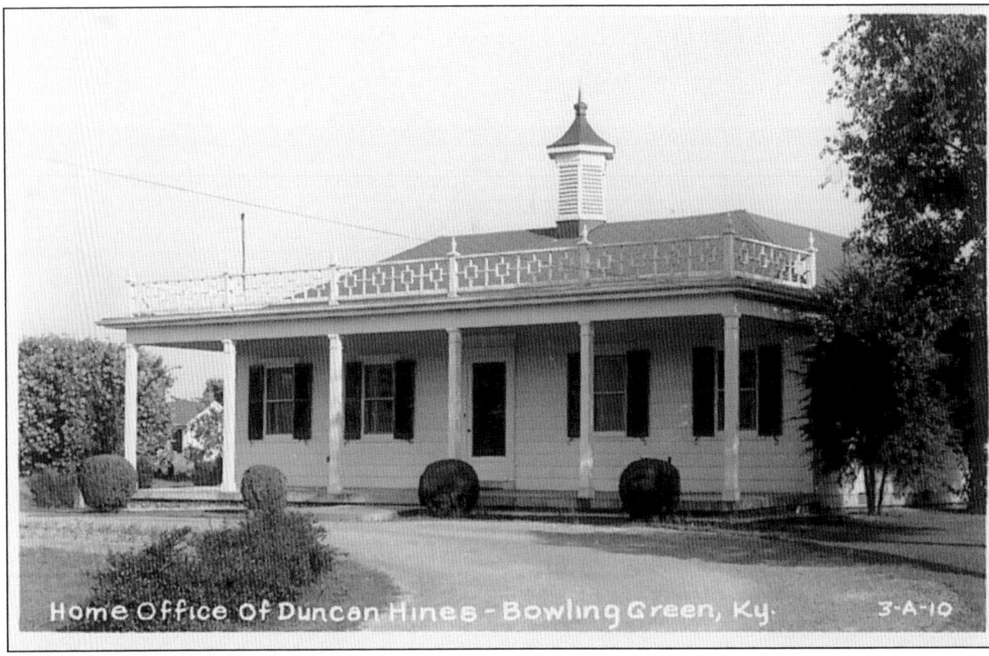

DUNCAN HINES HOME. Duncan Hines (1880–1959) moved his publishing business from Chicago to his hometown of Bowling Green in 1938. In 1940, he purchased four acres on the Old Louisville Road to build this attractive house/office. If you look closely, you can discern that Hines told his contractor that he wanted the facade to replicate the back portico of George Washington's Mt. Vernon. The patio built in the backyard was rather avant-garde for the period, but Hines was aware of a growing trend in which Americans were beginning to construct "outdoor rooms" for their leisure activities.

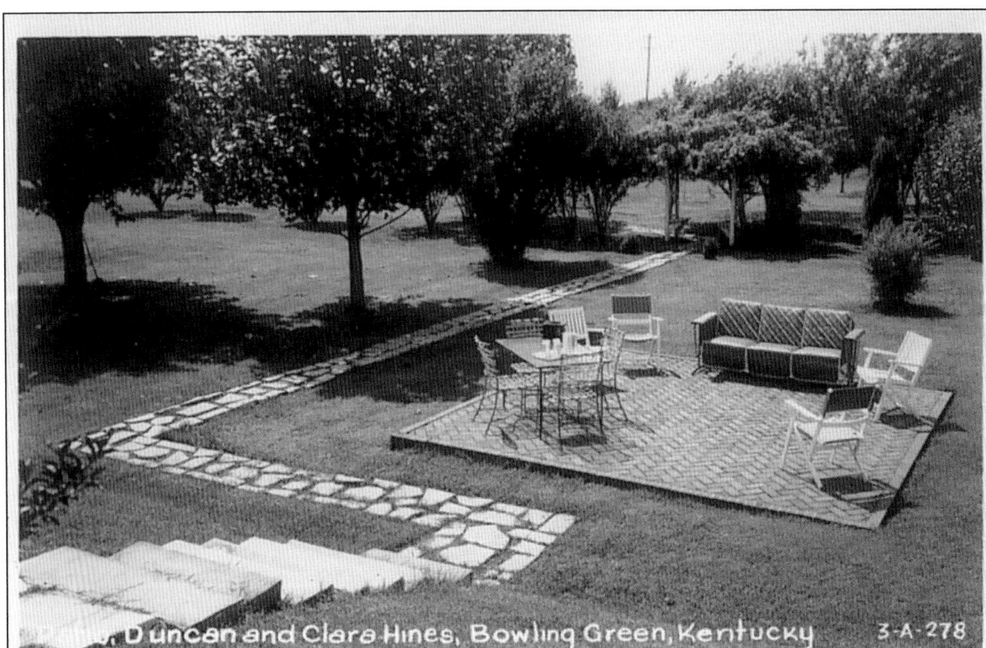

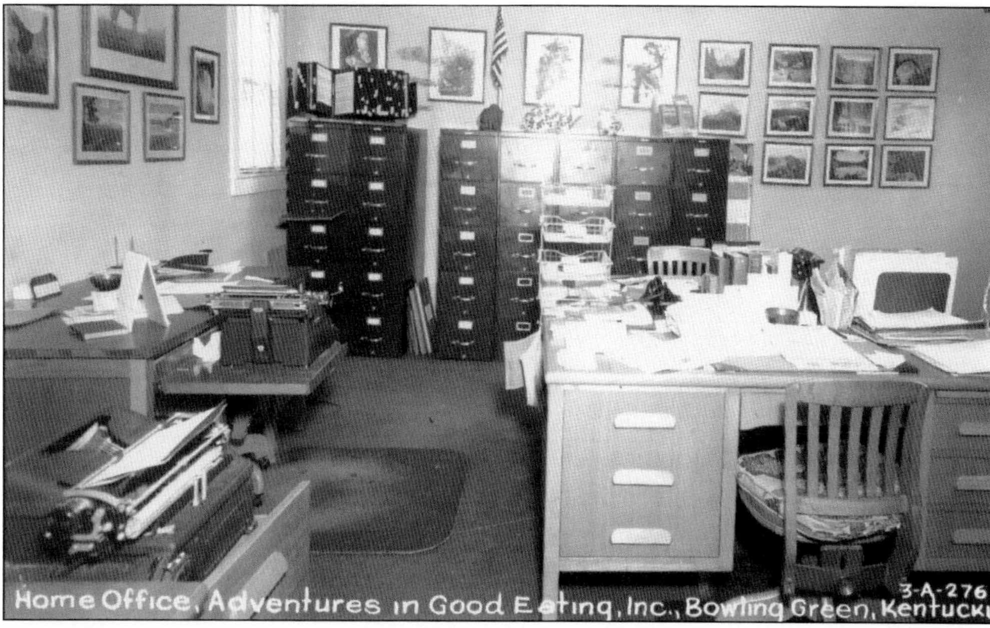

DUNCAN HINES HOME. Duncan Hines, the famed food and lodging critic, held court in this office from which he published numerous travel guides and rented his "Recommended by Duncan Hines" signs to restaurants and hotels. During his active years, Hines received up to 600 pieces of mail a day. Hines's name was eventually used on a whole line of food products ranging from bread to fruit cakes. Many homemakers still swear by his cake mix. Hines's kitchen featured a nice display of cutlery and other "modern" utensils of the day. Although Hines was a noted food critic, he himself rarely cooked.

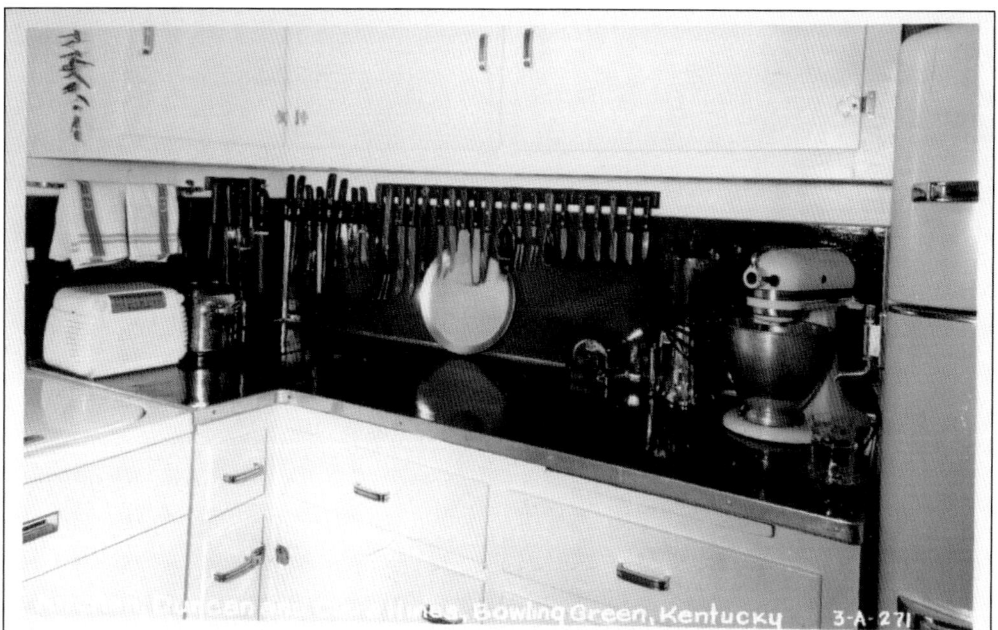

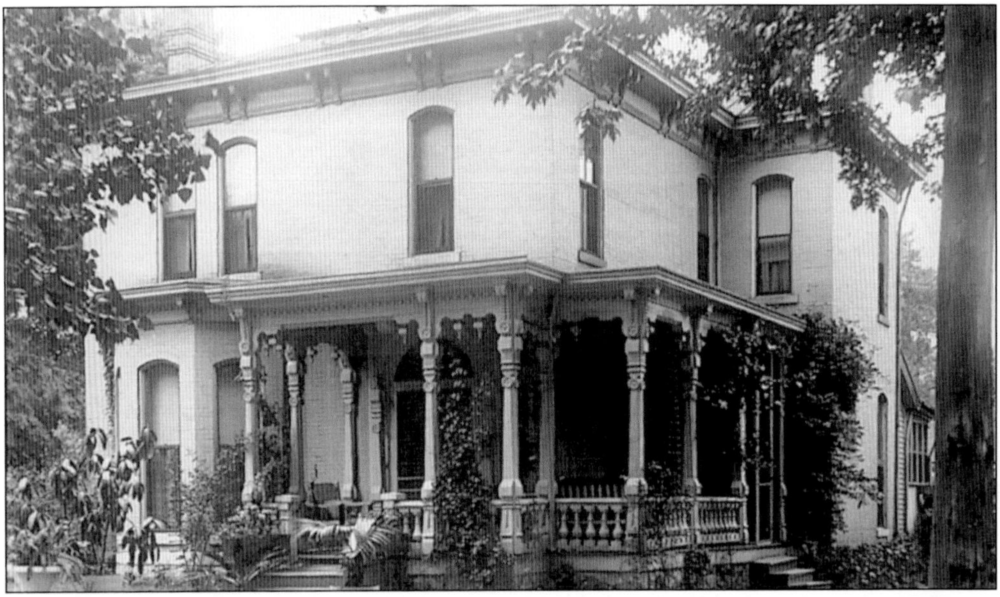

Potter Home. J. Whit Potter built this home at 1267 State Street sometime after 1877. It is Italianate in design, with bracketed eaves and decorative door surrounds. The ornate porch was removed in the early 20th century. Potter was part of an influential Bowling Green banking family, serving at one time as president of American National Bank and Potter Matlock Trust Co. Other influential owners have included the Spradlins, DeVashiers, Combs, and Walkers.

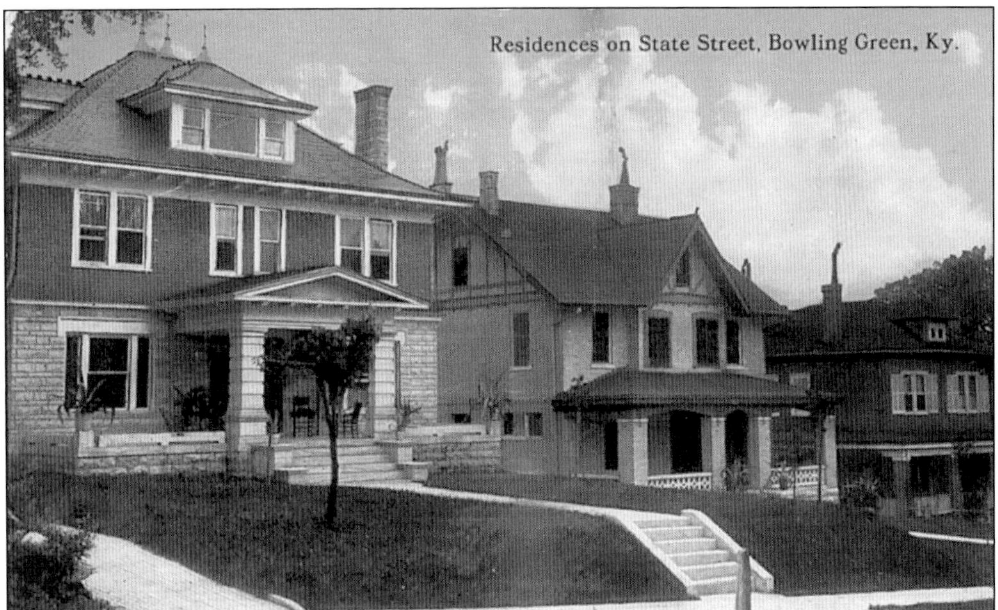

State Street Residences. Postcards of homes are not common, but these handsome residences in the 1400 block of State Street were noteworthy. They were homes for some prominent Bowling Green citizens. Pictured from left to right, these were the residences of M.O. Hughes, a banker; the Methodist manse; and Alex Duvall, a downtown merchant. The Duvall house was designed by Bowling Green native and noted architecture educator, Henry Kerr McGoodwin.

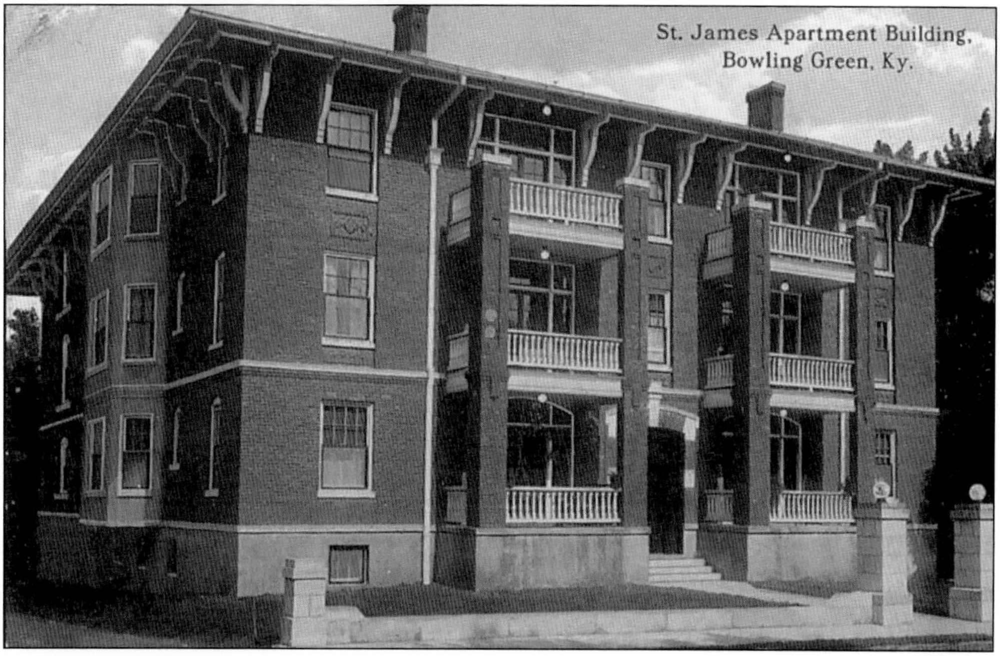

St. James Apartments. This attractive building at 1133 Chestnut Street was the first apartment building constructed in Bowling Green. The St. James Realty Co., consisting of several local businessmen, had the three-story brick building erected in 1912. The building features limestone detailing, projecting balconies with wood balustrades, wide bracketed eaves, and projecting bay windows on the side. The building was substantially renovated in 1984.

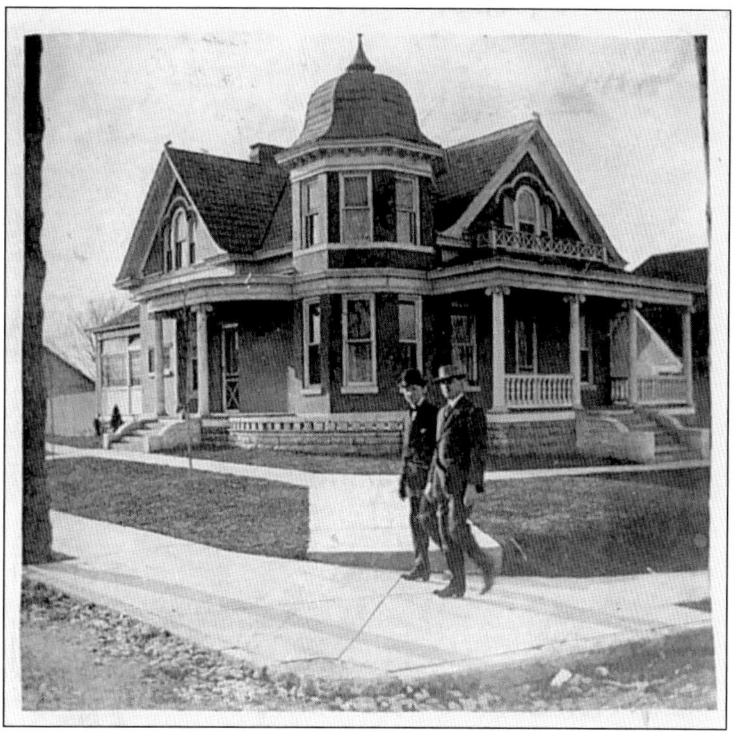

Jesse Home. Palmer C. Jesse came to Bowling Green in 1898 to establish the Planter Insurance office. Jesse was an avid hunter and a founding member of the Bowling Green Gun Club. He had this home built around 1900. The young woman who sent this postcard, obviously a student, penned this tongue-in-cheek message on the back: "This is a picture of my future residence. How do you like its looks? And also the two boys?"

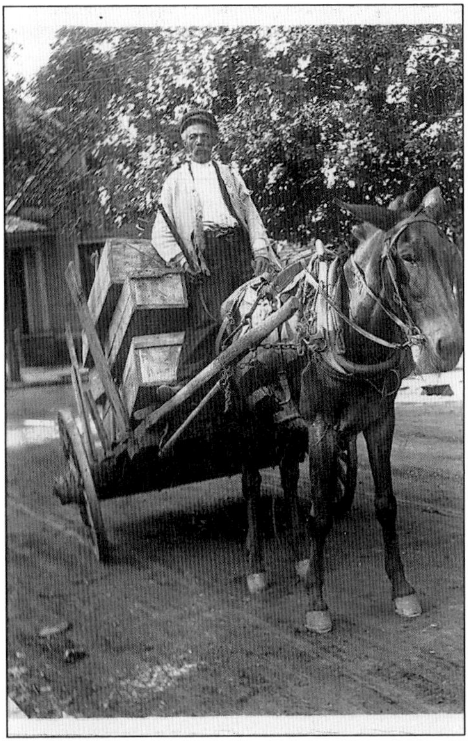

BILLY PORTER. Drayman Billy Porter was born a slave in Warren County. Local store owners hired him to haul freight from the boatlanding and from the railroad depot to their businesses. He employed his odd, two-wheel dray and mule long after the truck became the preferred means of hauling freight. He died in 1931 in his early 90s.

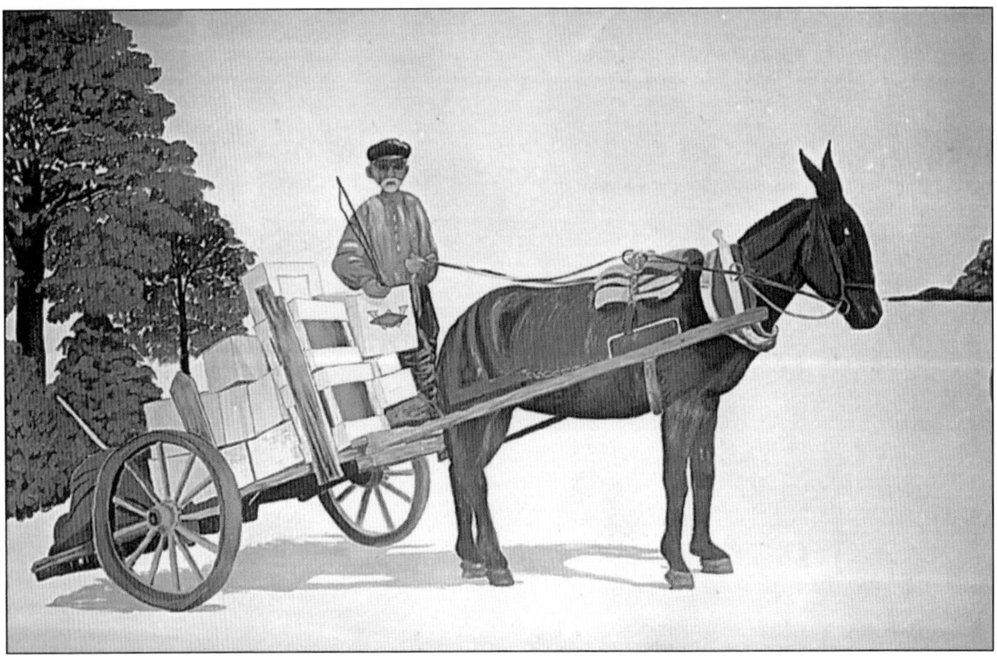

BILLY PORTER. Local artist Dorothy Reeves painted this representation of drayman Billy Porter in the form of a mural at her husband's grocery, Reeves Food Center in Fairview Plaza. Porter charged 25¢ per load to move packages from the depot to downtown mercantile establishments.

Two

BUSINESS AND INDUSTRY

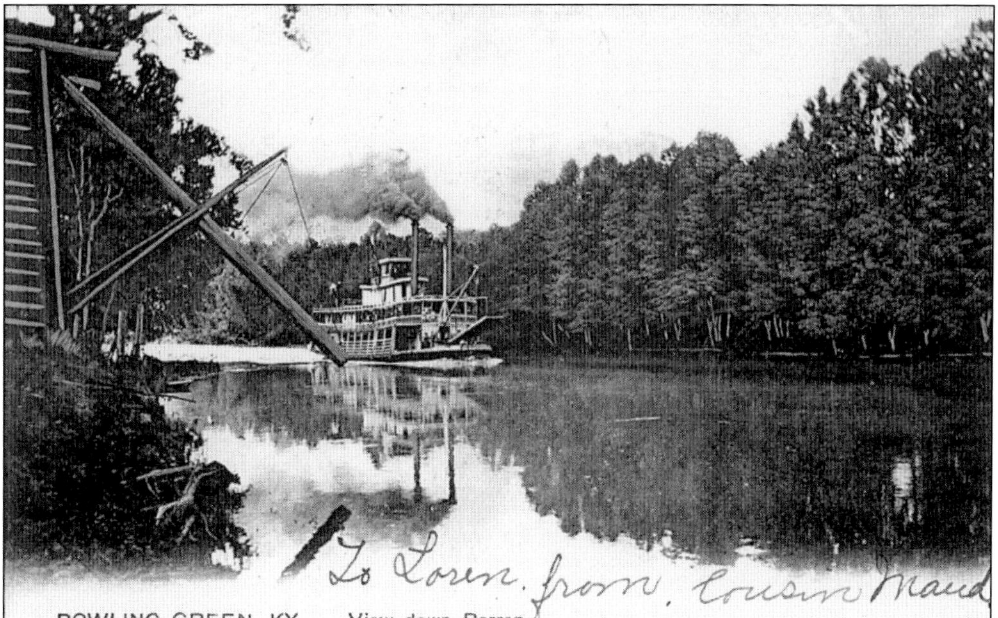

BARREN RIVER. The Barren River flows into the Green River in northeastern Warren County and is the Green's largest tributary. The river was made navigable to Bowling Green in the mid-1840s when a series of locks and dams was completed. The United States government assumed maintenance of this system in 1888. Passenger steamboat traffic died out in the early 20th century, but the river continued to be used for commercial transportation until the mid-1960s.

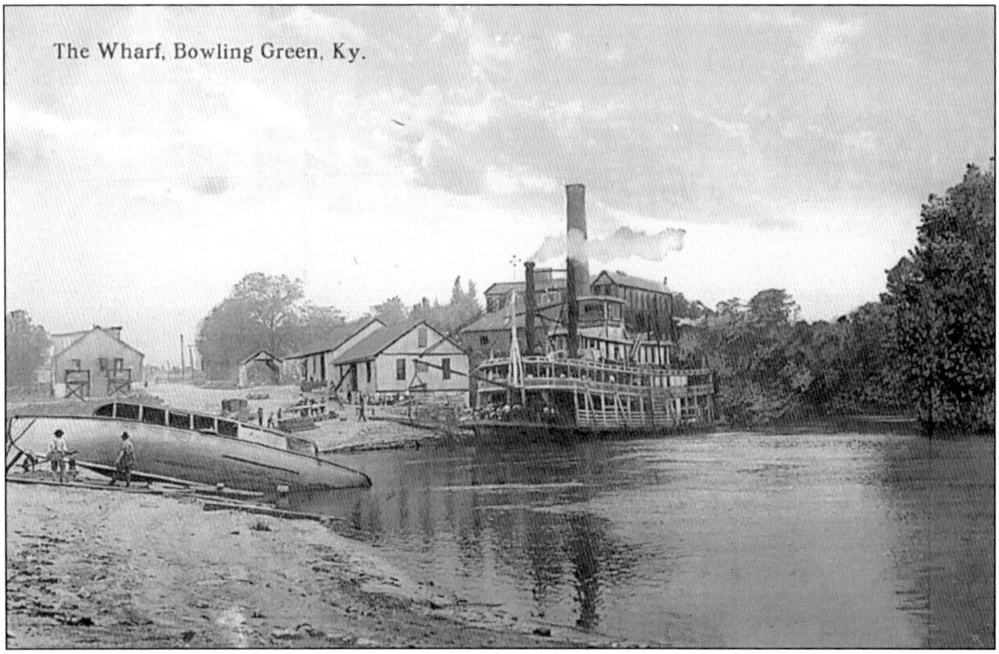

BOATLANDING AT BOWLING GREEN. The river was a critical commercial and passenger avenue for Bowling Green. The boatlanding was located one-and-a-half miles from downtown, and local entrepreneurs built a small rail line—known as the Portage Railroad—to link the river to downtown. These two postcards document some of the activities at the boatlanding—unloading freight, repairing boats, and warehousing. In the top card, the large Bowling Green Ice and Cold Storage facility looms in the background.

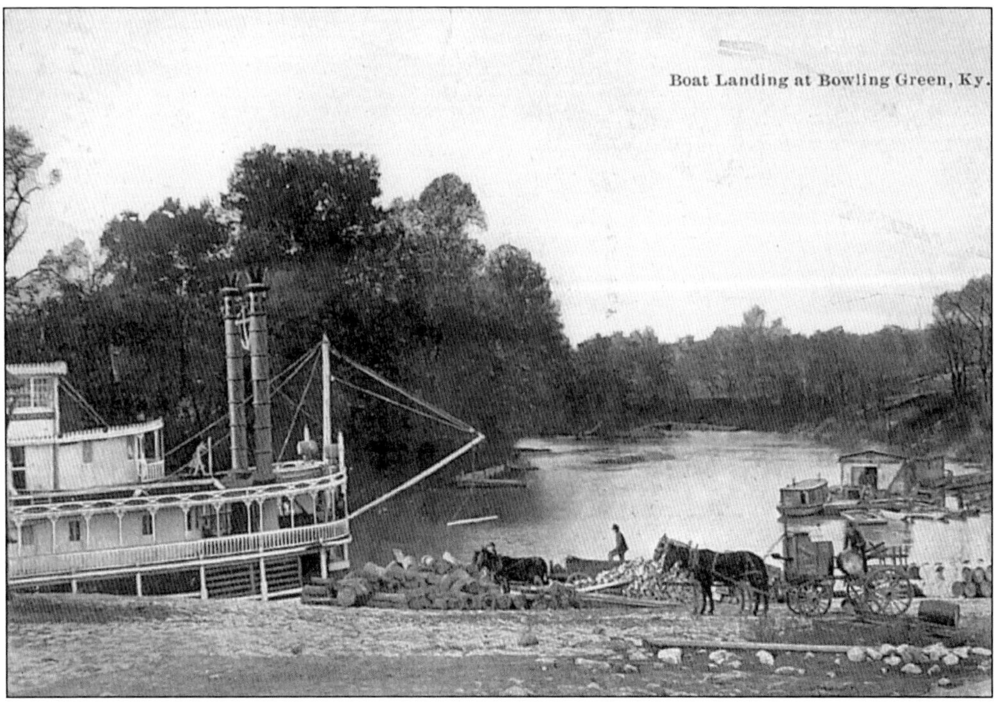

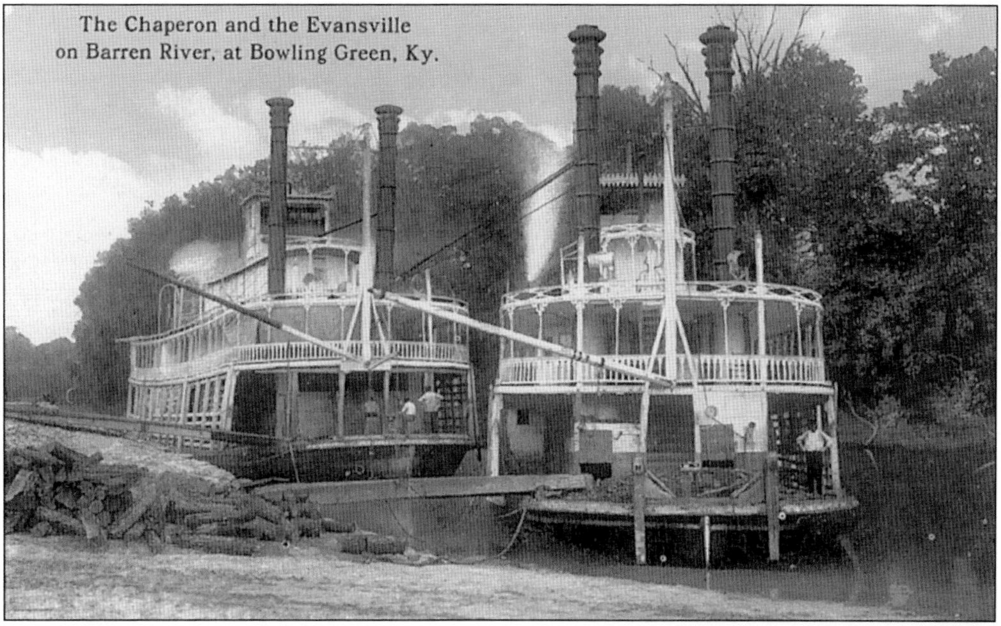

THE *CHAPERON* AND THE *EVANSVILLE*. These steamboats were used by the Evansville and Bowling Green Packet Co. The *Chaperon* was built in 1884 and measured 121 feet in length, and the *Evansville* was built in 1880 and was 120 feet long. Both boats burned; the *Evansville* caught fire at the Bowling Green Boatlanding in 1931, and the *Chaperon* burned in Mississippi in 1922.

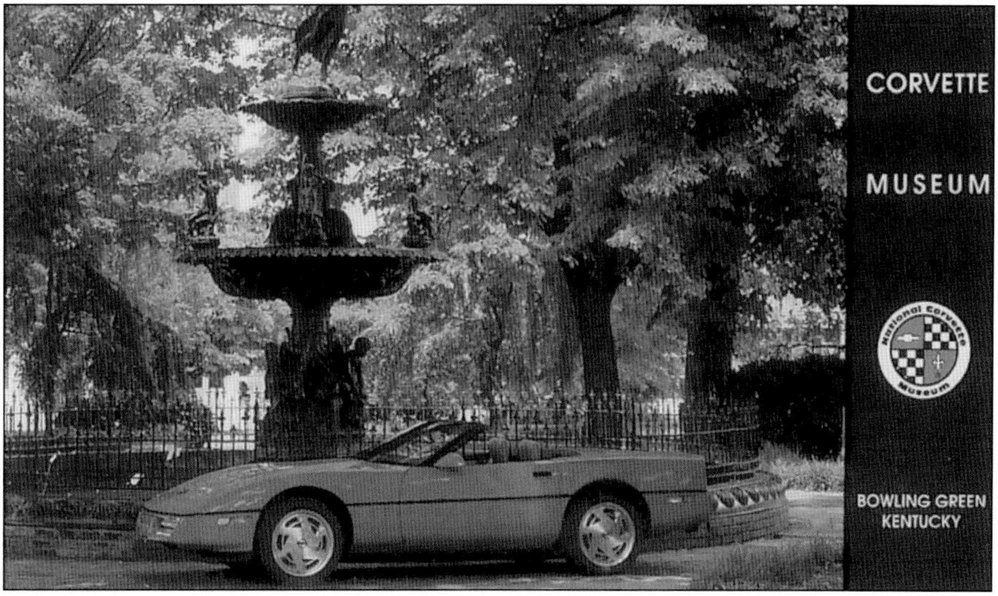

CORVETTES. Roads and air space now rule commerce rather than rivers and rails. One of the princes of the road is the Corvette. Operations of the General Motors Corvette Assembly Plant moved to Bowling Green in 1981 from St. Louis, where Corvettes had been manufactured since the 1950s. The over one-million-square-foot manufacturing facility is located adjacent to Interstate 65. The Bowling Green plant is the only General Motors facility that builds America's favorite sports car, the Corvette. Plant tours are a favorite tourist attraction.

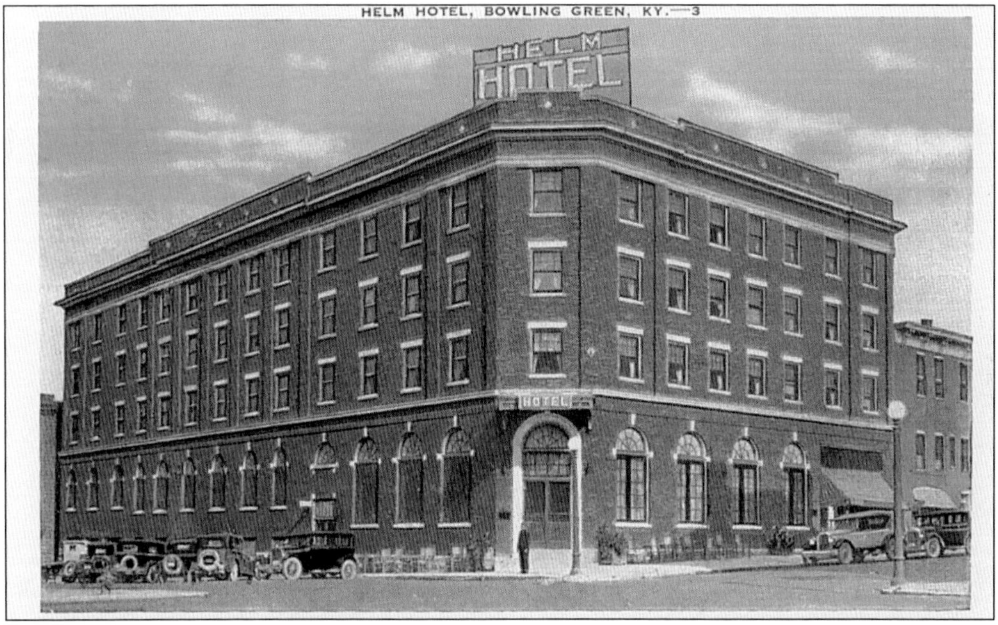

HELM HOTEL. The corner of State and Main Streets boasted a hotel from 1847 to 1970. Dr. T.O. Helm traded his Twelfth Street Hospital for the Morehead House Hotel in 1915. He and his son, T.O. Jr., operated the hotel during the hectic years of the Bowling Green oil boom. In 1923, the Helms hired Cincinnati architect, C.C. Weber, to design a new four-story hotel. The $300,000, 110-room Helm Hotel opened to guests in January 1924 and was called "Southern Kentucky's most complete hostelry." Guest rooms boasted steam heat, hot and cold running water, and telephones. The Helm family sold the hotel in 1969, and it was razed in January 1970 to make way for Citizen National Bank's new building. A former manager remembered, "Everything that happened in Bowling Green happened at the Hotel Helm, or it just didn't happen."

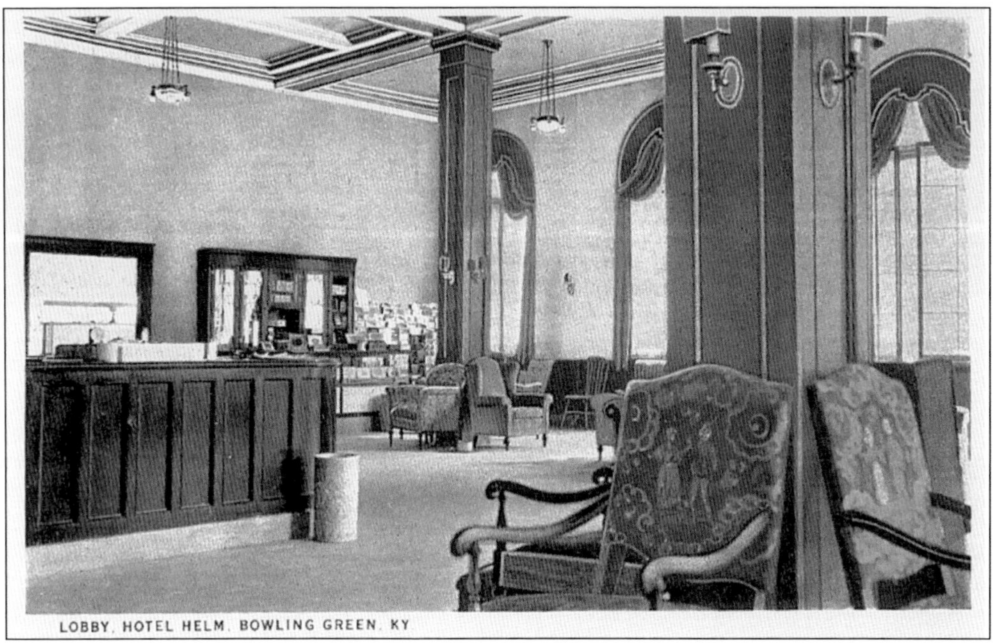

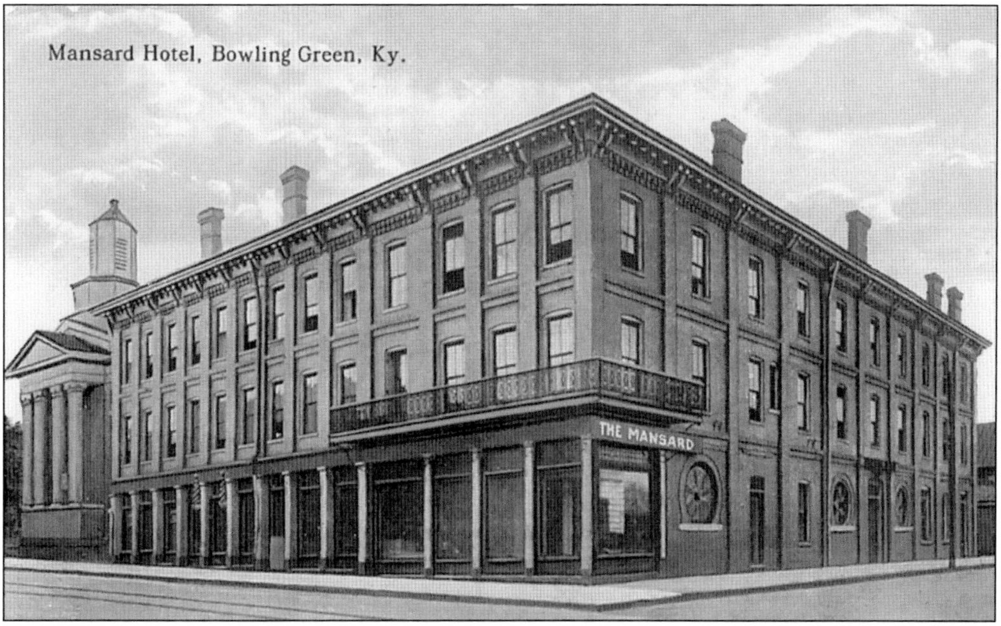

MANSARD HOTEL. In 1891, Joseph Winans purchased a building at the corner of Main and Center Streets to remodel into a hotel. He opened the new hostelry the following year and named it the Mansard Hotel, for the building's distinctive mansard roof. The building was remodeled several times and was particularly noted for its fine dining facilities located on the second floor. A special ladies entrance, which led directly to the dining room, was located on the building's eastern side The lobby postcard is from the oil boom period, 1917–1921. The sign over the glass case is for "The Kentucky Glycerin Co.," which sold oil well blasting supplies. The lobby postcard also features the ubiquitous scales and a convenient spittoon. A hotel employee was killed in the 1969 conflagration that destroyed the building.

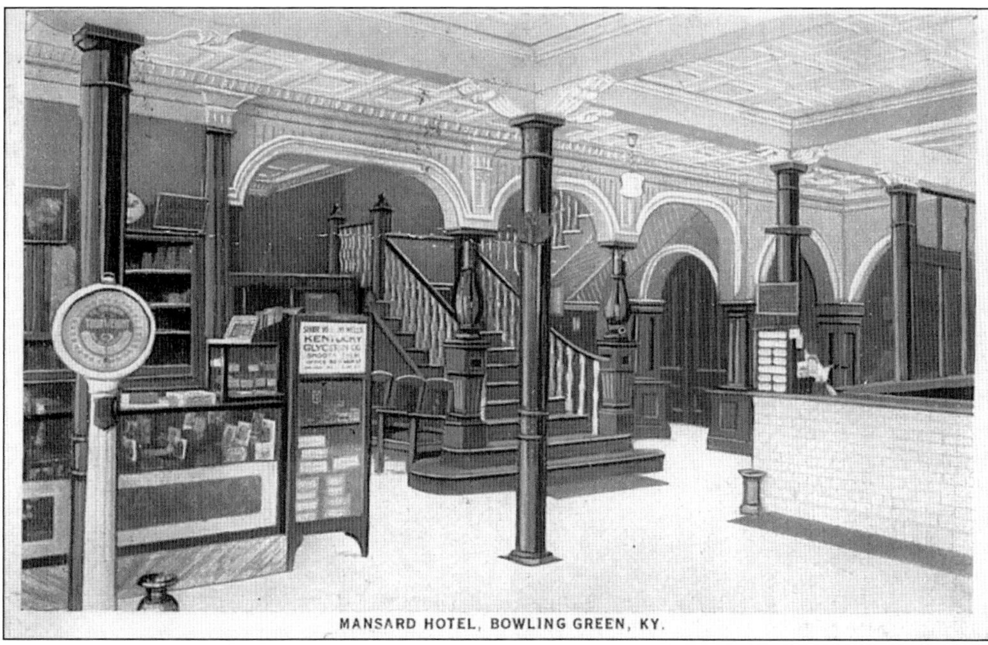

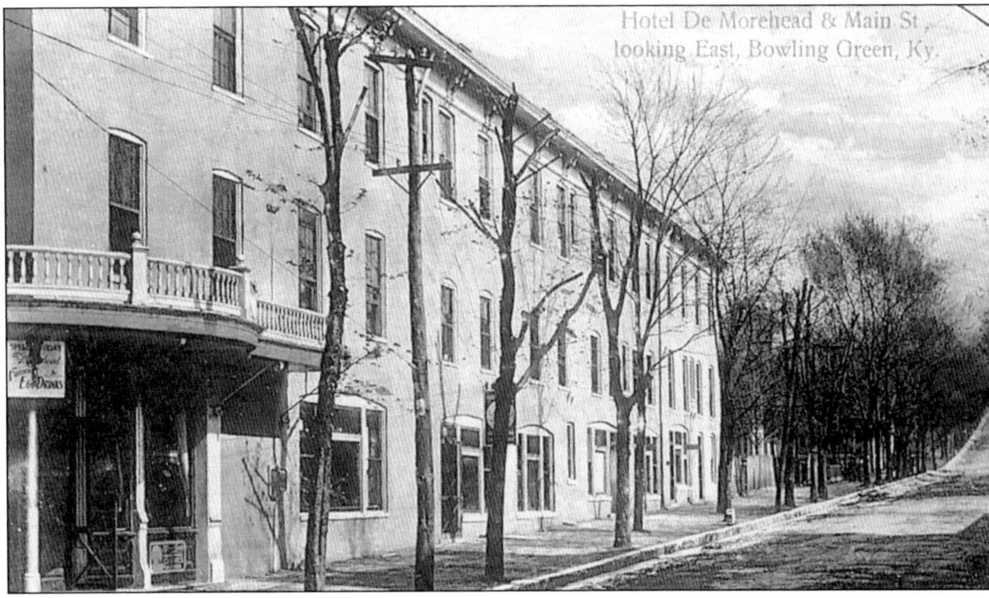

MOREHEAD HOUSE HOTEL. In 1847, Charles D. Morehead constructed this hostelry in a pattern that replicated the Quigley-Younglove Building across Main Street. From 1876 to 1897, the hotel and its dining facilities were operated by the Hess sisters who managed it quite successfully. The hotel was extensively remodeled in 1883 with an additional story added at that time. After a proud heritage, the Morehead was razed in 1923 to make room for the new Helm Hotel.

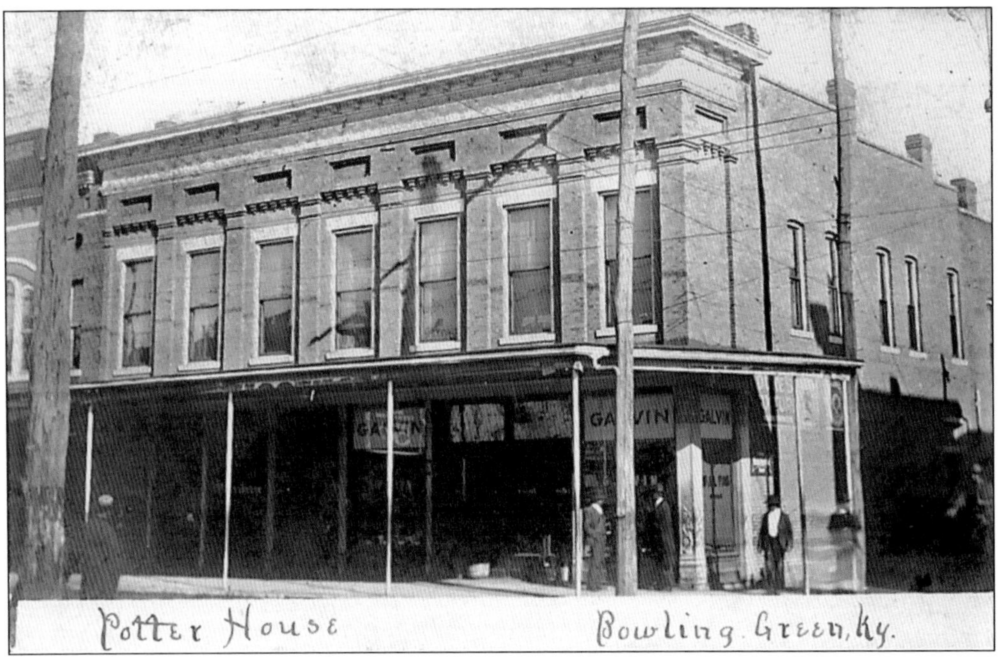

THE POTTER HOUSE. Downtown hotels such as the Potter House, located at the corner of Main and Center Streets, were local landmarks before the 1940s. Because of its lower prices, the Potter House attracted a working class clientele. An examination of any court docket in the 1910s and 1920s will also indicate that the Potter House had plenty of activity, some of it from local prostitutes.

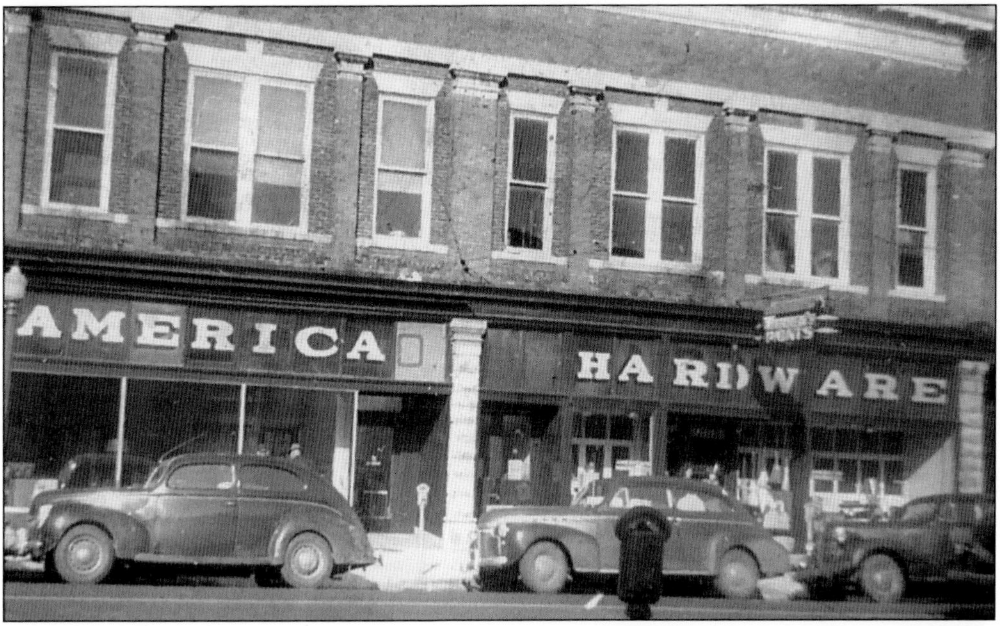

American Hardware. Located at 1023–1025 State Street, this retail establishment was one of south central Kentucky's largest hardware stores. Organized in 1910 by M.E. and B.S. Porter, W.L. Bray, and J.G. Dillard, the store successfully operated for nearly 50 years at this location. It was particularly noted for its farm machinery and auto parts departments. George McIntire built this masonry structure in 1911 after a conflagration destroyed the old Patterson Livery.

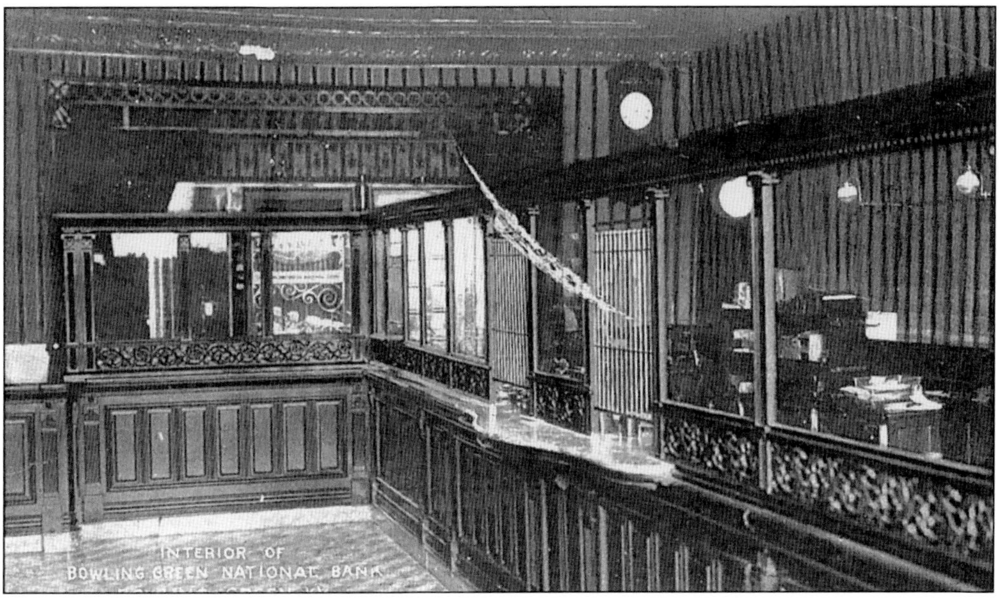

Bowling Green National Bank Interior. This banking institution was organized in July 1905 with a capital stock of $100,000. Located at the corner of Park Row and State Streets, the bank's interior featured brass wickets, a marble top counter, and beautiful walnut wainscoting. Their advertising noted that the "building throughout is thoroughly equipped and everything is safe-guarded to the limit." The bank only remained open six years, closing in July 1911.

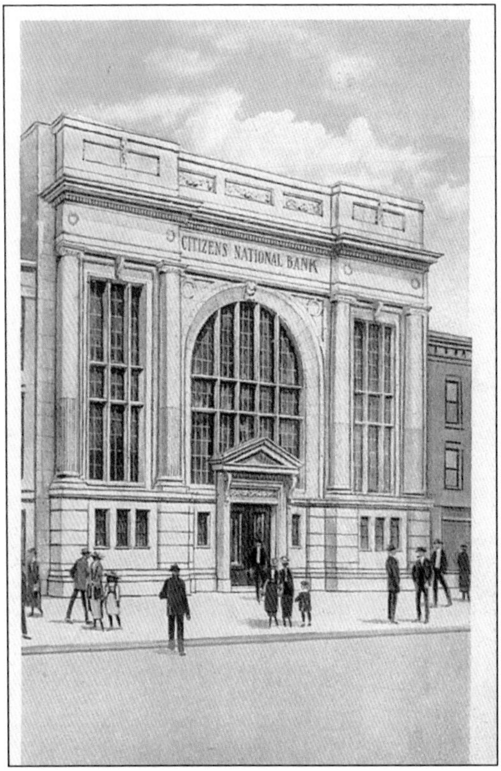

CITIZENS NATIONAL BANK. This longstanding Bowling Green bank opened for business on July 15, 1901, the first national bank in the city. The institution was housed in a substantial three-story building at 439 Park Row. In 1920 they razed that building and constructed this Beaux Arts structure. The newspaper called it "the ultimate in bank design."

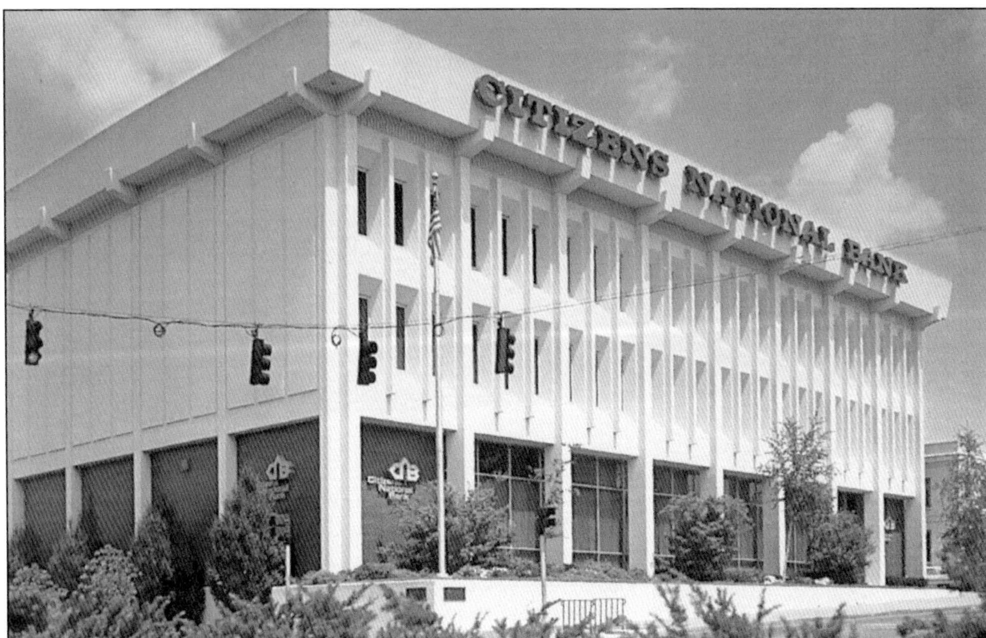

CITIZENS NATIONAL BANK. In 1972 the bank moved to its new facility, a post modern creation designed by H. Lloyd Hill of Atlanta, at the corner of Main and State Streets. In 1991, the bank merged with TransFinancial Bancorp and lost its name.

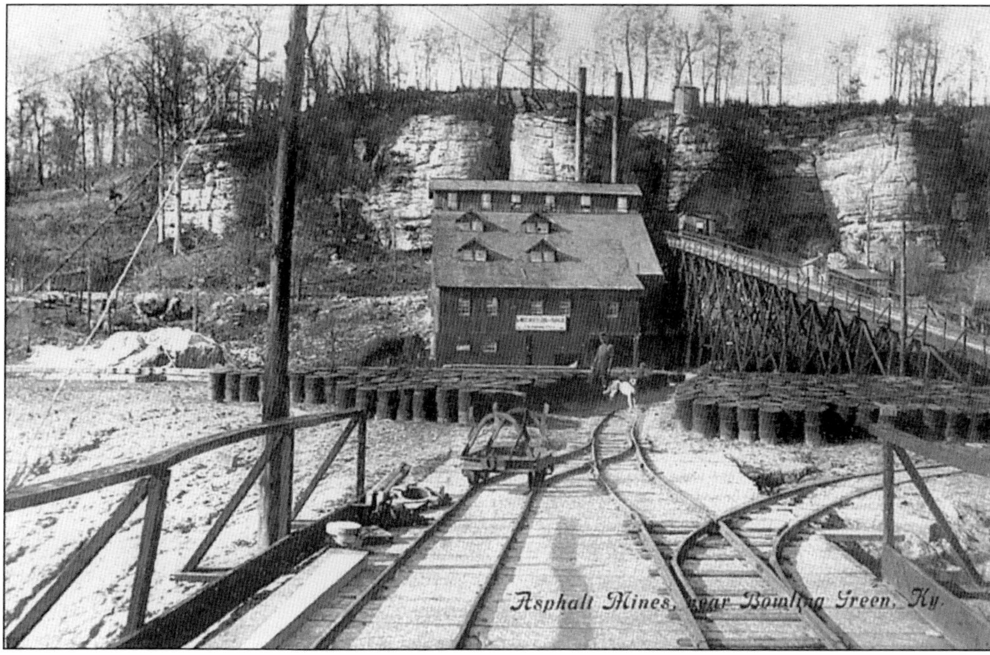

ASPHALT MINES. The largest asphalt mines in the area were located at Kyrock in adjoining Edmonson County. A great amount of this paving material was transferred to Bowling Green via river. From Bowling Green, the asphalt was distributed throughout the Midwest. Chicago at one time boasted that its main thoroughfares were paved with asphalt from Kyrock.

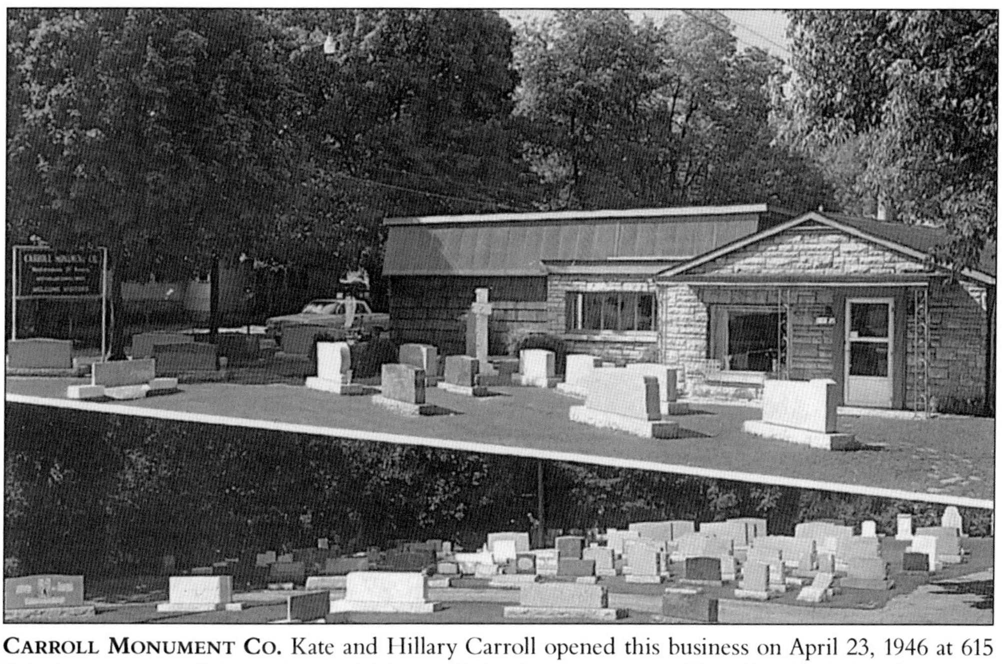

CARROLL MONUMENT CO. Kate and Hillary Carroll opened this business on April 23, 1946 at 615 Fairview to create "Masterpieces of Memory" for their customers. The Carrolls believed that any monument "should be accorded thoughtful deliberation before a final decision is made." At one time the business boasted three acres of monuments of granite or marble from which to choose.

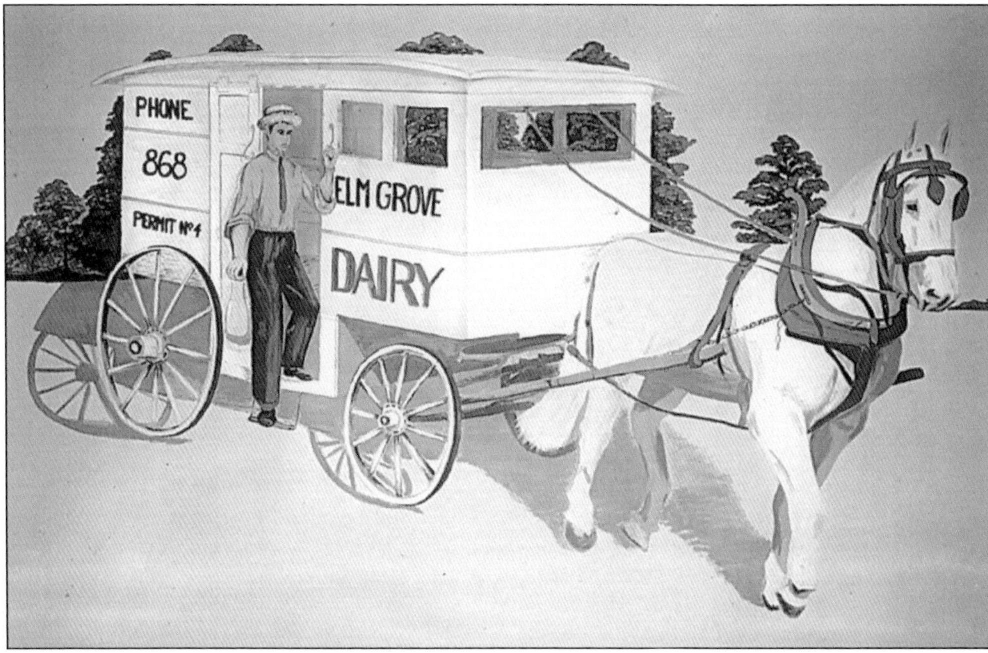

ENTREPRENEURS. Dorothy Reeves executed these murals of early Bowling Green businesses for Reeves Food Center in Fairview Plaza. Elm Grove Dairy was opened in 1922, and its dairy products were delivered by wagon. One horse, Dan, knew his route so well he could stop in front of each customer's house without any sign from the driver. Harry Stevens, one of the city's colorful fruit and vegetable vendors, made his rounds in a customized 1923 Ford truck. These murals were painted over in 1990 when the store was sold to Houchens Markets.

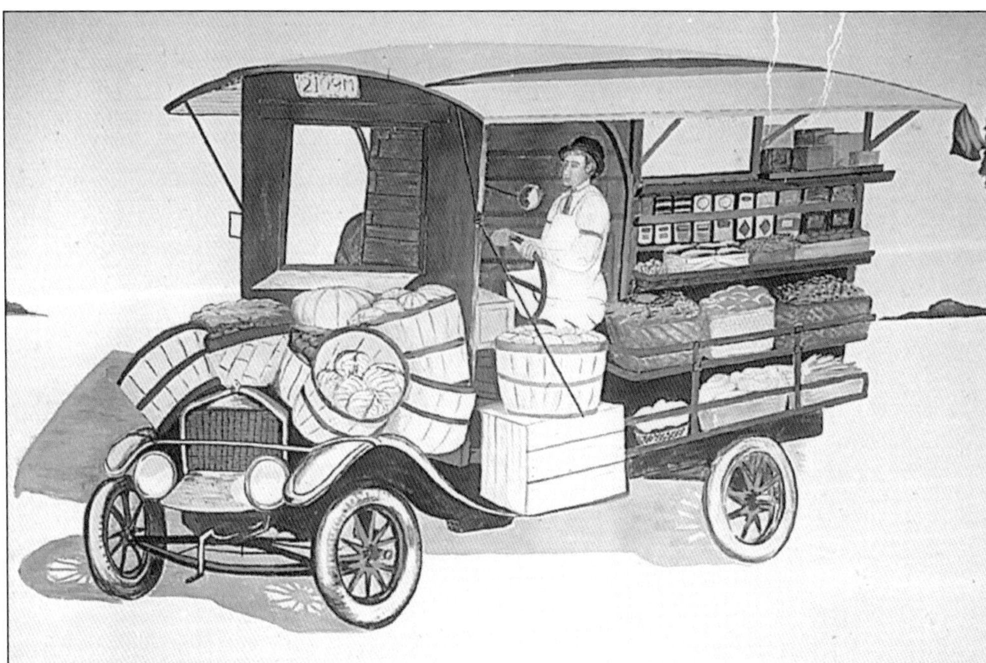

R.L. Morris Advertisement. This Art Nouveau advertisement melds the faces of two hugging women into the shape of a spoon. The card was produced in 1909 to advertise "LaFayette" flatware, which local jeweler R.L. Morris carried in his store. Morris worked for several jewelers before buying out his father-in-law Frank Maier's operation in 1911. Maier had been in the same location at 408 East Main Street since at least 1881.

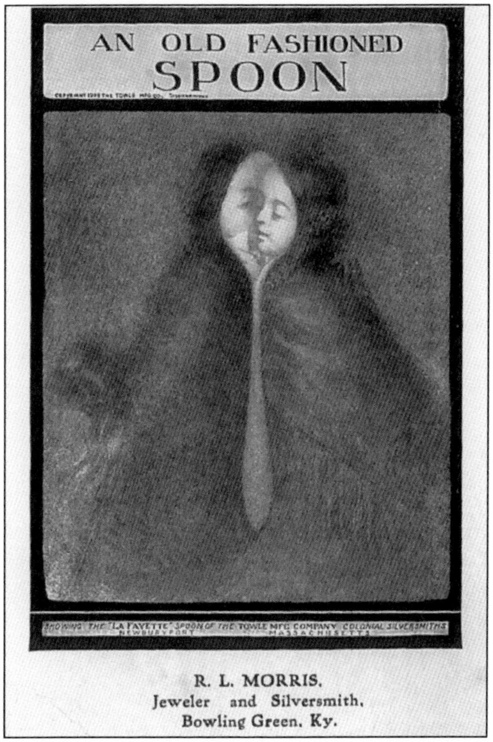

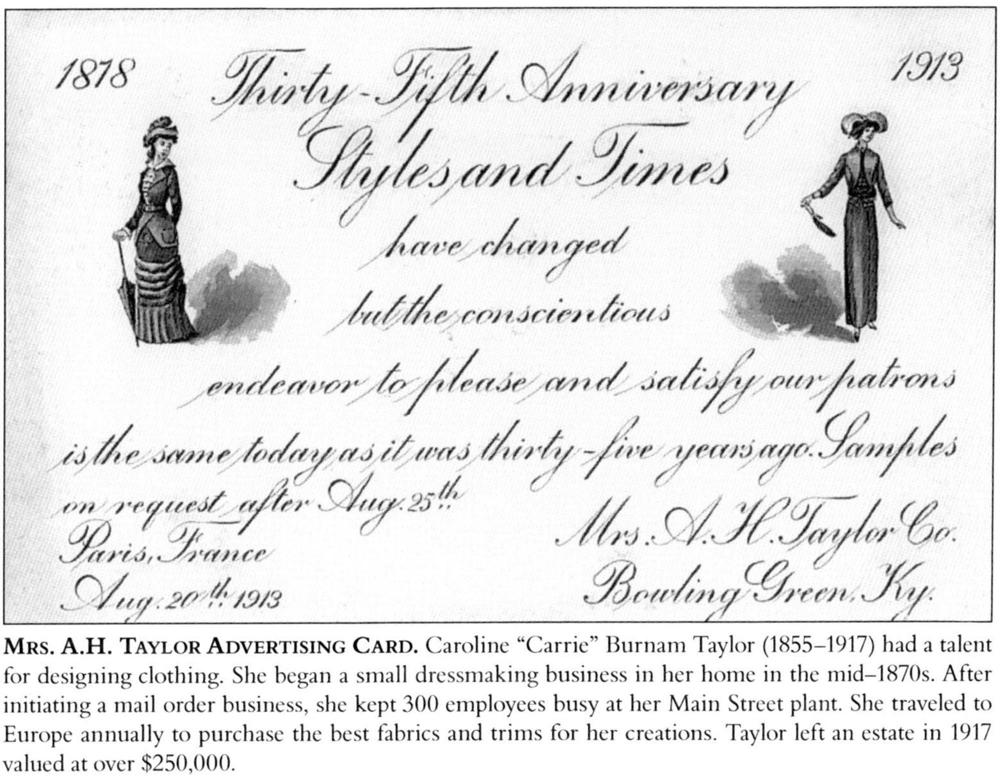

Mrs. A.H. Taylor Advertising Card. Caroline "Carrie" Burnam Taylor (1855–1917) had a talent for designing clothing. She began a small dressmaking business in her home in the mid–1870s. After initiating a mail order business, she kept 300 employees busy at her Main Street plant. She traveled to Europe annually to purchase the best fabrics and trims for her creations. Taylor left an estate in 1917 valued at over $250,000.

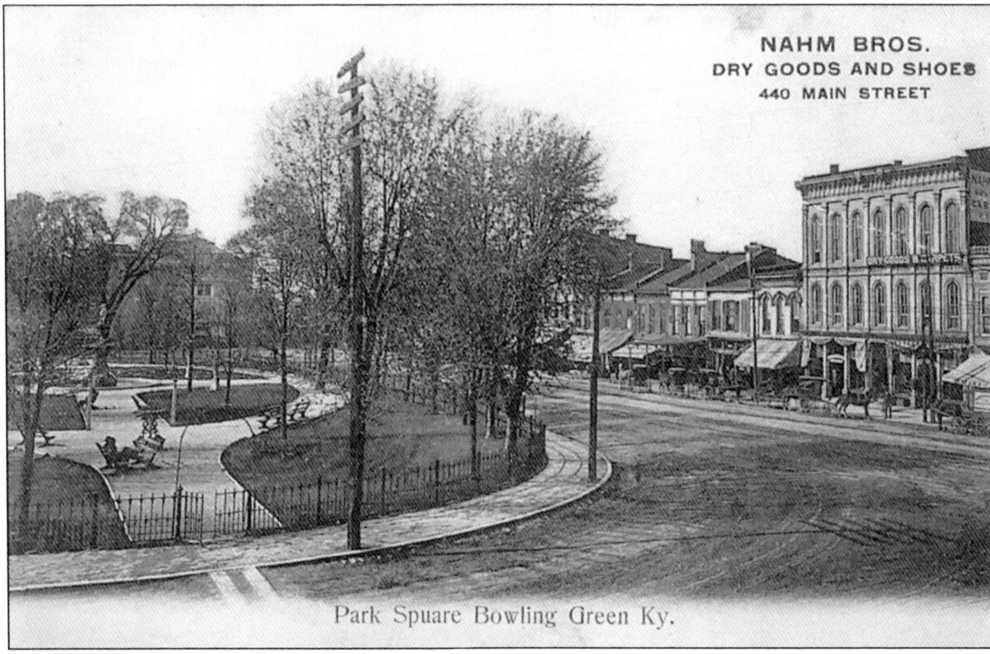

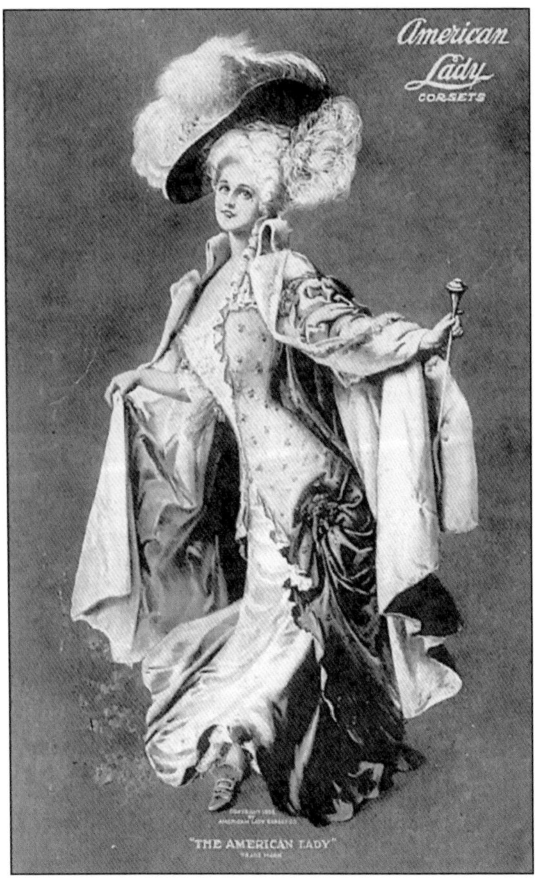

NAHM BROTHERS. The Nahm family were a part of Bowling Green's Jewish community and operated a successful dry goods store first at 440 East Main Street (the three-story building pictured in the foreground). If you look closely, you can see an advertisement painted on the side of the building. Eventually the Nahms constructed a new building several doors down that still bears their name in its attractive cornice.

"THE AMERICAN LADY CORSET." Postcards such as this one represented a continuation of an earlier genre of chromolithograph cards known as advertising cards. Sent in 1911, this postcard advertises a corset sold at Nahm Brothers. The postcard promises a woman that once she donned this contorting contraption she would "note the improvement" in her figure.

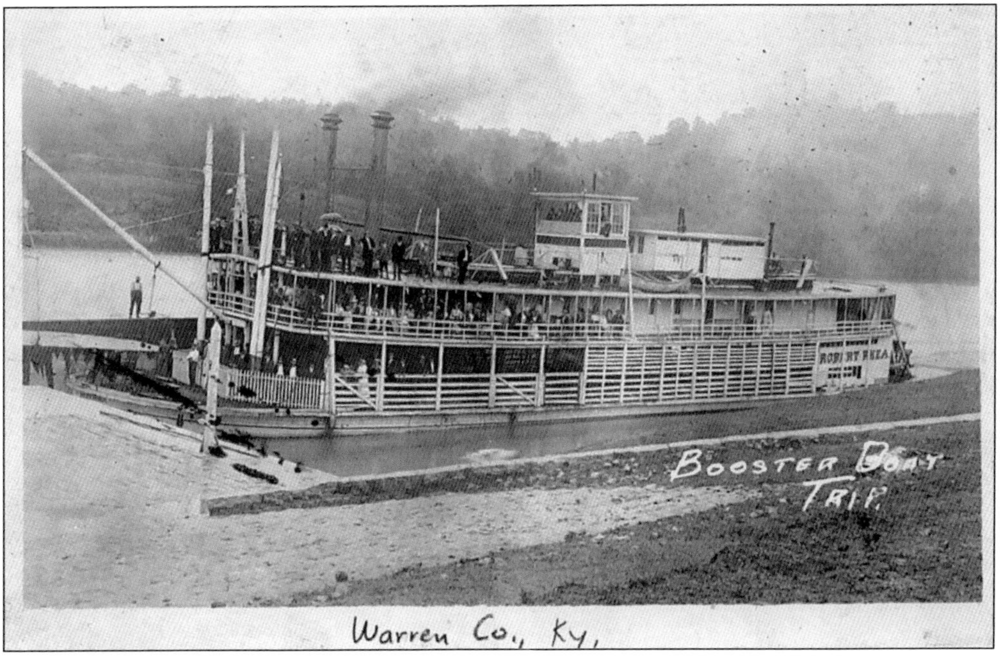

Booster Boat Trip. In the 1910s, local businessmen hired boats once or twice a year to ply the waters of the Green and Barren Rivers to drum up customers for their stores. The boats made stops in small communities along the rivers, where entrepreneurs spent time talking to locals about the products and services they offered in Bowling Green. Locals were encouraged to visit the city and "see for themselves." This particular crowd is aboard the *Robert Rhea* and has come out in the rain to stand on deck and watch the boat rise in one of the locks.

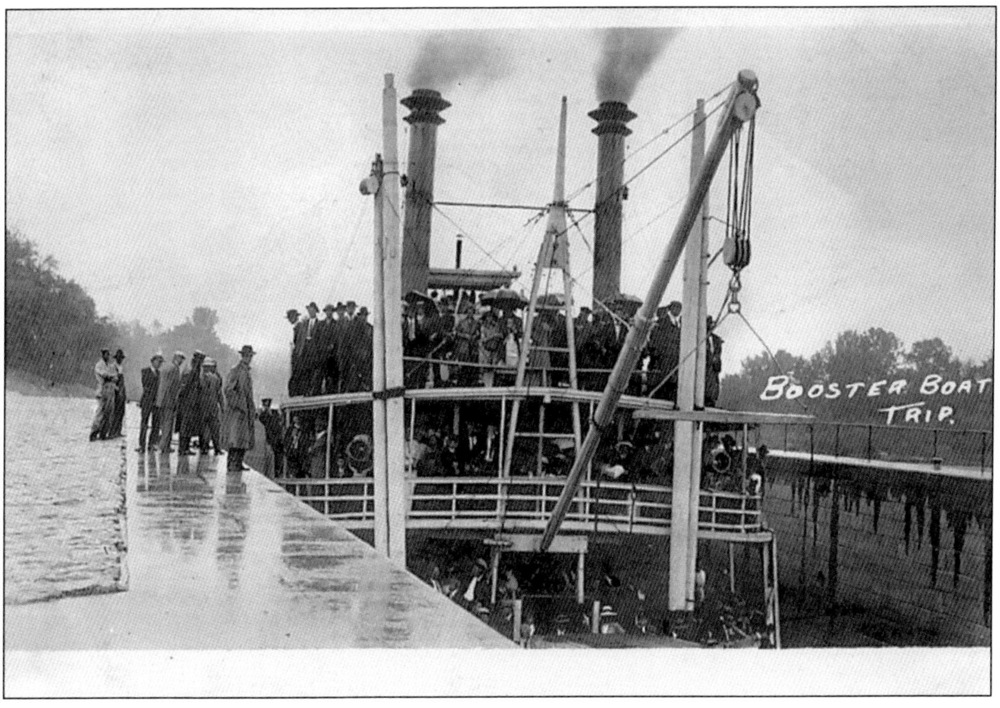

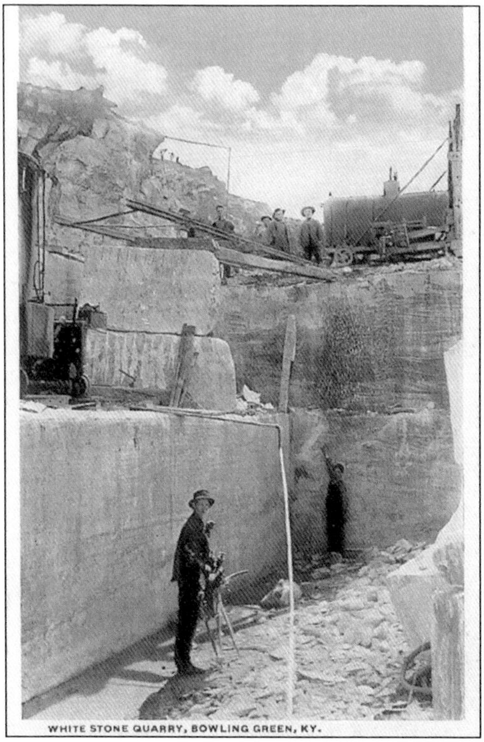

WHITE STONE QUARRY. At one time, Warren County boasted several limestone quarries that produced a superior building stone. Of these, the White Stone Quarry was the largest and supplied the best quality stone. Located approximately four miles west of Bowling Green, the quarry produced a stone noted for its durability, strength, ease of shaping, and its ability to bleach white when exposed to sunlight. Much of the heavy equipment at the quarry was steam powered.

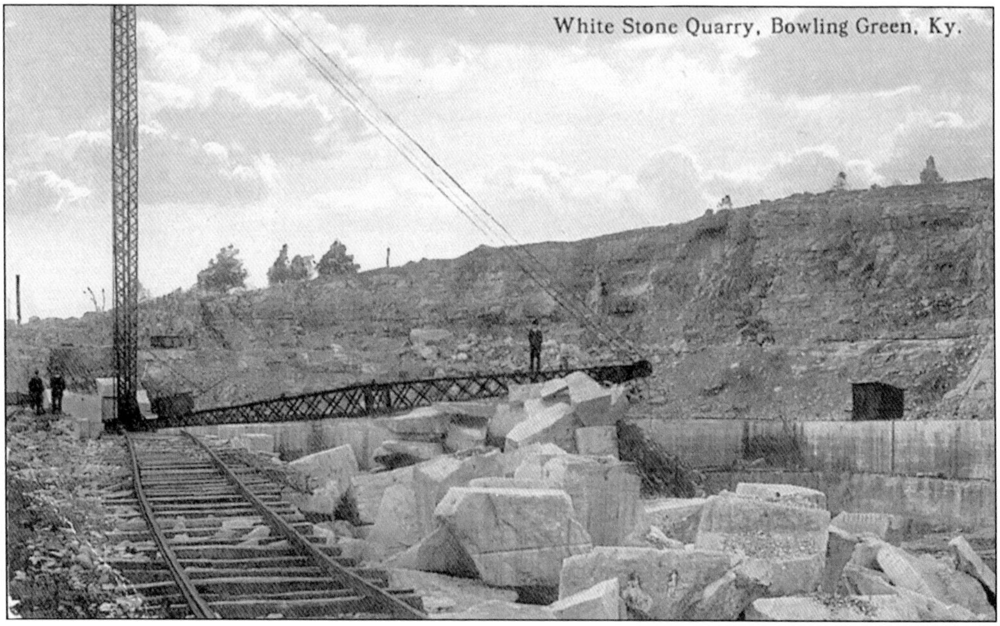

WHITE STONE QUARRY. Although opened in 1833, this quarry's capacity was not fully exploited until a railroad spur reached it in 1872. Tremendous amounts of the stone was shaped by the Southern Cut Stone Factory at its facility on lower Church Street. Architects preferred this wonderful building stone and specified its use for buildings in New York, Philadelphia, Washington, Cincinnati, Louisville, and many other locales. The quarry closed in 1928.

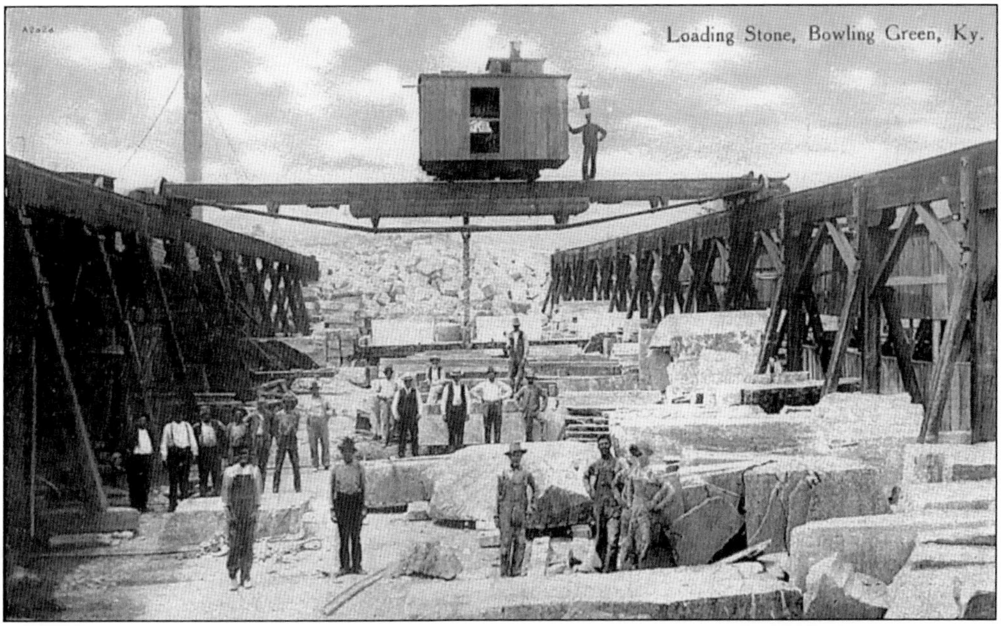

QUARRIES. Besides White Stone Quarry, Warren County boasted a number of smaller stone operations that produced a lesser quality stone. Although some of this stone was quarried specifically for building purposes, a larger amount was used for street and landscape curbing, outdoor ornamentation, and tombstones. Limestone was also quarried and roughly pulverized for gravel or finely ground for an additive to mortar and for a soil enhancement agent.

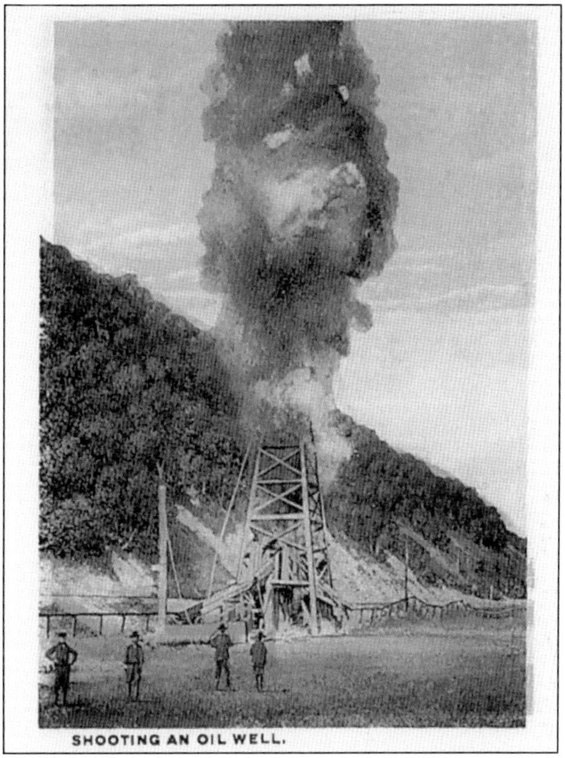

OIL BOOM. This small card, which appeared as part of an accordion Bowling Green "souvenir folder," documents an important but short-lived oil boom in Warren County. The peak period for the boom was from 1917 to 1921, when wildcatters unmercifully pierced Warren County's soil for black gold. Initial success led to the quick conversion of the old Baptist Church on Main Street into a temporary oil exchange.

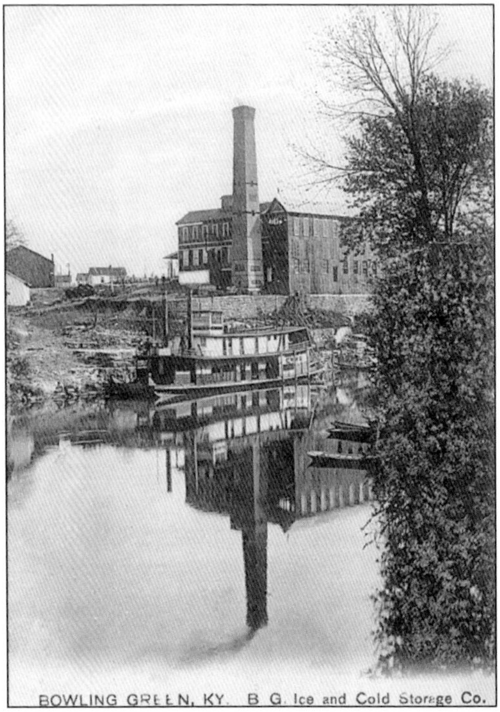

Bowling Green Ice and Cold Storage Co. John A. Robinson and E.B. Seeley established this large ice-making facility in 1888. Located on the boatlanding, the plant had a capacity of 15 tons per day when it was constructed. By 1924, the facility was churning out 100 tons per day. Most of the ice was used locally, but generous quantities were also shipped from here via steamboats and the railroad.

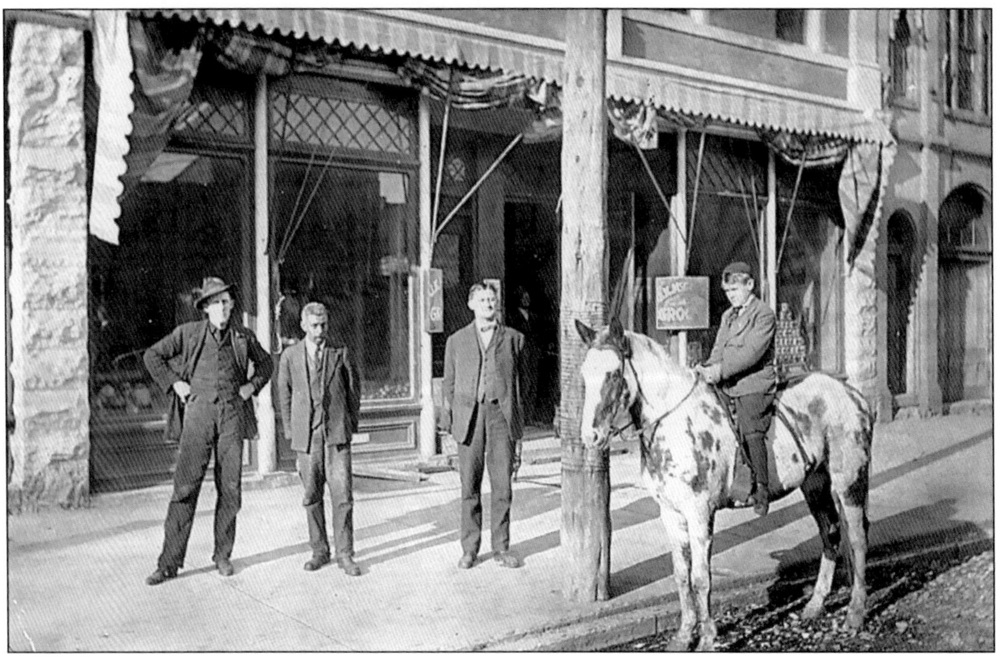

McGinnis Grocery. James Kiah McGinnis (1867–1914), located to the left of the telephone pole, conducted a grocery business at 831 State Street in the first decade of the 20th century. He is pictured with two of his employees and his son, Frank McGinnis (on the pony). McGinnis later served as the city tax collector and as a funeral home director. He seemed convinced that everything was avoidable but death and taxes.

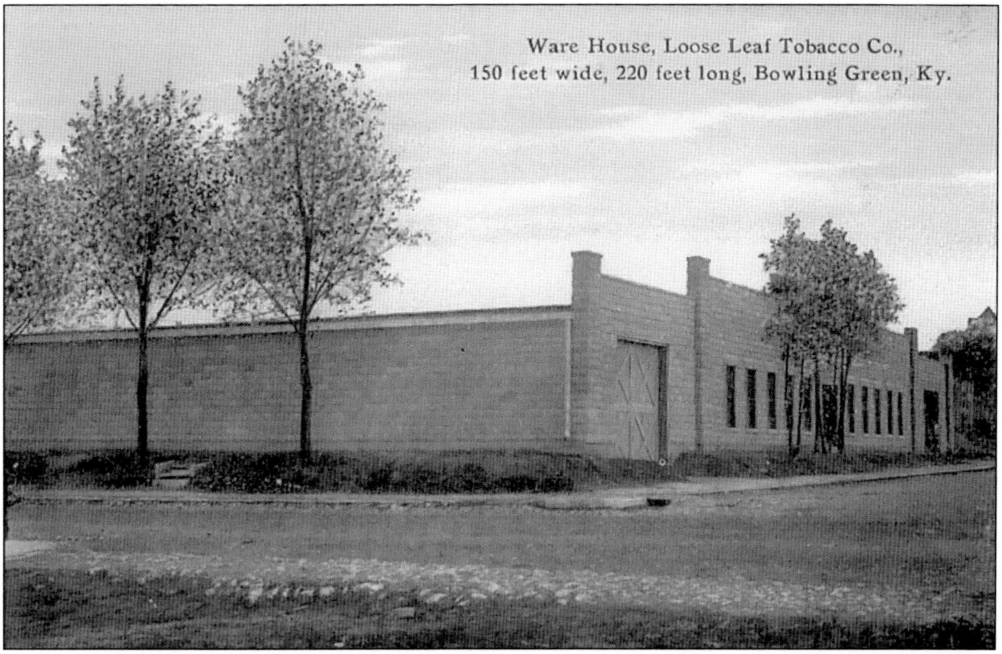

TOBACCO WAREHOUSE. A number of large tobacco warehouses and processing plants were located in Bowling Green. The buildings were, of necessity, large, and many times poorly constructed. Bowling Green was the site of a horrendous disaster in 1922 when a tobacco warehouse and factory owned by the American Tobacco Co. collapsed, killing three.

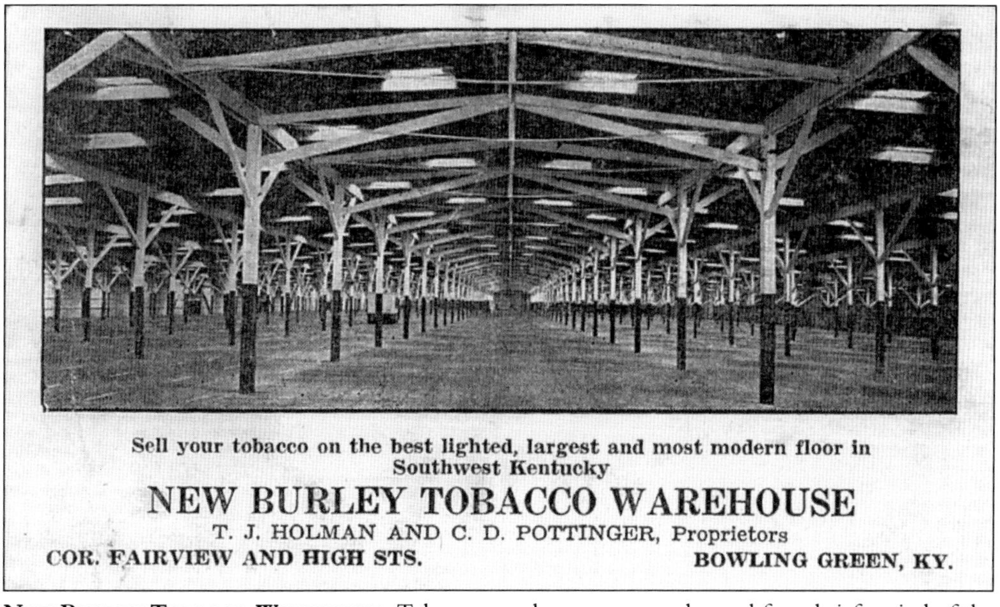

NEW BURLEY TOBACCO WAREHOUSE. Tobacco warehouses were only used for a brief period of the year, so some were not well constructed. This company promotes its facility as "the best lighted, largest and most modern floor in Southwest Kentucky." The postcard was sent to a grower with information on the back telling where his tobacco was located in the warehouse.

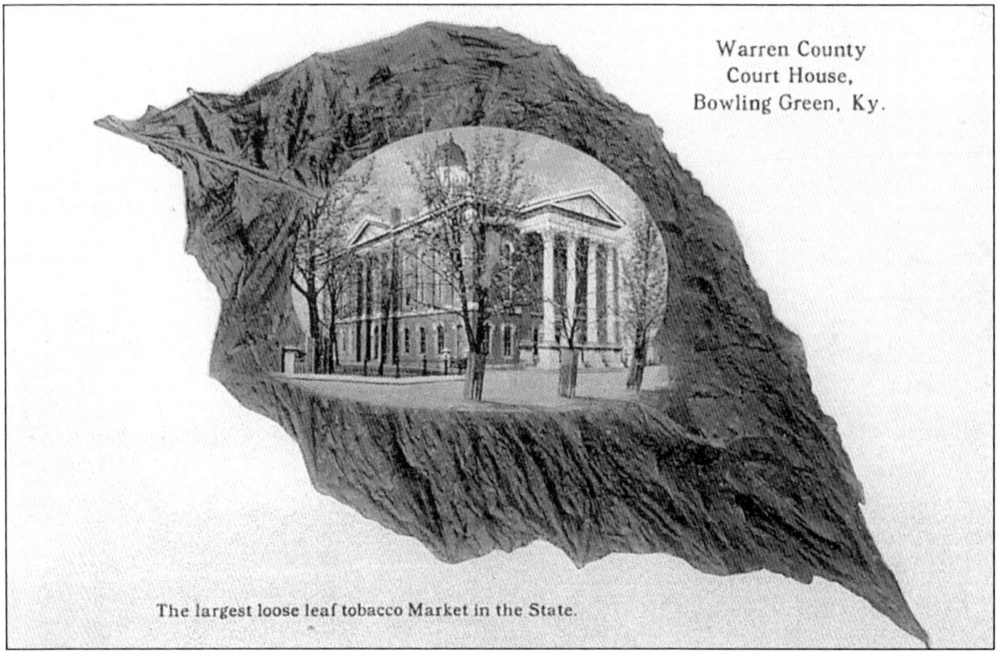

TOBACCO. This image documents how pervasive tobacco culture was in south central Kentucky. The card boasts that Bowling Green is "the largest loose leaf tobacco Market in the State." This was a high claim and difficult to substantiate in that time period, but Warren County has always been one of the state's major producers of burley tobacco.

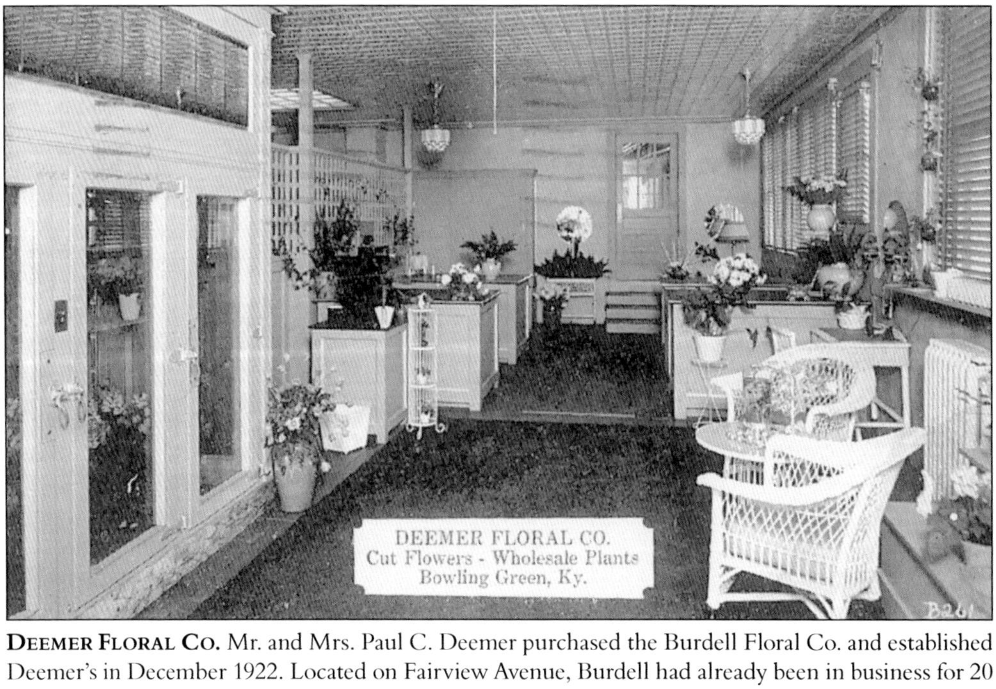

DEEMER FLORAL CO. Mr. and Mrs. Paul C. Deemer purchased the Burdell Floral Co. and established Deemer's in December 1922. Located on Fairview Avenue, Burdell had already been in business for 20 years. With extensive greenhouses, the Deemers operated a large scale nursery and floral shop, shipping flowers and plants throughout south central Kentucky via truck and rail.

PATSY'S PLACE. In 1889, Patsy Henry Fitzpatrick (1861–1927), an Irish immigrant, assumed operation of a 60-year-old family saloon in this building. In 1903, he hired Creedmore Fleenor to remodel the Slade building. The facade appears to be stone, but it is actually concrete. However, the beautiful side entrance is Bowling Green limestone. During Prohibition the operation evolved into an ice cream parlor, "Patsy's Fountain of Youth."

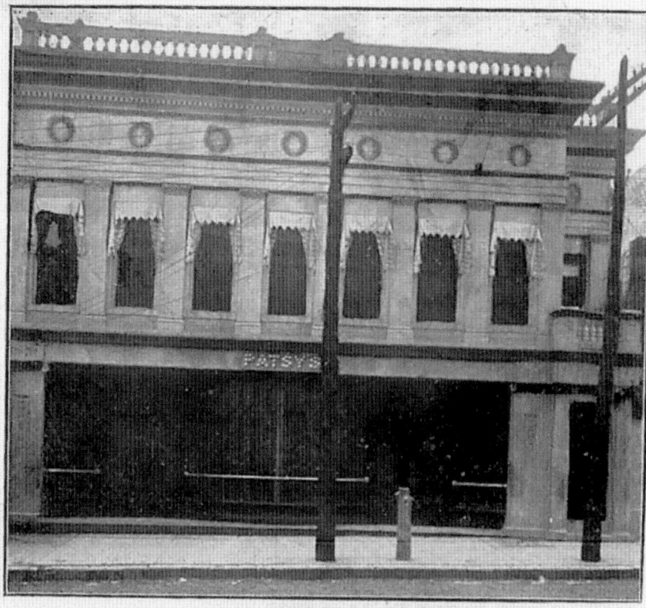

PATSY'S PLACE. Bowling Green, Ky.

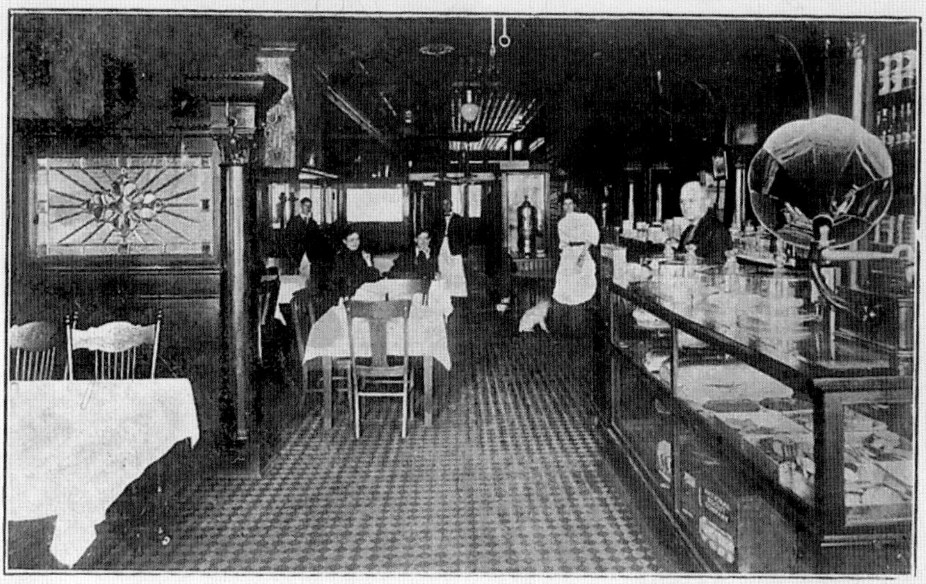

JOE'S RESTAURANT, 443 Park Place, Bowling Green, Ky.

JOE'S RESTAURANT. Located at 443 Park Row, this restaurant was obviously short-lived. It does not appear in any of the post-1905 city directories, and we know that Woolworth's took over that location in 1910. The dress of those pictured indicates a time around the beginning of the 20th century. Look carefully at the foot of the standing woman, and you will see that the cafe had its own cat to keep away unpaying mice.

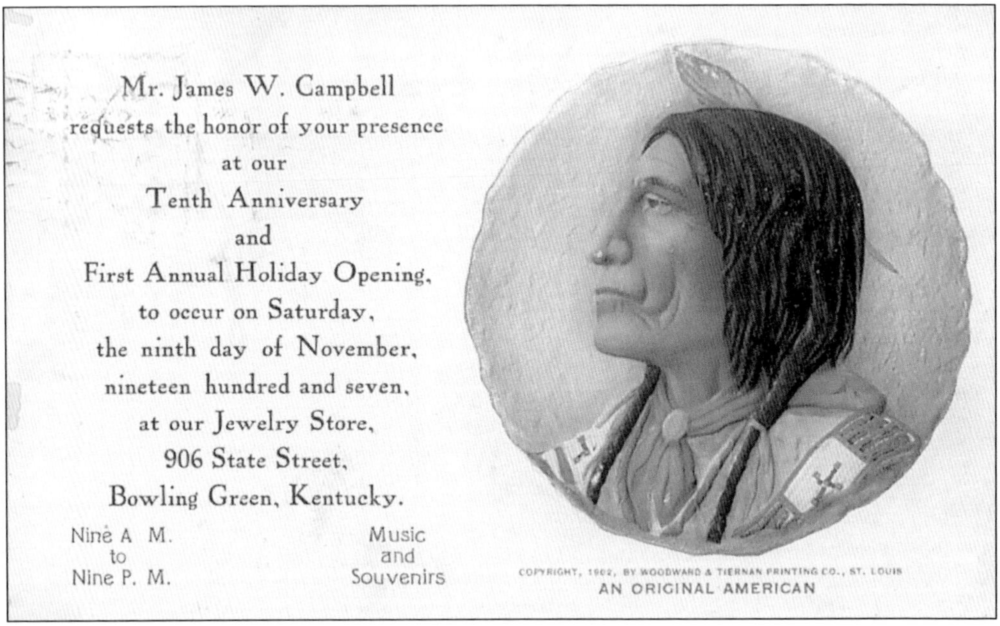

CAMPBELL JEWELRY. Located at 906 State Street, the Campbell Jewelry store used this stock postcard to send a sales announcement to its prized customers. The 1907 sale was to commemorate their 10th anniversary and the beginning of the holiday shopping season. James W. Campbell operated this store into the mid-1940s when it became Howard's Jewelry.

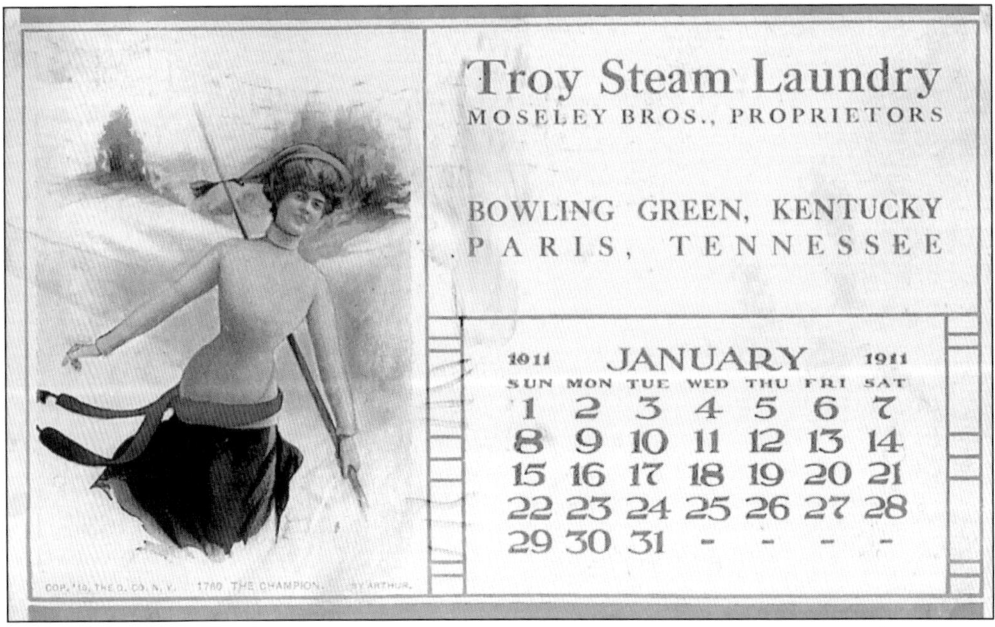

TROY STEAM LAUNDRY. The Moseley Brothers, owners of the Troy Steam Laundry, sent this postcard to customers directly after the holiday season to remind them that proper care of clothing extends its life. The card noted that "Christmas gifts" of "lingerie, handkerchiefs, neckwear, and shirts can't lose their prettiness sooner than by careless laundering." They even suggested sending the business a postcard and they would call to pick laundry up.

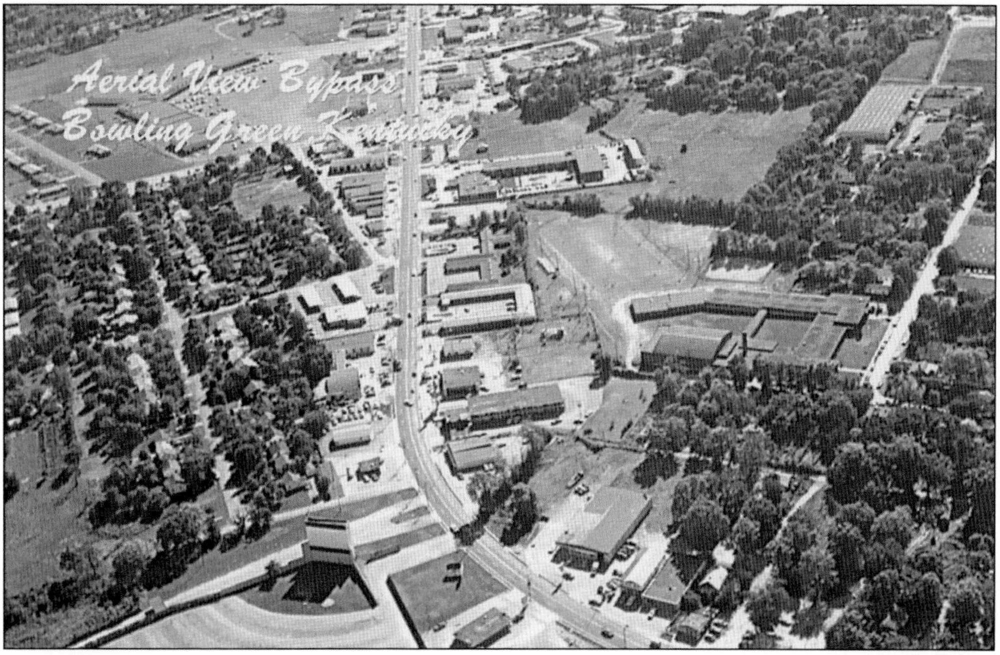

The 31-W By-Pass. The completion of the by-pass in the late 1940s around the eastern part of Bowling Green allowed for a business boom away from downtown. It wasn't long before the area was populated with court motels, car washes, service stations, strip malls, and restaurants, which provided respite for the tremendous number of travelers using the Dixie Highway. In the left foreground is the old Riverside Drive-In, which opened in 1950 and closed in 1985.

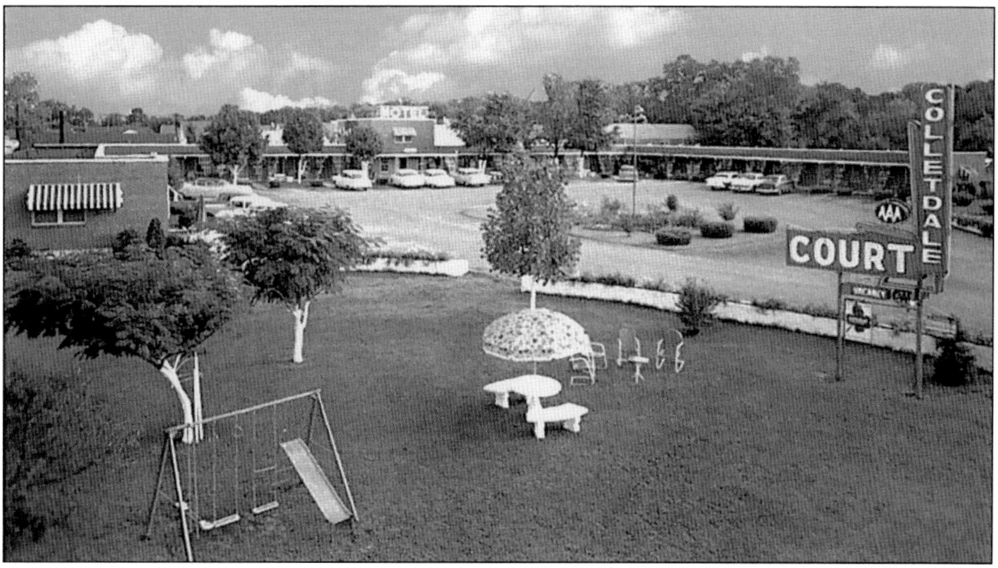

Colletdale Court. The Colletdale Court was built in the late 1950s on the new 31-W By-Pass. The Colletdale's 31 air-conditioned rooms were advertised as having "free TV in rooms, ceramic tiled baths, tub and shower in each room, and carpeted floors." Developers replicated this horseshoe court hotel in cookie cutter fashion along the by-pass and the Dixie Highway. People loved driving their automobile right up to the door of their room.

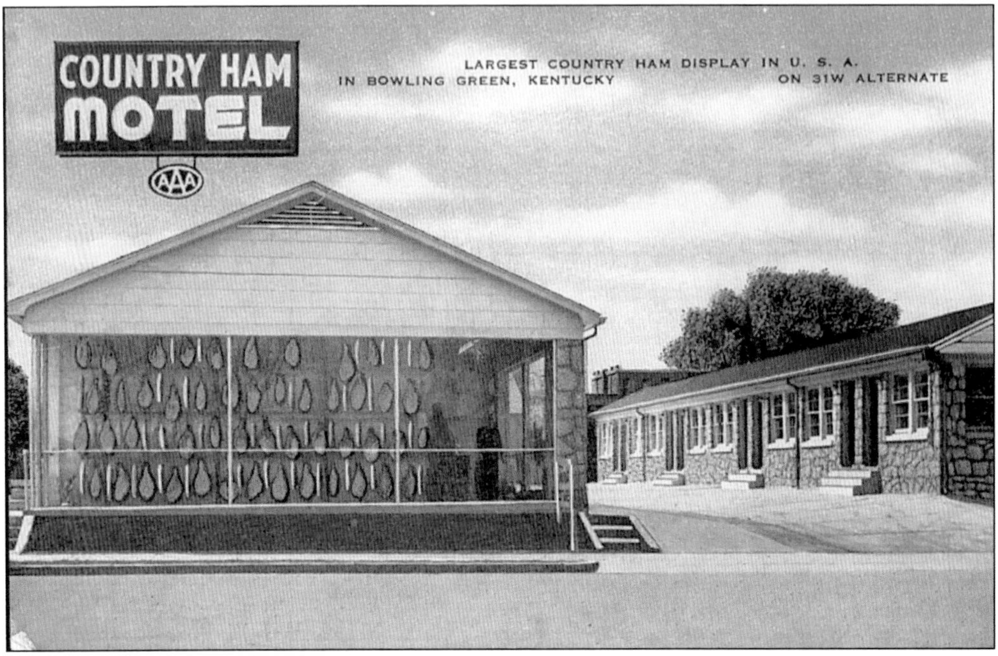

COUNTRY HAM MOTEL. Jimmie Siddens combined his court motel, located at the lower end of the 31W By-Pass, with a Kentucky favorite, the hickory smoked country ham. This delicacy judiciously blends the meat's natural sweetness with the salt used for curing. Smoking adds the delicate wood bouquet. These prices are from the early 1950s. Siddens's ham business was a local institution for years, because his advertising was correct—"Everybody likes 'em."

OLD KENTUCKY COUNTRY HAMS

"EVERYBODY LIKES 'EM"

Real Hickory Smoked—Size 15 to 30 Pounds

6 Month Old Country Hams — 80c per Lb.
One Year Old Country Hams 90c per Lb.
Two Year Old Country Hams 98c per Lb.
Lean Hickory Smoked Bacon, 4 to 10 lb. Slab 55c per Lb.
Real Country Smoked Sausage, 3 to 5 lb. Bags 55c per Lb.
Sliced Country Ham, Two Years Old $1.45 per Lb.

FINE GIFTS FOR NOW OR CHRISTMAS

We Ship C. O. D. or Send Check. Guaranteed Good. Order Now!

Jimmie Siddens Country Ham Motel

Motel Phone 6171 — On Alternate 31-W Route
Business Phone 5141 — 521 First Street
Residence Phone 5141 — Bowling Green, Ky.

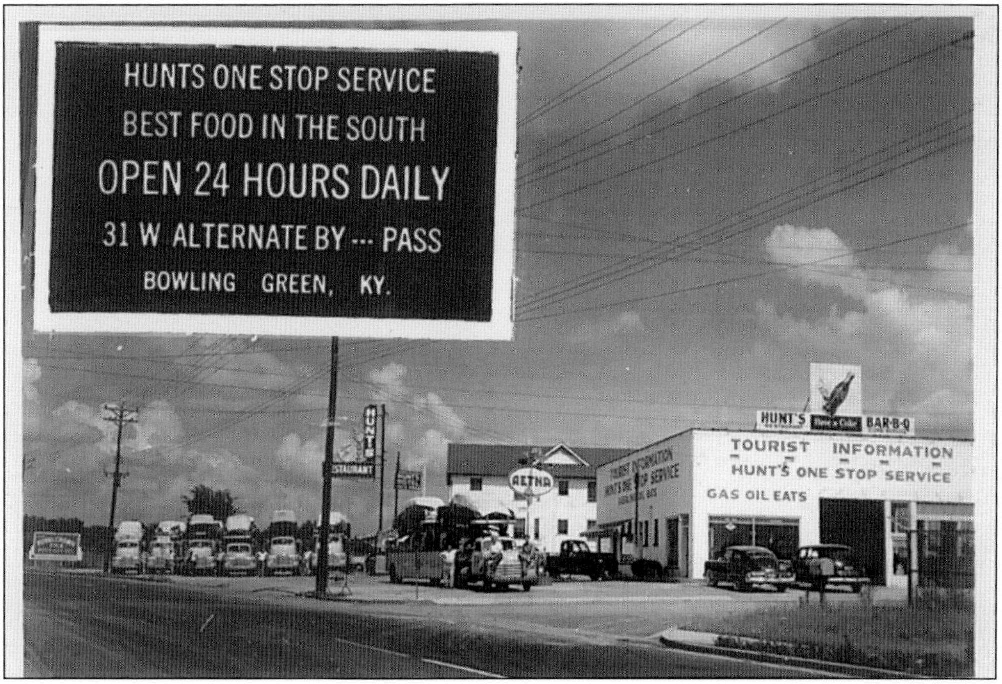

HUNT'S ONE STOP. Convenience was the name of the game for the American traveler when the by-pass began to develop in the early 1950s. At Hunts One Stop you could stop 24 hours a day to service your car, eat a barbecue dinner, pick up food items at the grocery, get tourist information, or check into the Hunt's Motel at 1516 Laurel Avenue.

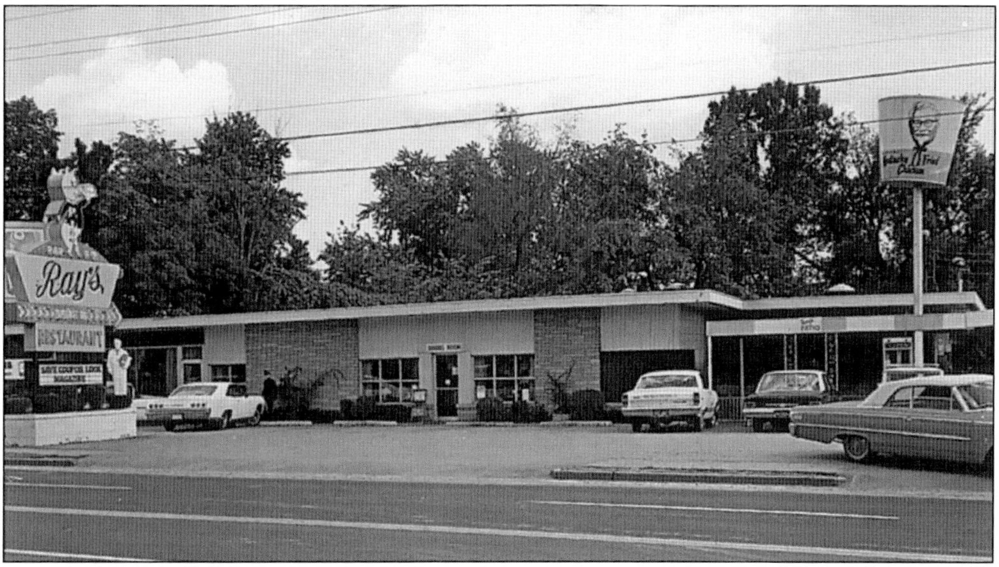

RAY'S DRIVE-IN. Charles Ray Woosley opened a restaurant at 736 College Street in the mid-1960s. When he saw the number of cars traveling on the by-pass, he opened a drive-in on lower Laurel Avenue. He advertised real pit barbecue and service at your car. Woosley was an early Kentucky Fried Chicken franchisee, and the Colonel and his bucket are prominently displayed. Woosley later operated a successful catering establishment.

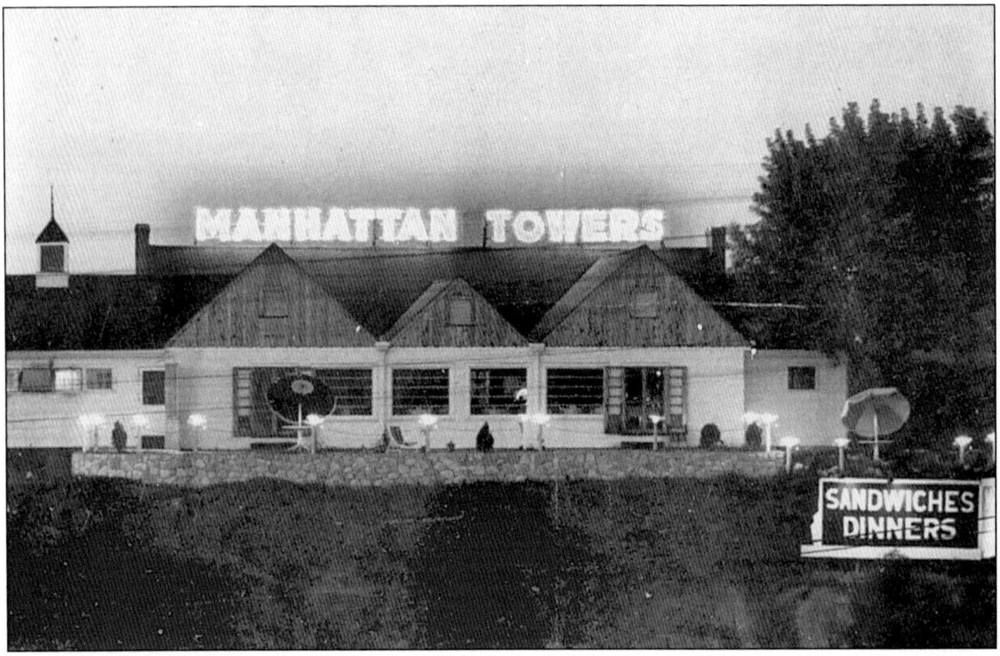

MANHATTAN TOWERS. This unique supper club at 109 Old Louisville Road was designed, owned, and operated by Frank McDaniel. It opened for business on February 18, 1950 and featured a lovely skyline of Manhattan in the dining room. Organ music was played nightly for many years, and local radio station WKCT broadcast the concerts. Its food was feted as highly original and delicious. The lights were turned off for good in 1970.

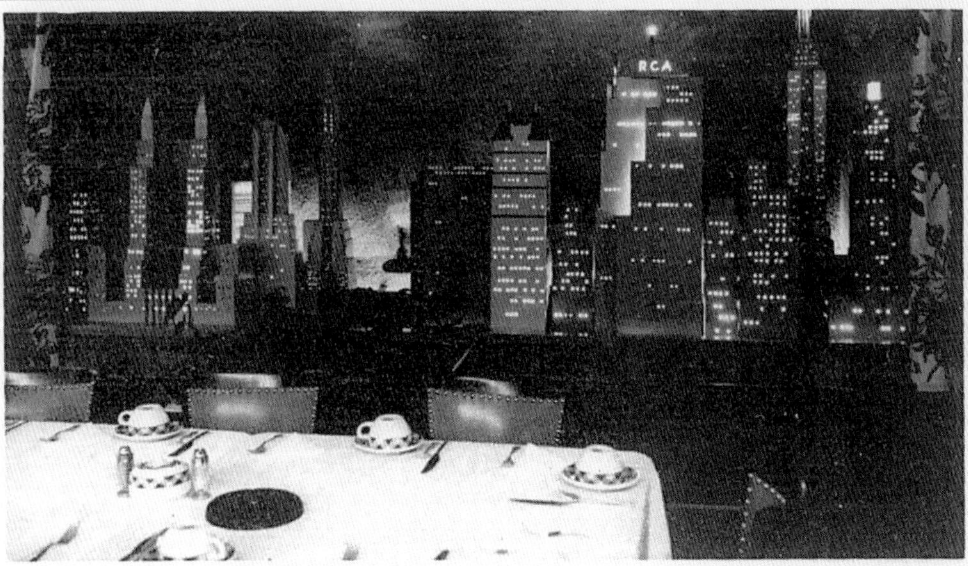

Panaroma of New York Skyline - MANHATTAN TOWERS - Bowling Green, Ky.

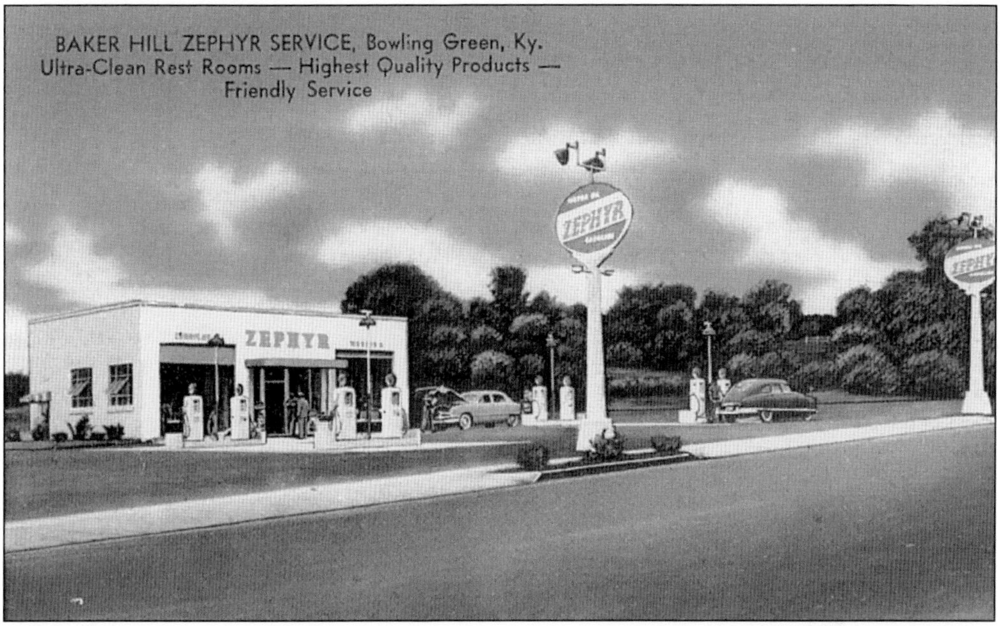

SERVICE STATION. This Zephyr Service Station was located at the foot of Baker Hill. It guaranteed "Ultra-Clean Rest Rooms, Highest Quality Products and Friendly Service." It was a convenient stop right off the Louisville Road. The owner also noted on the back of the card the historical significance of its location, as it had been "used as a fort during the war between the states."

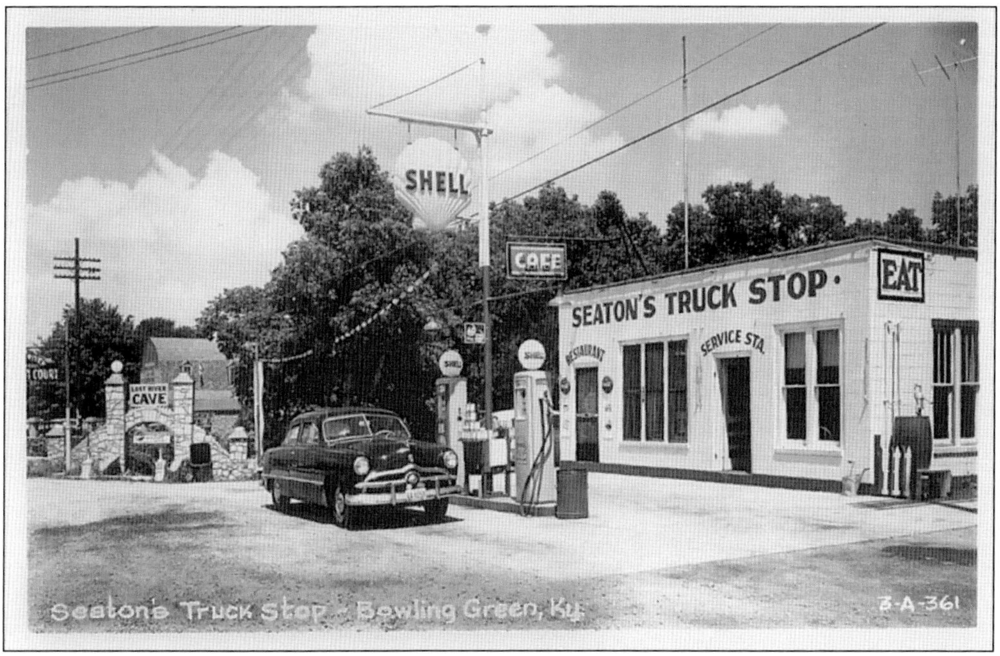

SEATON'S TRUCK STOP. This all-purpose service stop was located at the top of Lost River Cave. Patrons could eat at the restaurant, fill up with gas, or stretch out in comfortable lawn chairs under trees behind the facility.

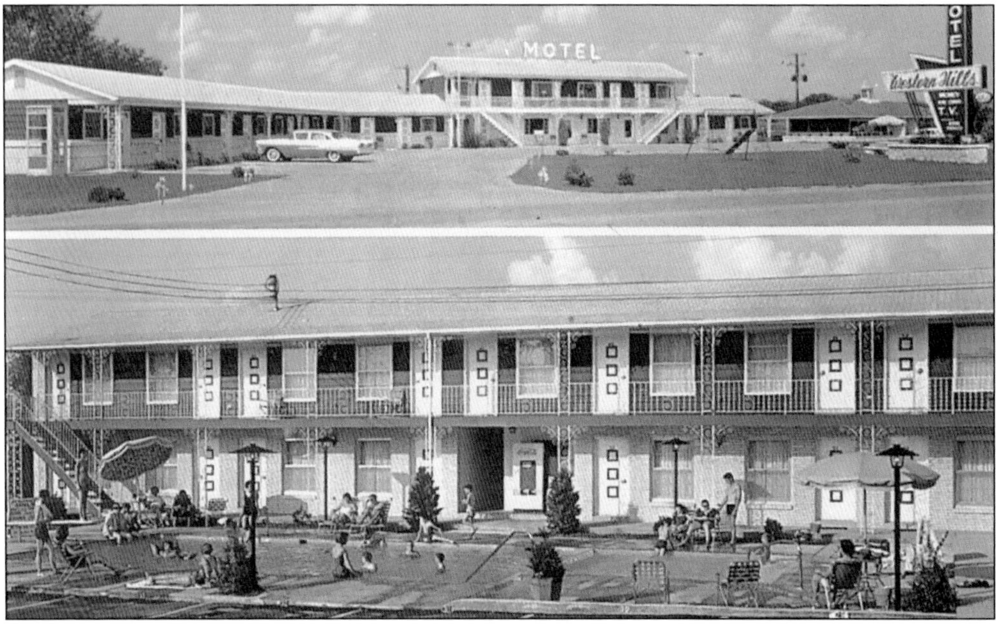

WESTERN HILLS MOTEL. This 42-room hotel was built close to Western Kentucky University to help house guests near the school. Most of the city's other hotels were downtown or on the 31-W By-Pass. Western Hills's advertising always mentioned its large swimming pool in capital letters. The adjacent restaurant became a favorite student hangout in the 1960s and 1970s. The distinctive metal and neon sign was removed in the middle-1990s.

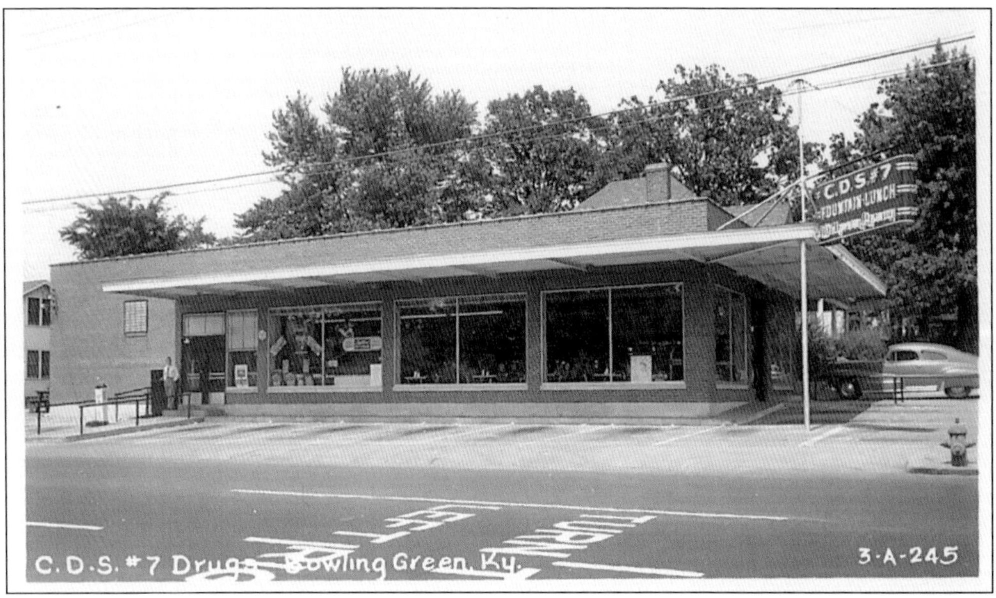

C.D.S. DRUGSTORE. The Carpenter Dent Sublett chain of drugstores was founded in 1912 in Bowling Green, and the number of outlets eventually numbered 10. The store pictured here, C.D.S. #7, was built in 1949 at the corner of Broadway and Laurel Avenue. It was remodeled and a floor was added for professional offices in 1954. One of its favorite amenities was a full-service lunch counter. It was razed in 1999 and replaced by a Walgreen's.

Three

WESTERN KENTUCKY UNIVERSITY

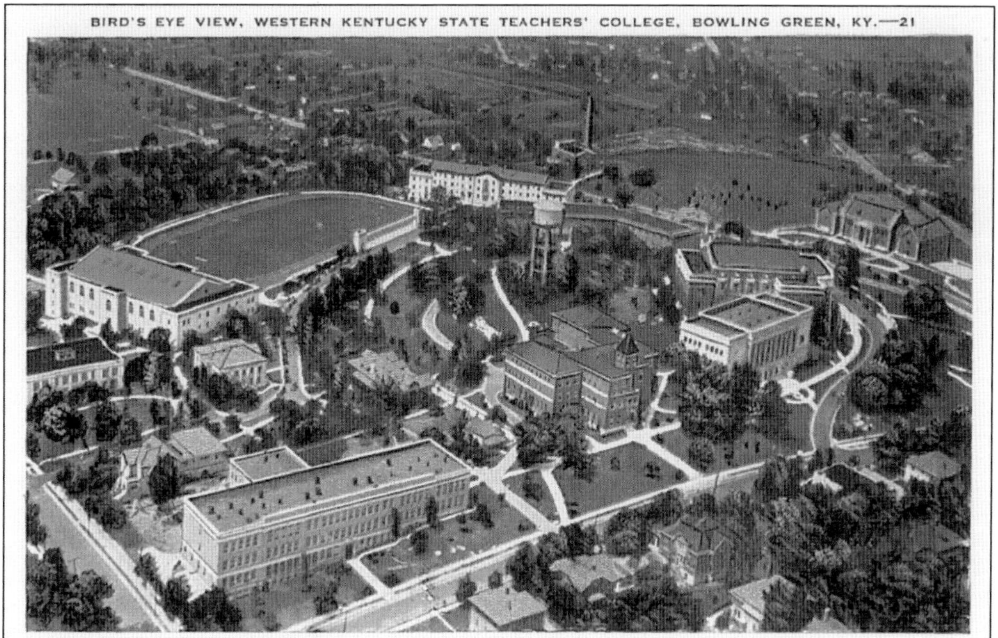

WESTERN KENTUCKY UNIVERSITY (WKU). This aerial view demonstrates the planned circular arrangement of building's at WKU, which allowed each building to dominate its own location around the hill's perimeter. It also preserved the old Civil War fort—known as Fort Albert Sidney Johnston—at the center of campus. This postcard was made just before the razing of the old Recitation Hall, which was replaced by Cherry Hall in 1937.

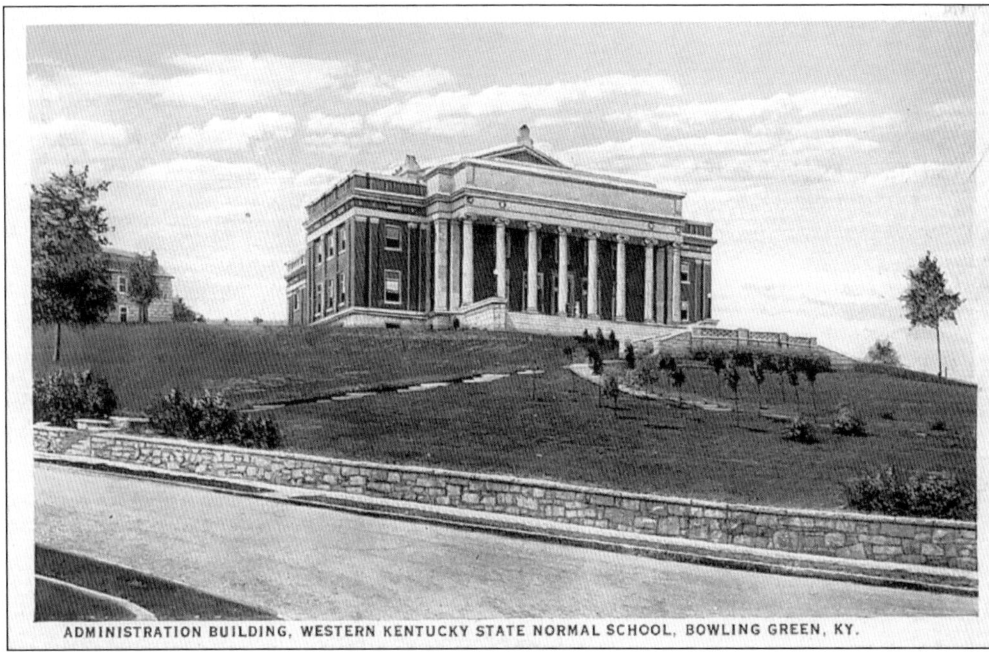

VAN METER. Perched atop College Heights, Van Meter Auditorium has been the gathering spot for educational, social, and arts events at WKU since its dedication on May 5, 1911. Its Classical Revival style is accentuated with a stately portico, graceful Ionic columns, and limestone detailing. WKU named the building for Capt. Charles J. Van Meter, an early riverboat captain and the school's first chancellor. The building, resembling a Greek temple atop College Heights, initially held administrative offices and a fine 1,600-seat auditorium, where students gathered for chapel. Even today, there are few scenes in Bowling Green more spectacular than coming out of Van Meter after an event in the winter and viewing the valley of twinkling lights.

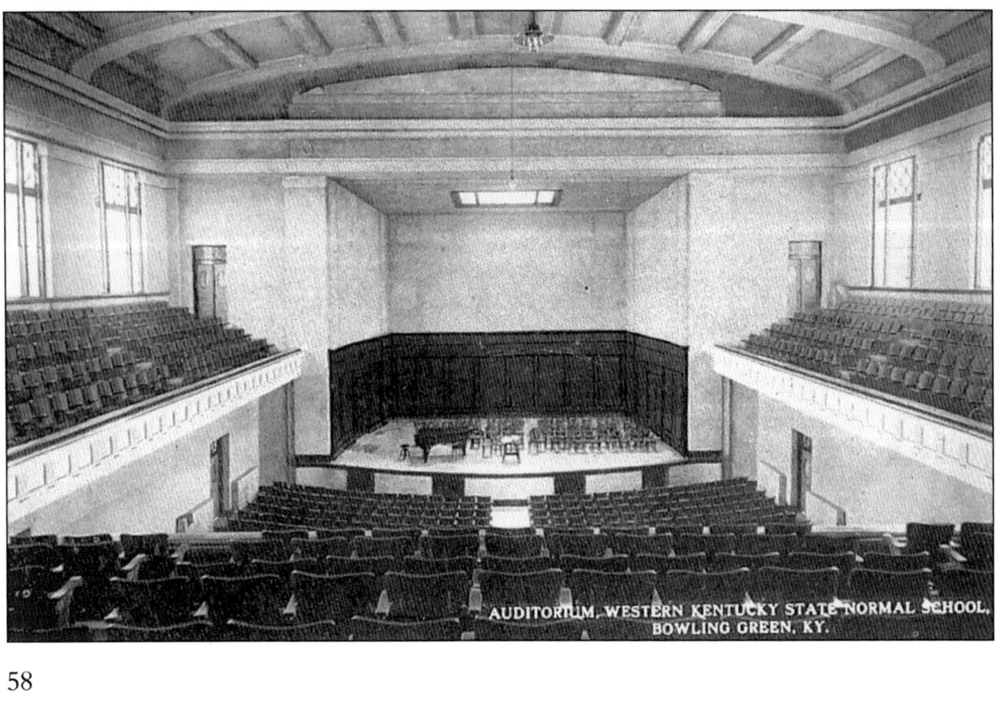

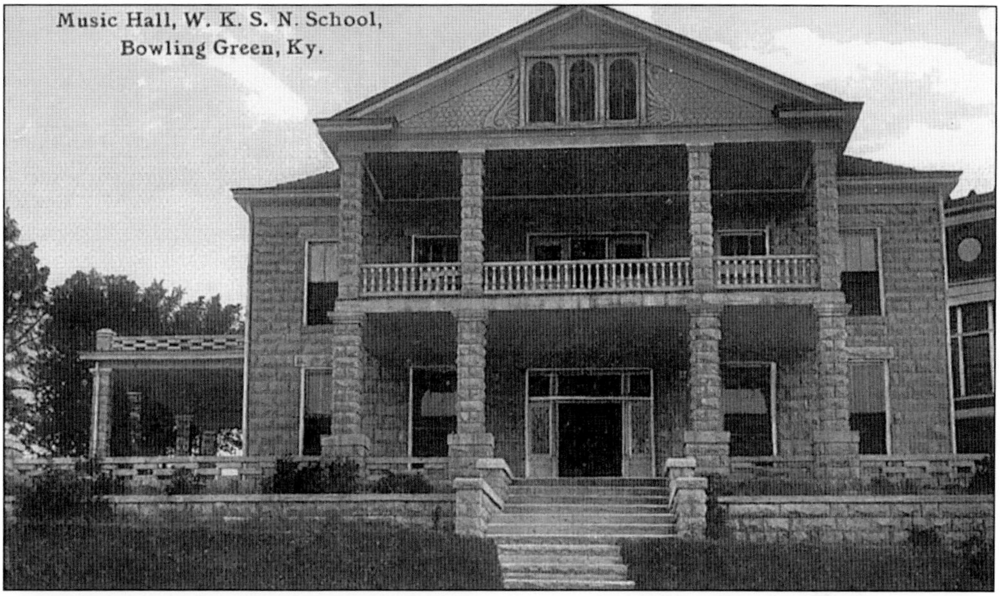

CABELL HALL. This building was originally constructed as the home of B.J. Cabell, the president of Potter College. When WKU moved to the hilltop in 1911, the home was used for music and home economics classes. In 1927, this area of campus was commandeered as a space for the new library. Architect Brinton B. Davis used salvaged material from this home to construct the new Home Economics building, which was razed in 1982.

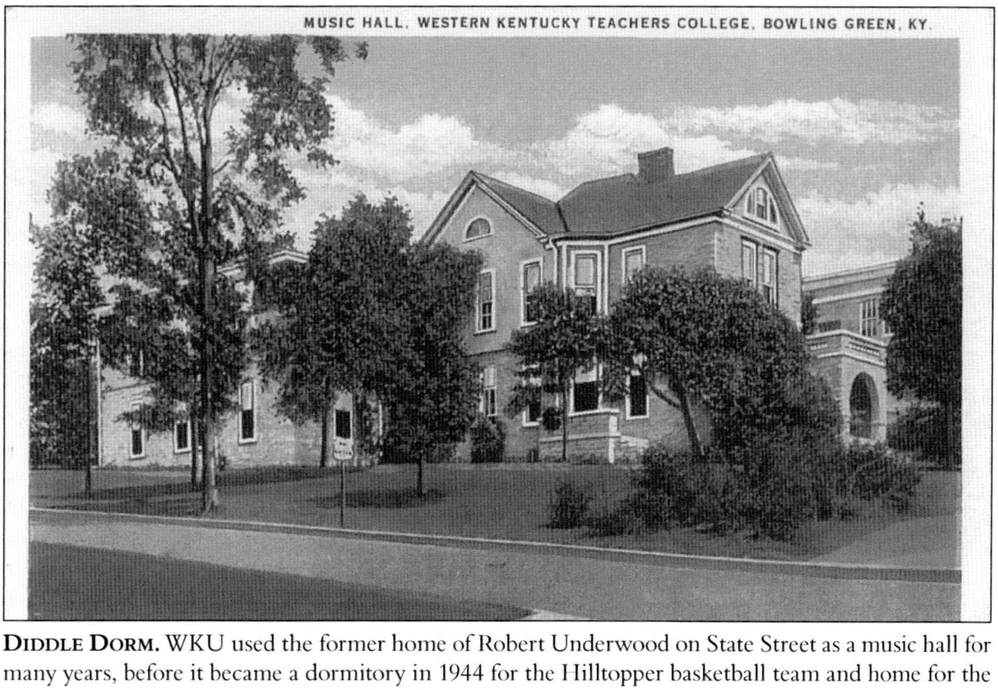

DIDDLE DORM. WKU used the former home of Robert Underwood on State Street as a music hall for many years, before it became a dormitory in 1944 for the Hilltopper basketball team and home for the team's legendary coach, Edgar A. Diddle. The building was razed in 1994; however, one of the attractive stone arches from the front porch was re-erected in an idyllic pocket park on the site as a memorial to Diddle.

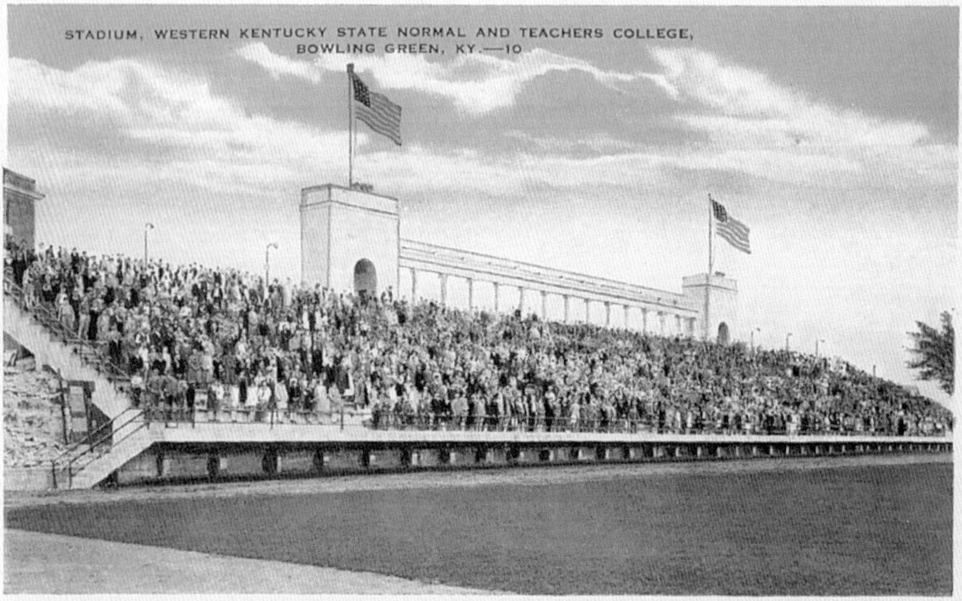

STADIUM. This 4,000-seat stadium (top) was constructed in 1927 on the site of a former rock quarry. Architect Brinton B. Davis masterfully crowned the stadium with a lovely Ionic colonnade that still attracts the eyes of WKU visitors. Lockers and bathrooms were located under the seating area. Before the explosive campus growth of the 1960s and 1970s, the stadium afforded a beautiful panoramic view of the undulating Kentucky countryside. L.T. Smith Stadium (below), which seats over 17,000, was constructed in 1968 to replace the old football stadium. Instead of razing the older facility, administrators refurbished it for use as an amphitheater.

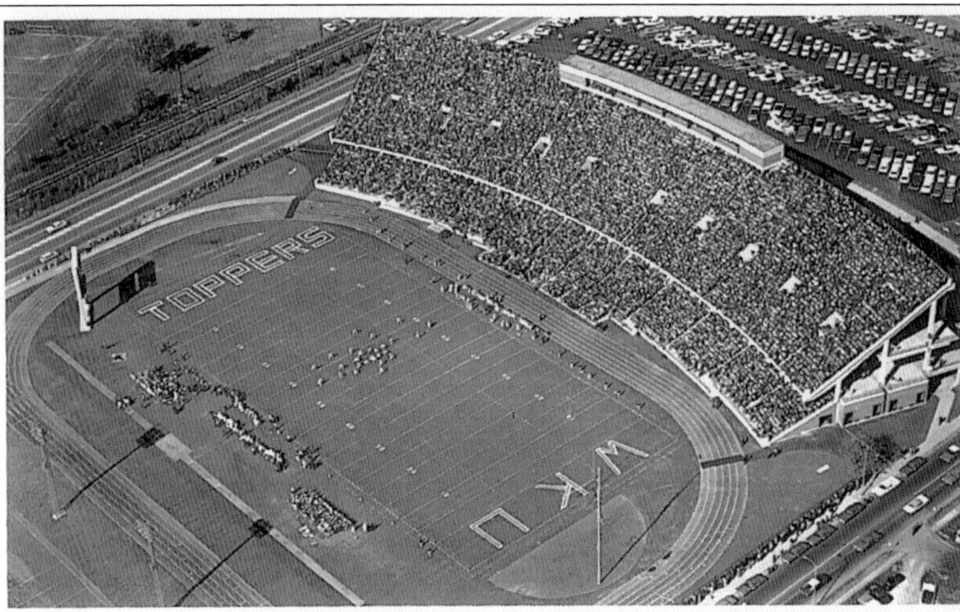

L. T. Smith Stadium, Western Kentucky University

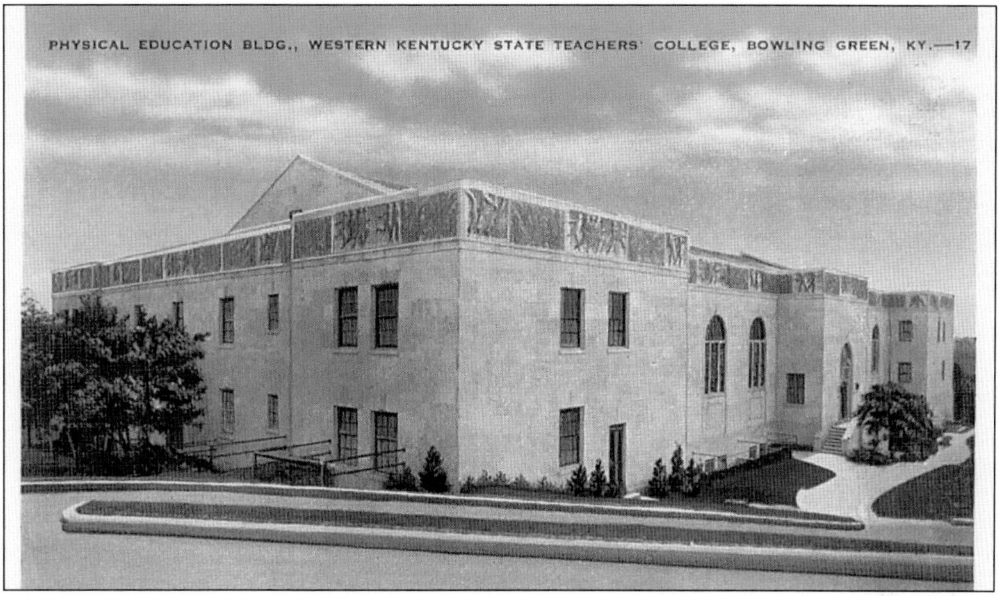

GYMNASIUM. Besides physical education classrooms and a large multi-purpose gym, the Physical Education Building erected in 1930 also housed a clinic, a band practice room, and ROTC offices. Designed by Brinton B. Davis, the building is truly eclectic in style and boasts an unusual terra cotta frieze, which at one time included nude athletic figures. These "unseemly" characters were removed when the building was converted into the university's main library in 1965.

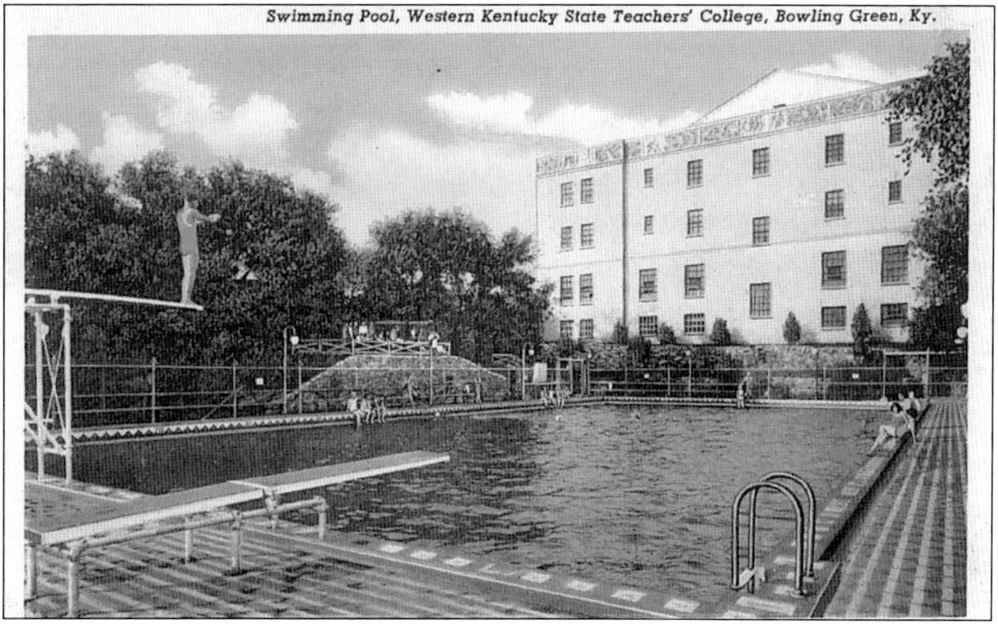

SWIMMING POOL. WKU's pool, built in 1931, was attached to the southern end of the school's new gymnasium. Dr. Cherry, an avid swimmer, wrote to architect Brinton B. Davis that the students' desire for a pool "was very, very great." Being Bowling Green's first public outdoor swimming facility, the pool was an instant success. Many an older Bowling Greener remembers the scratchy, sagging, wool swimming suits that were required attire at the pool.

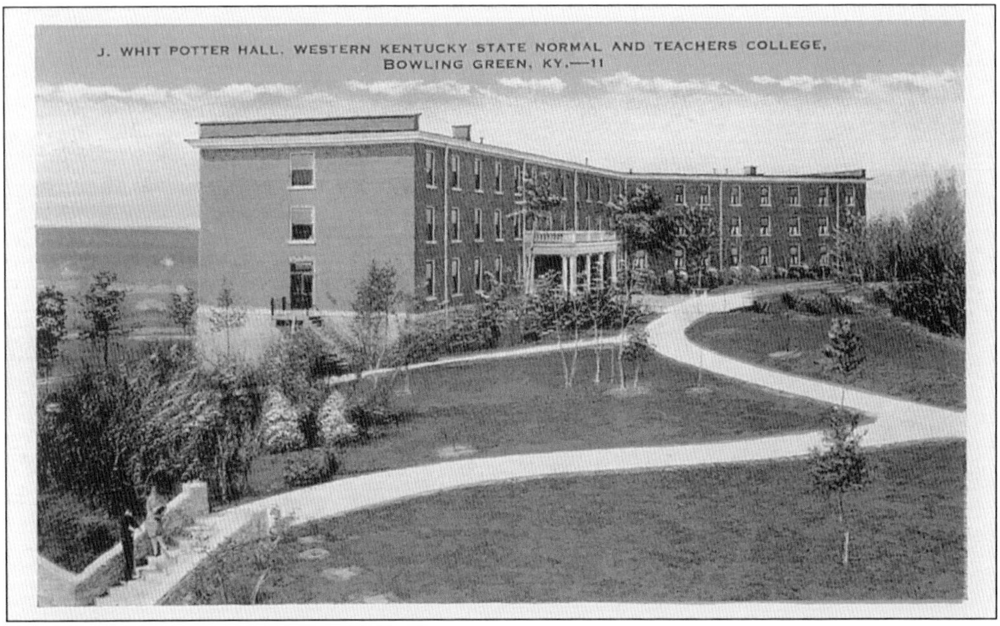

POTTER HALL. Designed by D.X. Murphy of Louisville, this building was erected as a women's dormitory in 1920. Bowling Green experienced an oil boom during the early 1920s, creating a severe housing shortage in town. The new dormitory was named for a Bowling Green native who went on to become president of one of New York City's largest banks. The building was extensively remodeled in 1998 for use as student service offices.

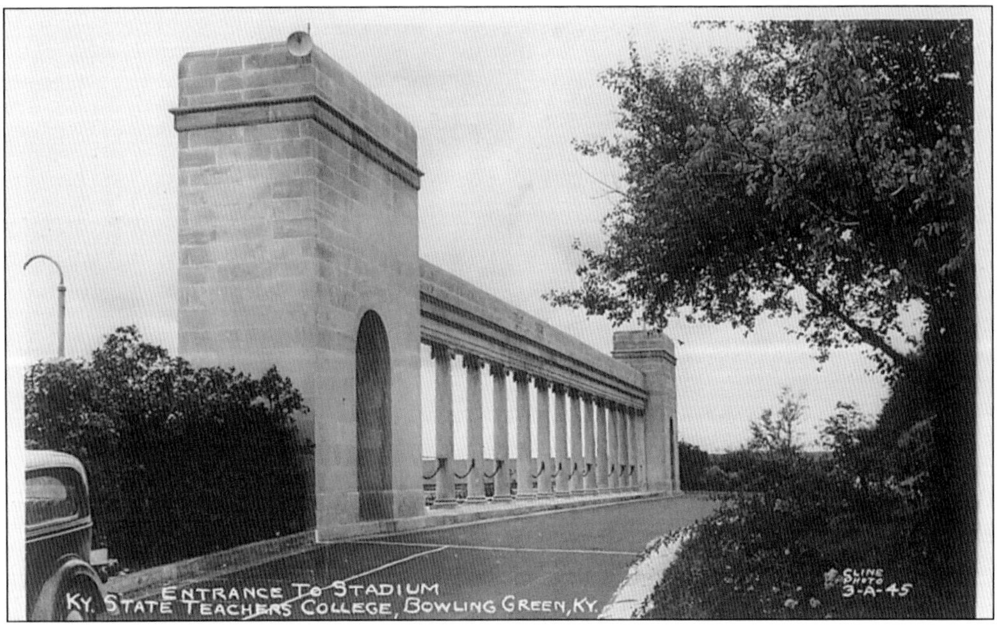

COLONNADE. This Classical Revival colonnade once served as the entryway to an athletic stadium. Lights were installed in 1946 and metal bleachers replaced wooden bleachers in 1963. Constructed of limestone, this colonnade contributes significantly to the character of the campus, and the stadium continues to serve as an amphitheater.

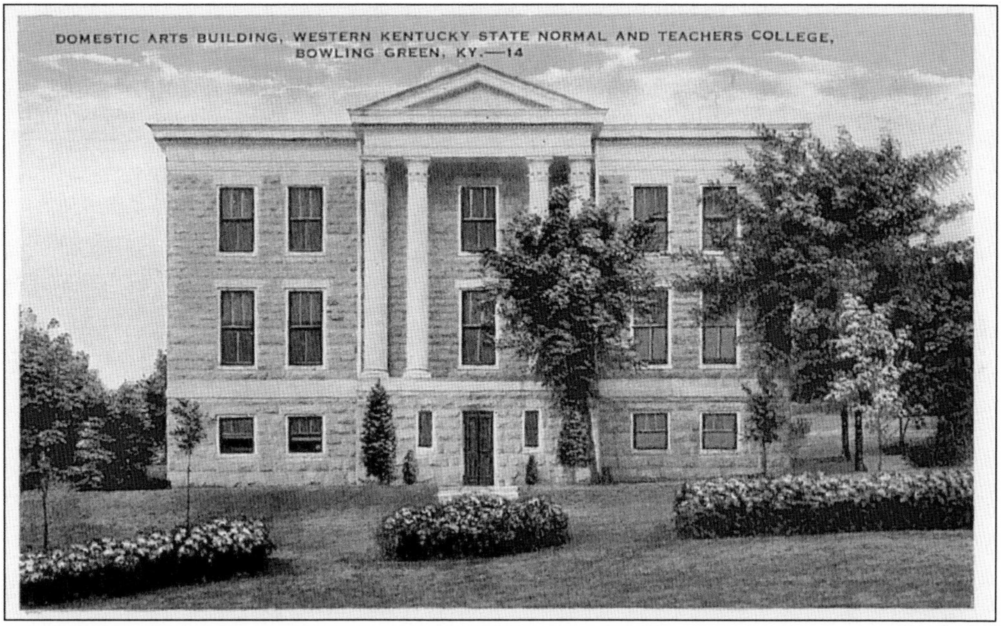

HOME ECONOMICS BUILDING. Architect Brinton B. Davis designed this building for the growing "domestic arts" program at WKU. The building was constructed from salvaged materials of the old B.F. Cabell home at the crest of College Heights. WKU had the building razed in 1982 to make way for a parking lot. A portion of the stone was used as a retaining wall for the new lot.

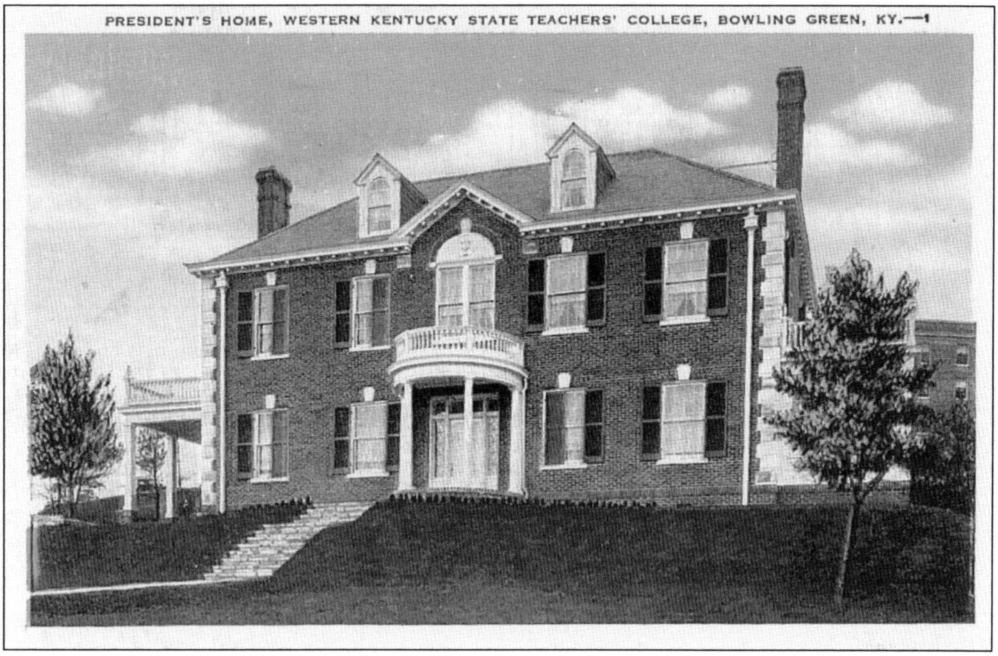

PRESIDENT'S HOME. WKU built a home for its first president, Henry Hardin Cherry, in 1929. The Federal style house, designed by Brinton B. Davis, exhibits outstanding architectural features including limestone quoins, dormers, bracketed eaves, a rounded portico, a hipped roof, paneled chimneys, and lovely balustrades. The home was converted into the Alumni Center in 1960.

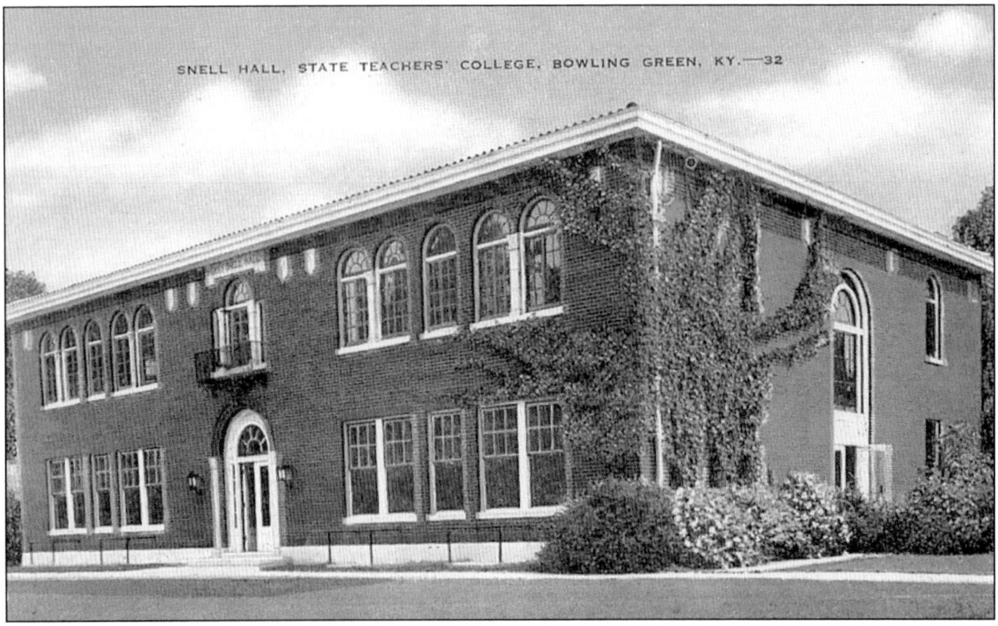

SNELL HALL. Brinton B. Davis designed Perry Snell Hall as a science classroom and auditorium building for Ogden College in 1924. C. Perry Snell was a Warren County native and alumni of Ogden who made a tidy fortune in the Florida real estate market. WKU acquired the building in 1928. Snell Hall is the only Italian Renaissance building in Bowling Green. Noted landscape architect Henry Wright designed the Italian garden (bottom) outside Snell Hall. WKU erected the statuary of the Four Seasons in 1931. They were removed in the late-1990s after one of the beautiful Art Nouveau lasses was vandalized.

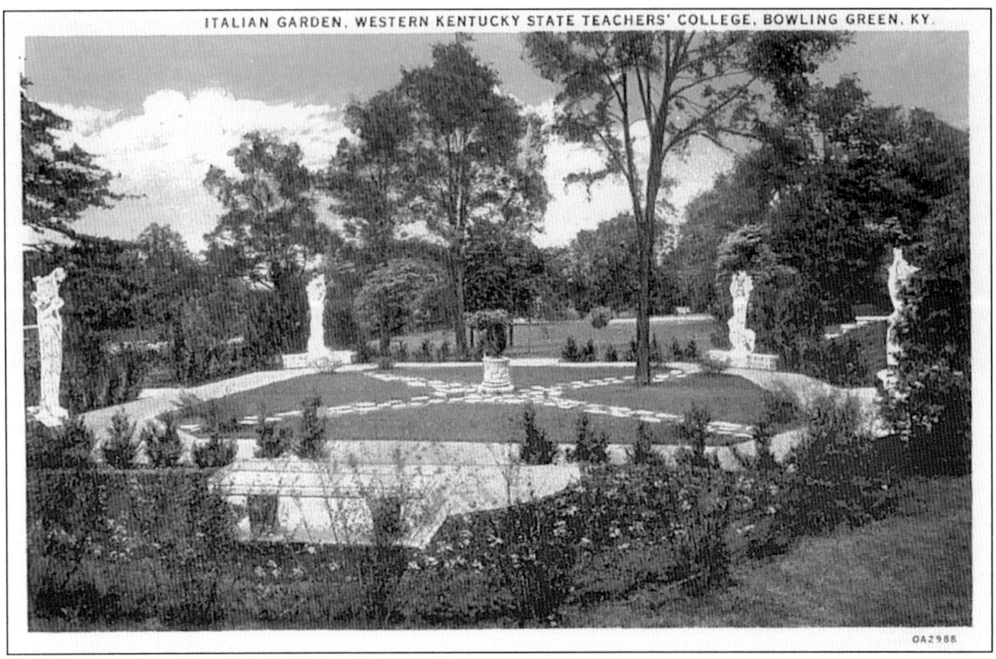

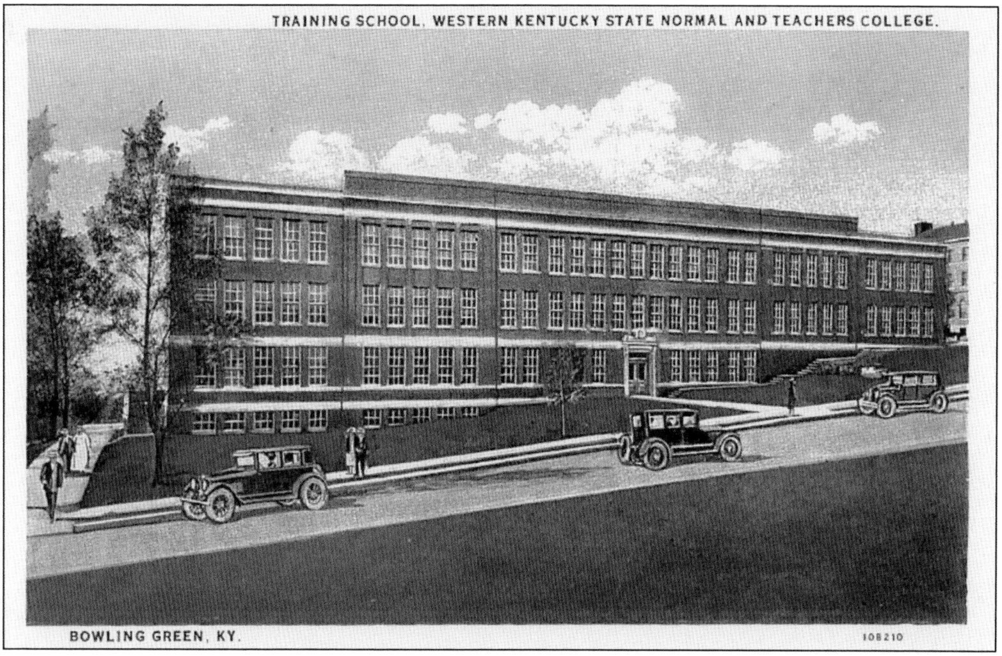

TRAINING SCHOOL. This structure was built in 1925 to accommodate a demonstration school that began as a cooperative effort between WKU and Bowling Green city schools in 1906. The city ties were severed in 1920, the same year that secondary level classes were added. The school's upper level became affectionately known as College High and enjoyed an intense rivalry with Bowling Green High School. The utilitarian structure pictured was designed by Atlanta architect Ten Eyck Brown. WKU closed the Training School in 1970, and the building became Science and Technology Hall. The Training School's seventh grade class from 1913 is pictured below with their teacher, Miss Todd. The girls in the back are actually standing on chairs.

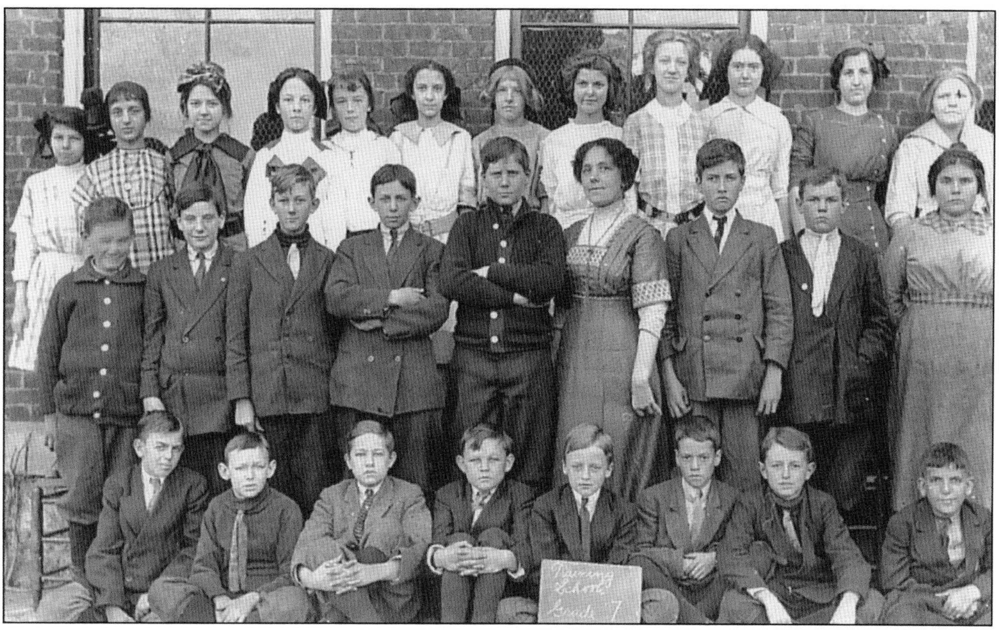

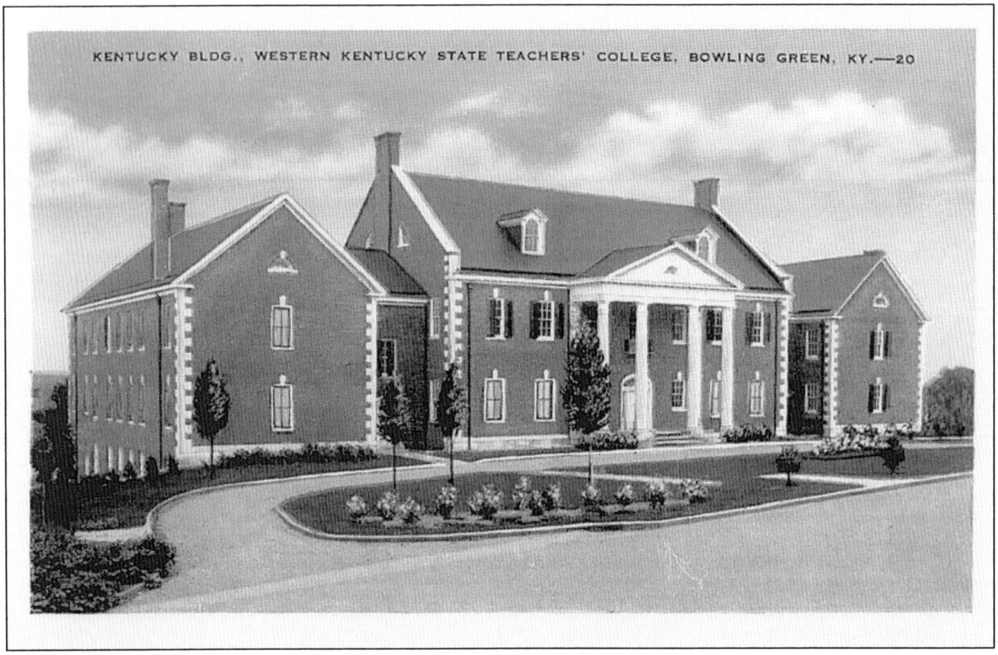

KENTUCKY BUILDING. Construction began on the Kentucky Building in 1929, but the Depression delayed its completion. With money from the Public Works Administration, the building was completed and dedicated in 1939. Its purpose was to serve as a repository for Kentuckiana material, an idea developed by Dr. H.H. Cherry and other WKU faculty. The building features a massive portico with each individual column turned from one shaft of stone.

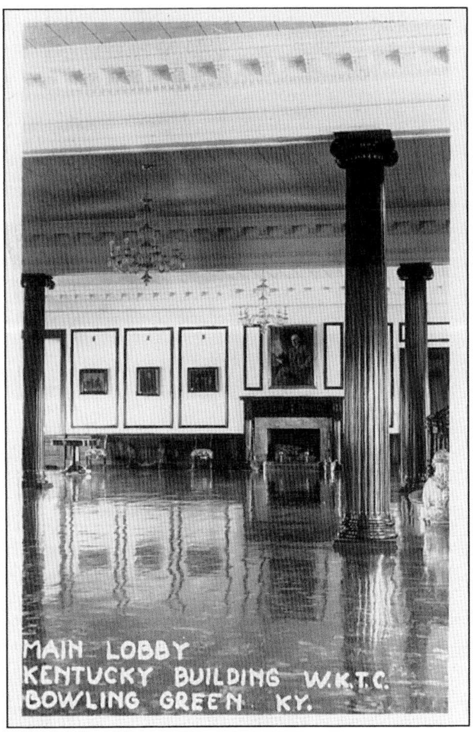

KENTUCKY BUILDING EXHIBITS. The 1939 building contains several impressive exhibit areas like the one shown here. The Kentucky Library and Museum mount exhibits related to the cultural heritage of the Commonwealth. A major addition in 1979 doubled the size of the imposing structure, which welcomes over 25,000 tourists, school children, students, and scholars annually.

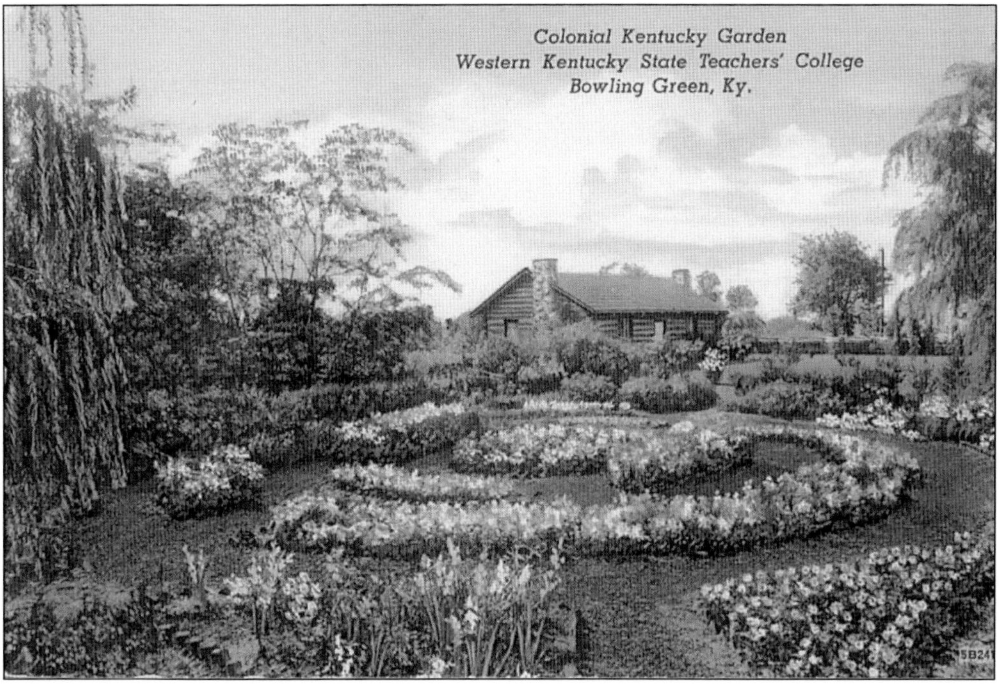

KENTUCKY BUILDING GARDENS. The Kentucky Building was once surrounded by Edenic gardens representing plants indigenous to the state accented with formal flower beds. The plantings were largely the work of faculty member Elizabeth Woods. This view highlights the pioneer log cabin, designed by Brinton B. Davis as a replica of the housing available to early Kentuckians. Most of the gardens were removed when the Kentucky Building was expanded in 1979.

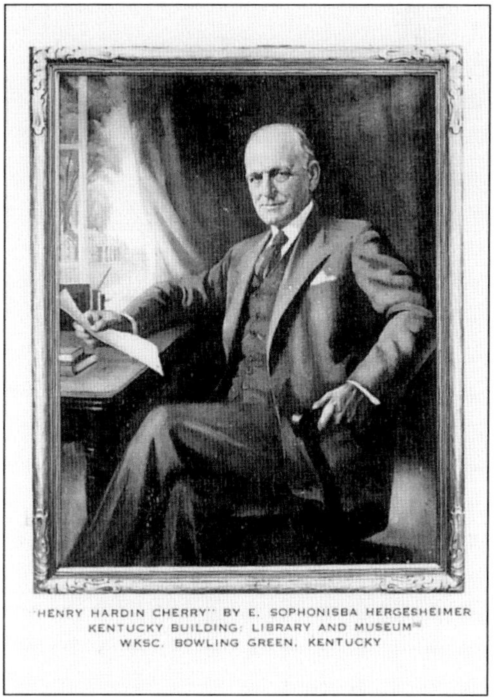

HENRY HARDIN CHERRY PORTRAIT. Sophonisba Hergesheimer painted this portrait of Dr. Henry Hardin Cherry for the Kentucky Building in 1929. Cherry, born in Warren County in 1864, attended A.W. Mell's Southern Normal School. He and his brother, T.C. Cherry, purchased the school in 1892. Cherry was instrumental in getting the school designated as a state normal school in 1906 and remained WKU president until his death in 1937.

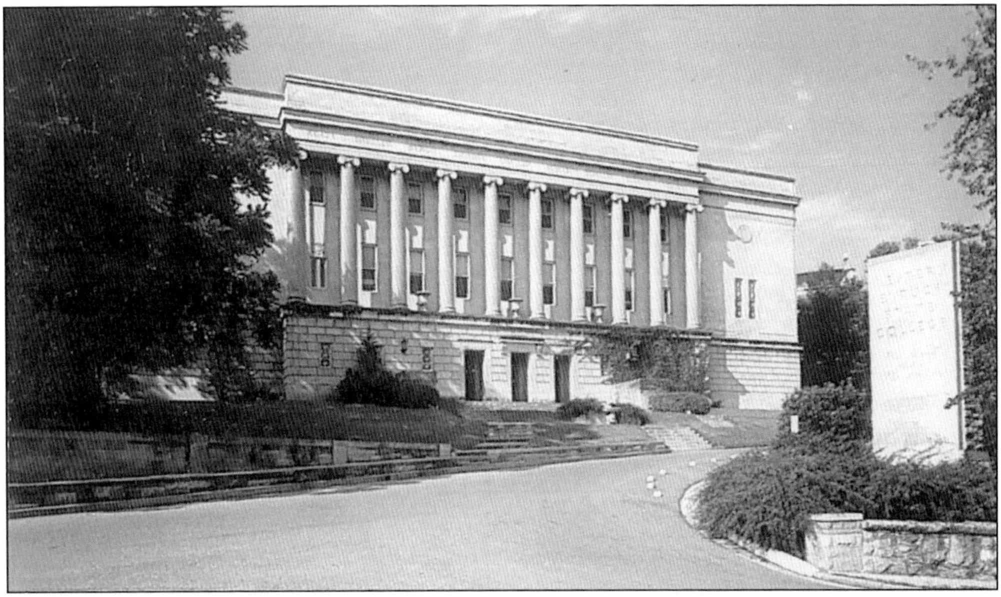

GORDON WILSON HALL. This beautiful neo-classical, limestone-clad building was constructed in 1927 as the campus library. The rusticated base, Ionic colonnade, and attractive siting made Gordon Wilson one of WKU's most striking buildings. Names of classical writers were incised in the building's frieze to denote its use as a library. When the library was moved to the old gymnasium, this building was named Gordon Wilson Hall in honor of a longtime English faculty member.

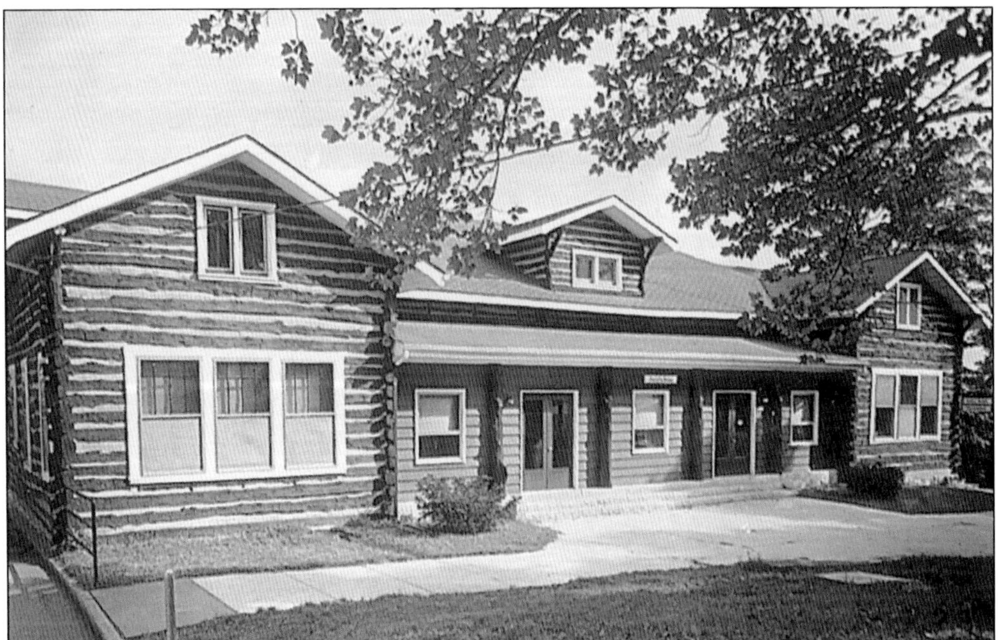

FACULTY HOUSE. D.X. Murphy of Louisville designed this building in 1921. It was constructed by WKU students who used cedar logs cut from university property in its construction. The building originally served as a student center. It was later adapted as the school's library and filled this role until the new library was completed in 1927. It was designated as the faculty house in 1959.

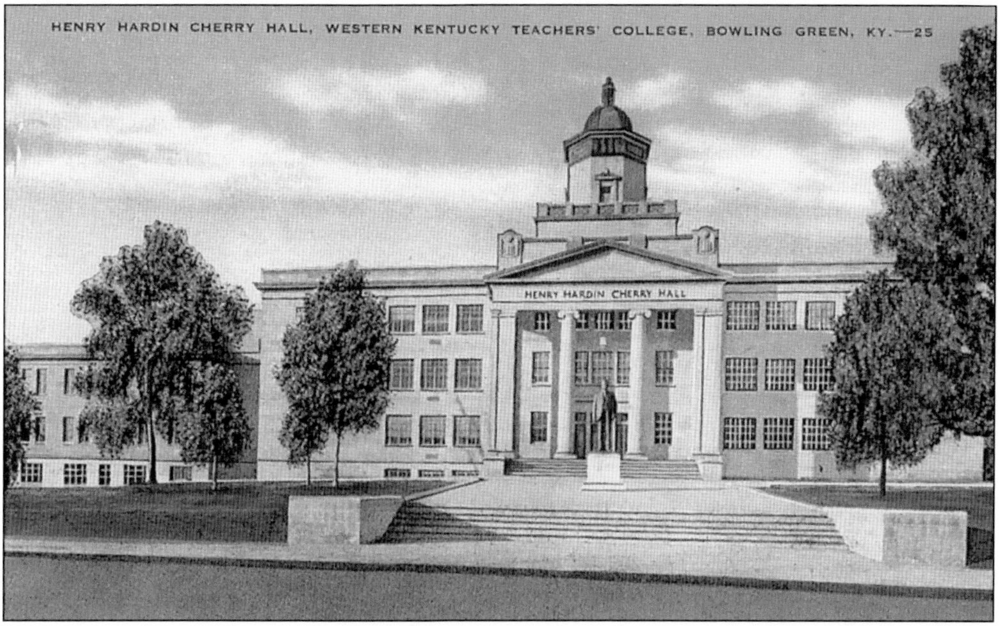

CHERRY HALL. Constructed in 1937 with funding from the Public Works Administration, Cherry Hall boasts a temple front with a commanding presence atop College Hill. The building is crowned with a masterful copper cupola that has become one of the university's most recognized symbols. The limestone used in this building came from Bedford, Indiana, not local quarries. The two large bas-reliefs on the building's facade represent the arts and the sciences.

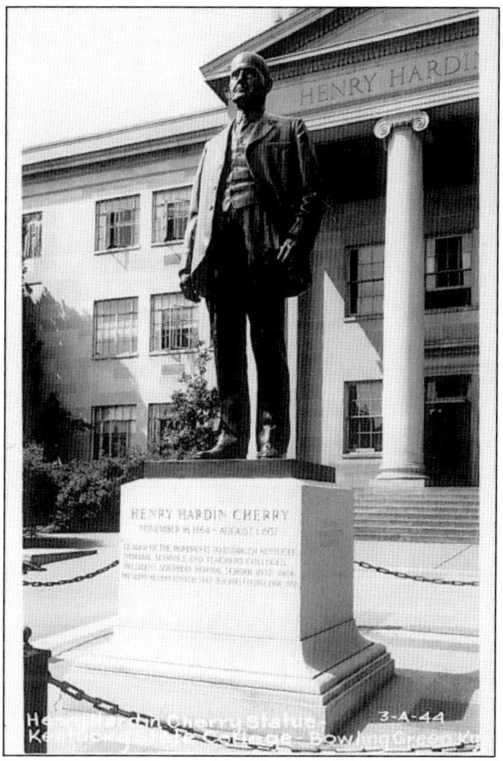

CHERRY STATUE. Cherry Hall is guarded by a 10-foot statue of Dr. Henry Hardin Cherry, which was executed by famed sculptor Lorado Taft. Faculty and staff spearheaded an effort to erect the statue through public subscription. Taft felt Cherry was larger than life, so he sculpted this likeness bigger than life size. The stance—with one thumb in a pants pocket—was familiar to anyone who knew Cherry.

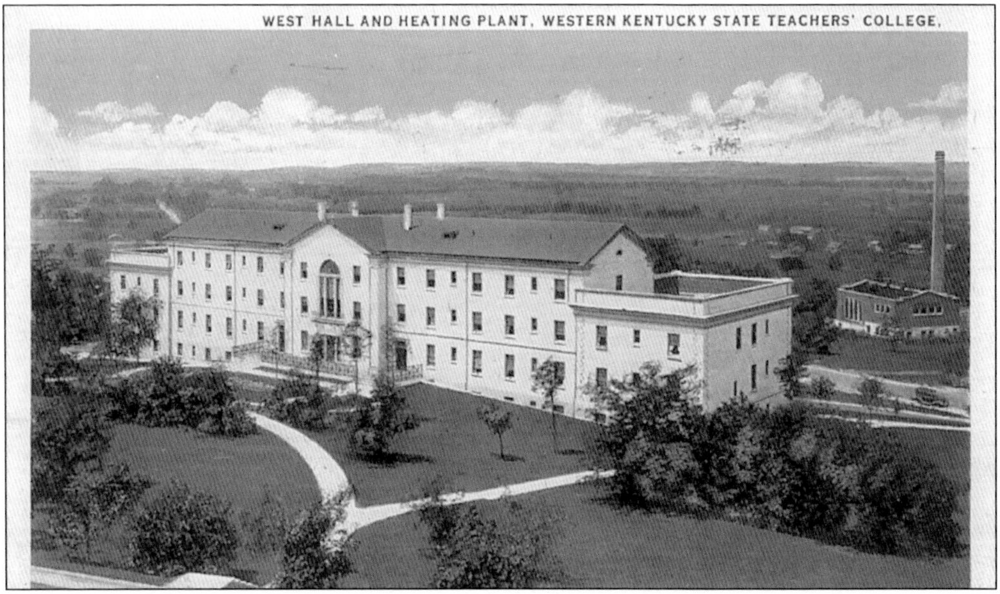

WOMEN'S DORMITORY. Constructed of Bowling Green limestone, this building has been known as White Stone Hall, West Hall, and was named Florence Schneider Hall in 1969 for WKU's long-time bursar. Designed in 1929 by Brinton B. Davis, the building was for many years a women's dormitory, but it is currently co-ed. Its central location makes it a prized campus address. To the left of the dormitory is another Davis design, the 1927 Heating Plant, which is still in use.

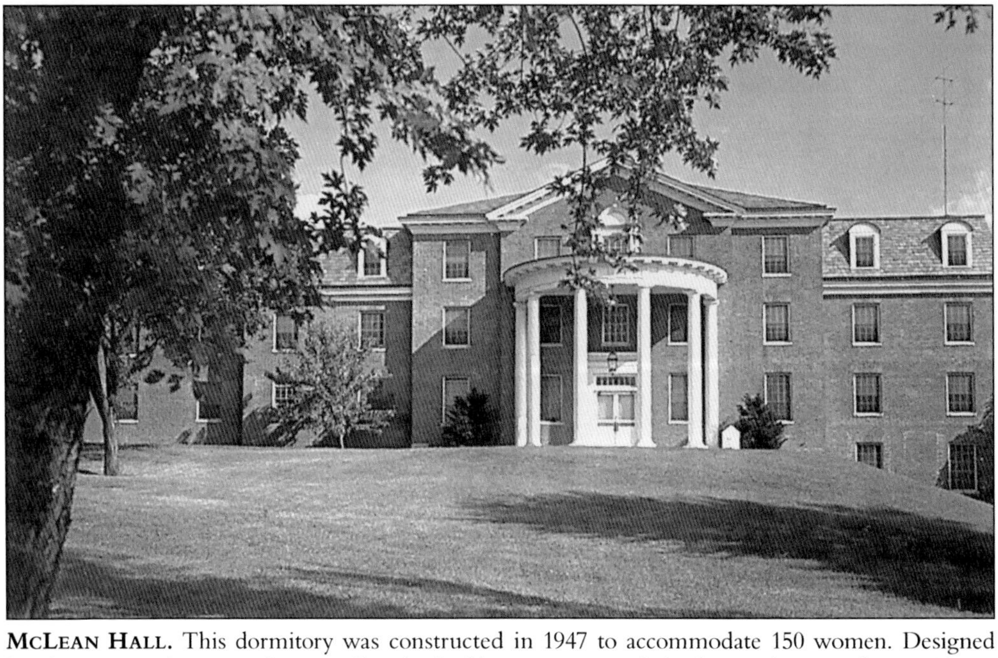

McLEAN HALL. This dormitory was constructed in 1947 to accommodate 150 women. Designed by the Arrasmith Firm of Louisville, the building was one of the last architecturally significant dormitories built on the WKU campus. The building is situated on a lovely rise and is accented with a Federal rounded portico with Doric columns. The building was named for Dr. H.H. Cherry's longtime secretary, Mattie McLean.

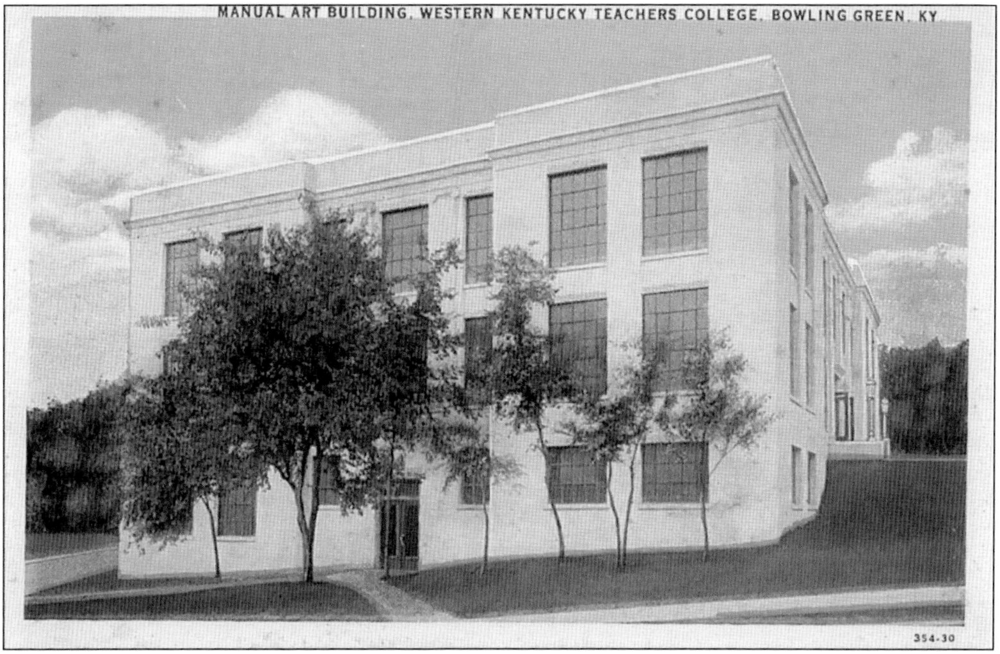

MANUAL ARTS BUILDING. Tucked on the eastern slope of College Hill, this building of Bowling Green limestone has housed the Department of Industrial and Engineering Technology since its construction in 1928. It replaced a frame building that burned. The building is utilitarian in design with large windows for natural lighting. The building's only architectural ornamentation is its Ionic pilasters.

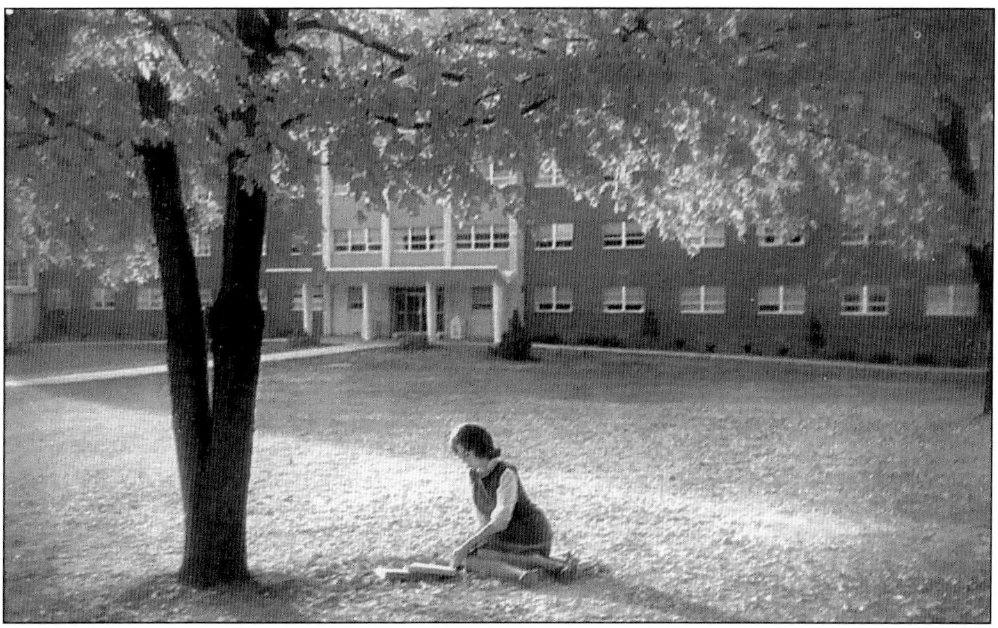

WKU CO-ED. This young lady takes advantage of some shade on a bright autumn day to catch up on school work in front of McCormack Hall, built to house 494 students. The building was first named State Hall, but its name was changed in 1969 to honor Dr. W.R. McCormack, a Bowling Green physician who served as the Hilltoppers team physician for many years and as a university regent.

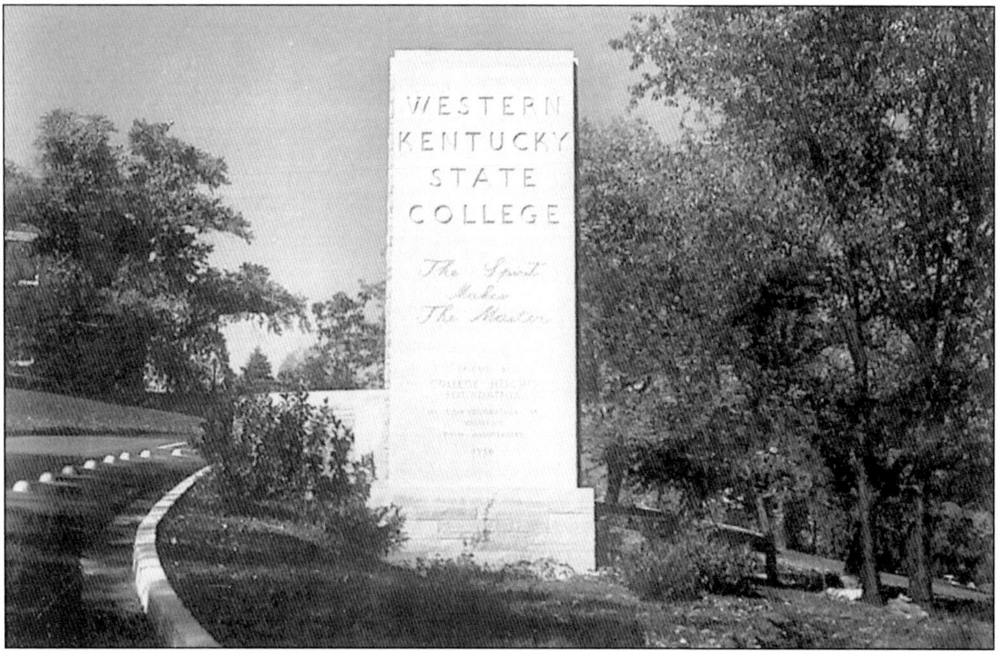

WELCOME PYLON. The College Heights Foundation had this limestone pylon erected in 1956 to commemorate WKU's 50th anniversary. "The Spirit Makes the Master" was one of Dr. Henry H. Cherry's clever phrases that was eventually adopted as the school's motto. The school achieved university status in 1966.

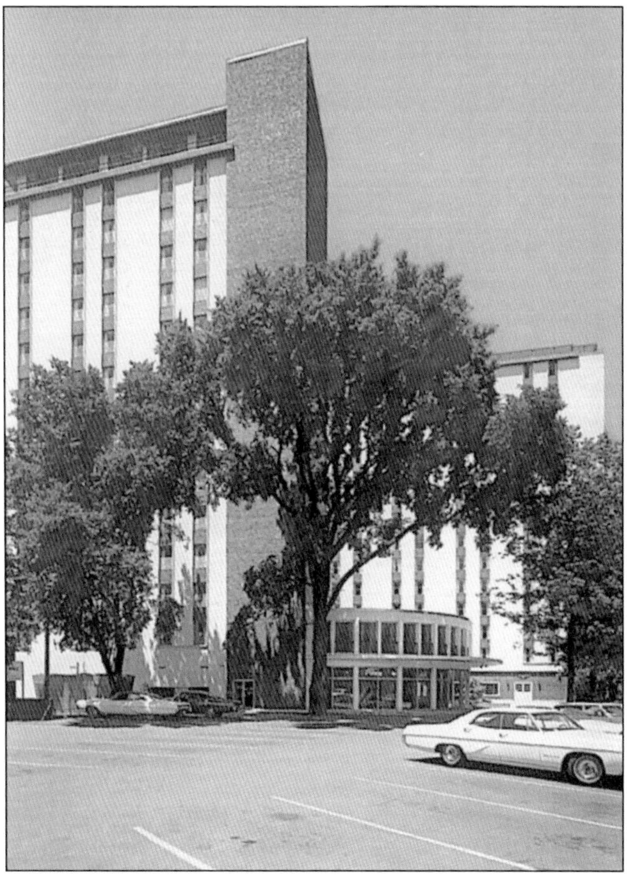

WESTERN TOWERS. This high-rise complex was constructed in 1967 by private investors on the site of the old Bowling Green Business University. It contained 187 suites capable of housing 816 students. The building's air conditioning was a major attraction. The name of the complex was changed in 1978 to Bowling Green Towers and is now operated as a subsidized housing facility for the elderly.

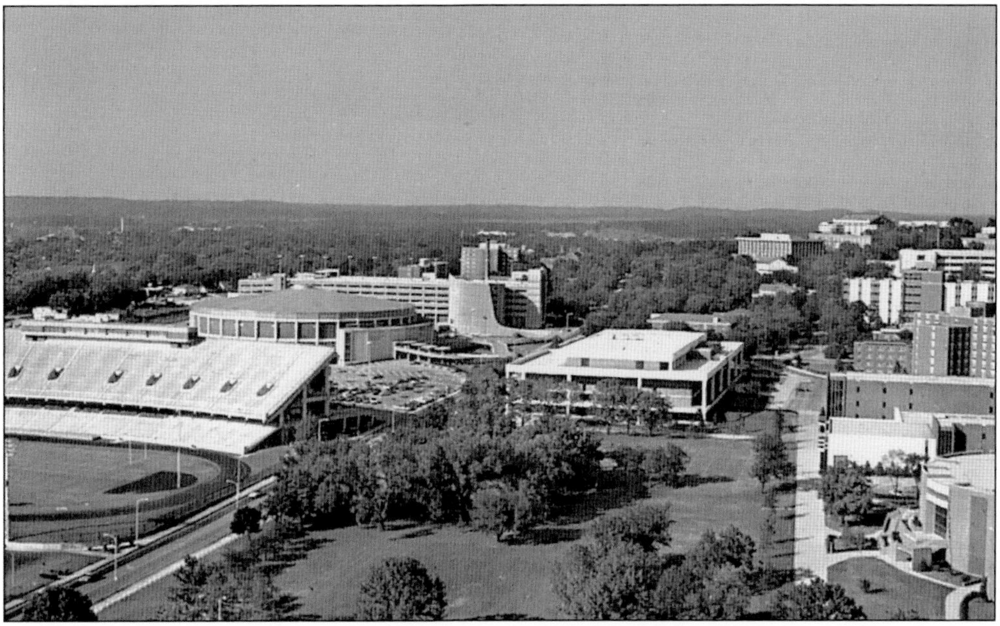

WKU. The WKU campus grew tremendously in the 1960s and 1970s. Almost every building in this view, except Van Meter, which crowns the hilltop in the background, was built during this time. This 1975 photo was taken from atop Pearce-Ford Tower, the 27-story high-rise dormitory at the south end of campus. Prominently displayed are (to the left) L.T. Smith Stadium, Diddle Arena, and the 1,000-car parking structure.

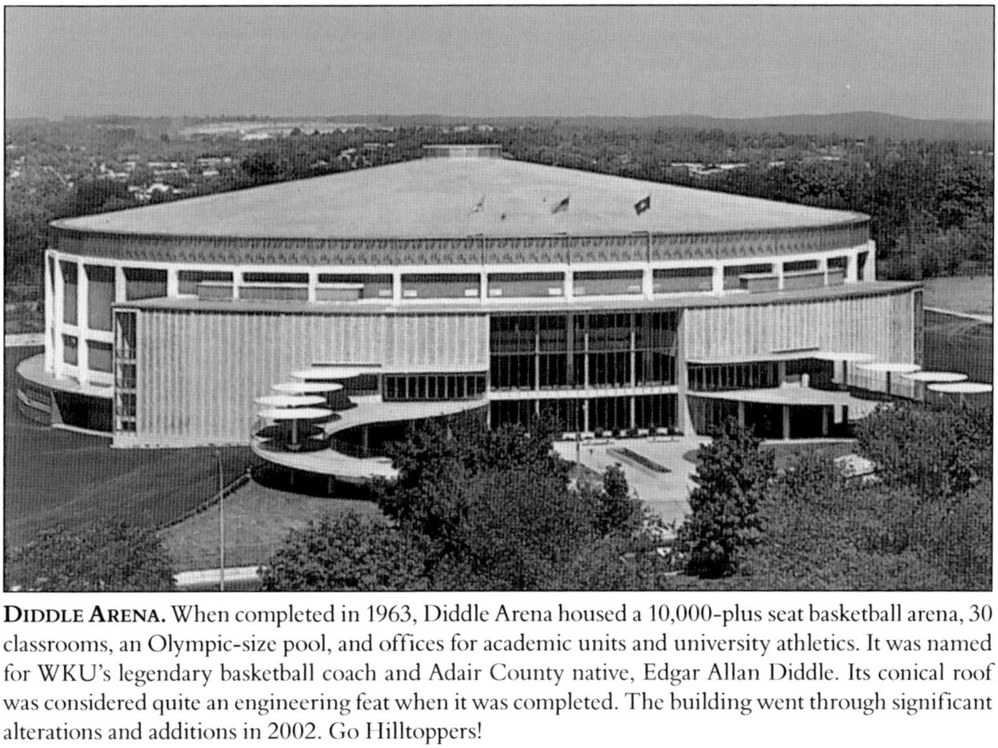

DIDDLE ARENA. When completed in 1963, Diddle Arena housed a 10,000-plus seat basketball arena, 30 classrooms, an Olympic-size pool, and offices for academic units and university athletics. It was named for WKU's legendary basketball coach and Adair County native, Edgar Allan Diddle. Its conical roof was considered quite an engineering feat when it was completed. The building went through significant alterations and additions in 2002. Go Hilltoppers!

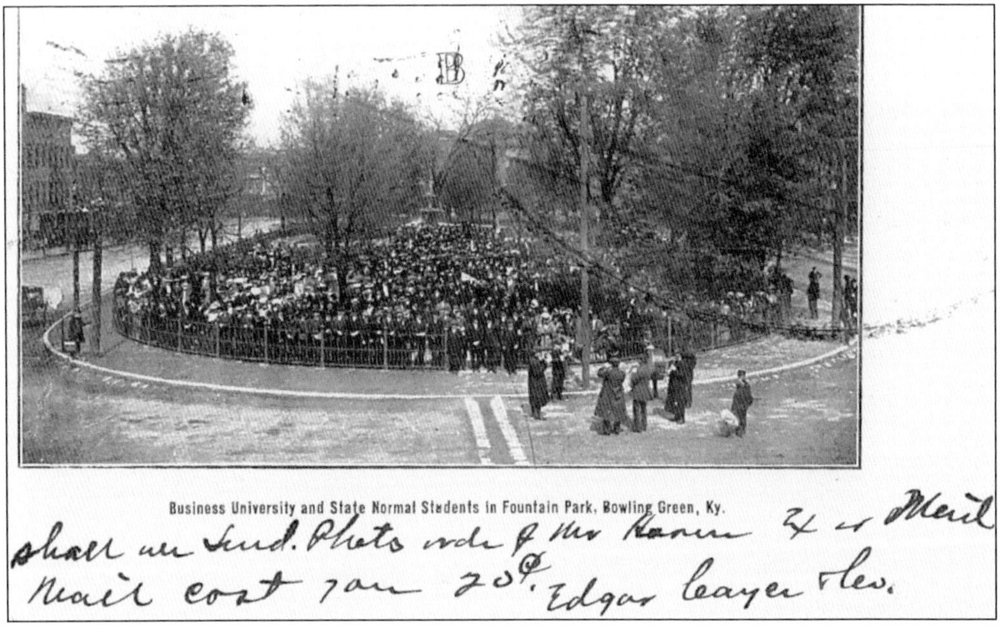

STUDENTS. Edgar Cayce took this photograph of a mass student gathering at Fountain Square in 1906, the same year that the Southern Normal School became Western Normal College. The card is marked Cayce & Co. on the back. The front message is actually signed "Cayce & Co." and indicates that the postage for sending a photograph in 1907 was 20¢. A band is performing in the foreground.

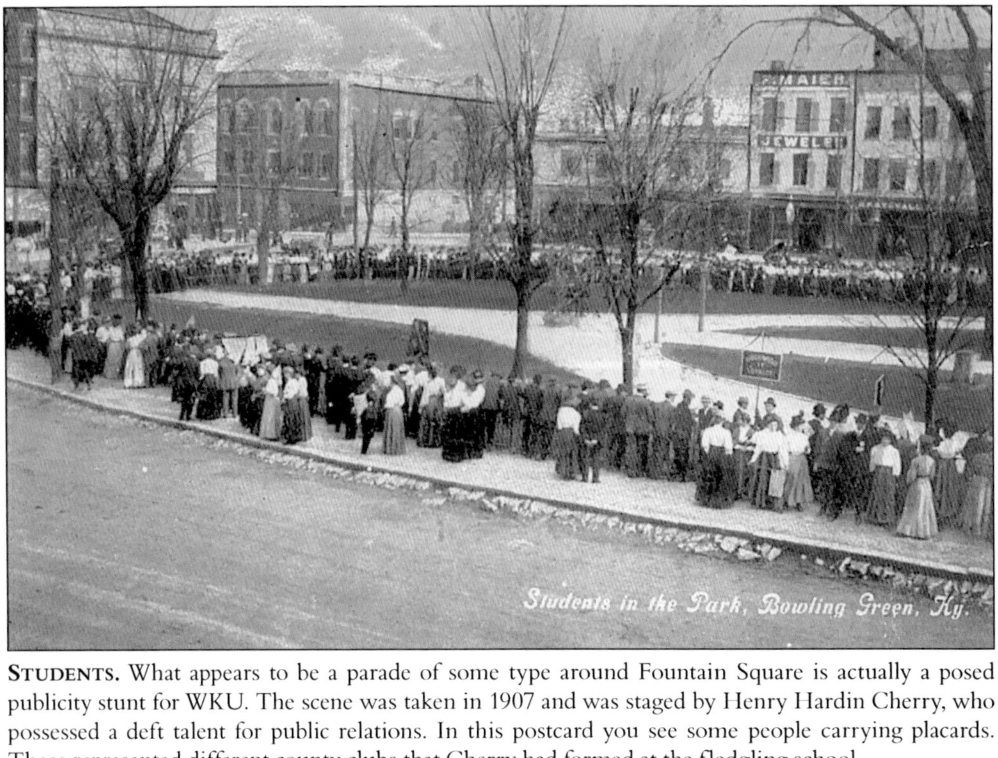

STUDENTS. What appears to be a parade of some type around Fountain Square is actually a posed publicity stunt for WKU. The scene was taken in 1907 and was staged by Henry Hardin Cherry, who possessed a deft talent for public relations. In this postcard you see some people carrying placards. These represented different county clubs that Cherry had formed at the fledgling school.

Four

RELIGION AND EDUCATION

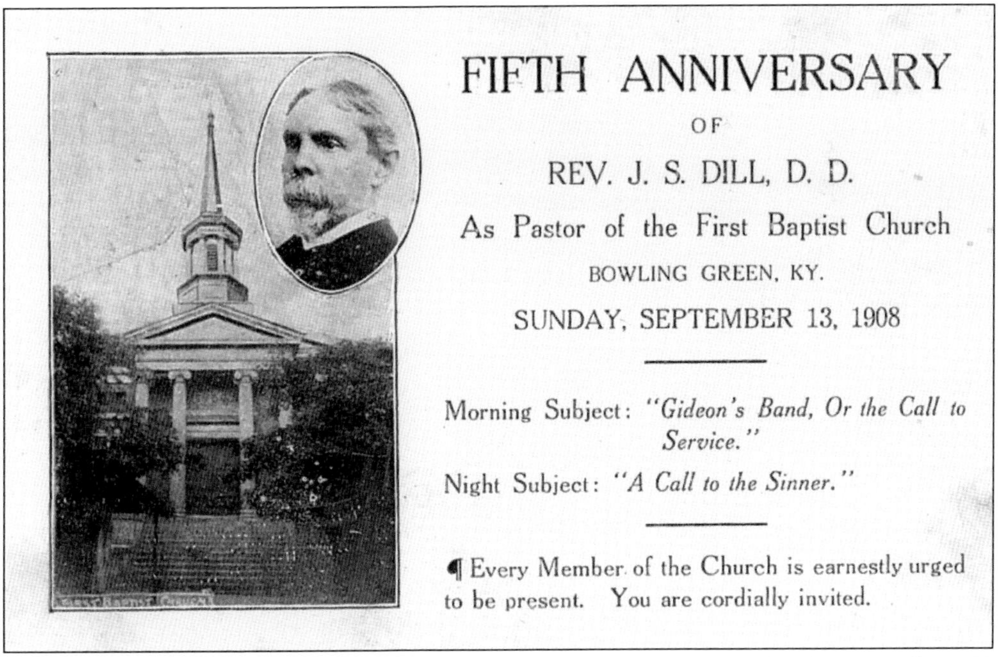

FIRST BAPTIST CHURCH. Postcards were popular and cheap ways to advertise church events. This 1908 card is an invitation to Jacob Smiser Dill's fifth anniversary as pastor; he served the church from 1903 to 1911. This postcard of the Main Street Church is a rare image of the building with its full steeple. This building served as the oil exchange during Bowling Green's brief oil boom.

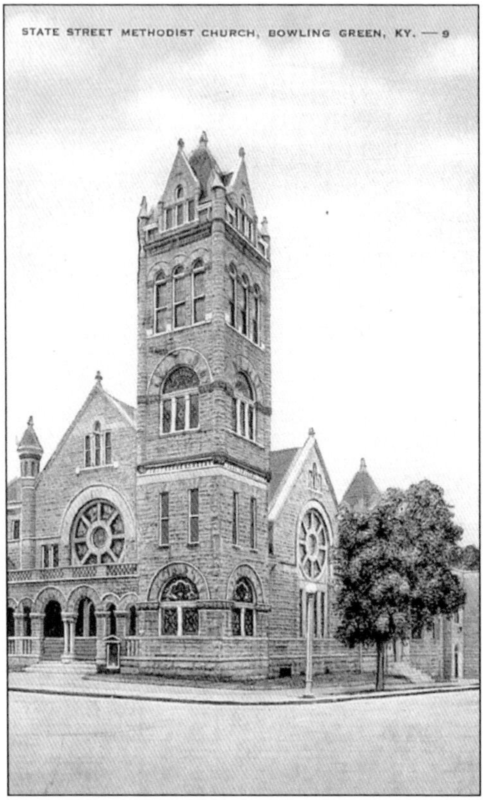

STATE STREET METHODIST CHURCH. Methodists first organized in 1819 in Bowling Green. Slavery split the church into a northern and southern faction in 1844, but the groups re-united in 1939. Ruben Hunt designed this beautiful Romanesque limestone structure in 1896, and it was built for $20,400. Those familiar with the building know that the front entrance was drastically altered in a 1950s renovation. The architect included a five-staged bell tower, variegated window shapes, and artistic massing to make this an architectural treasure. He chose to clad the building in rough ashlar Bowling Green limestone. One of the church's 77 stained glass windows features a representation of the congregation's previous building at 816 State Street, where the Treasure Seekers class had their photograph taken.

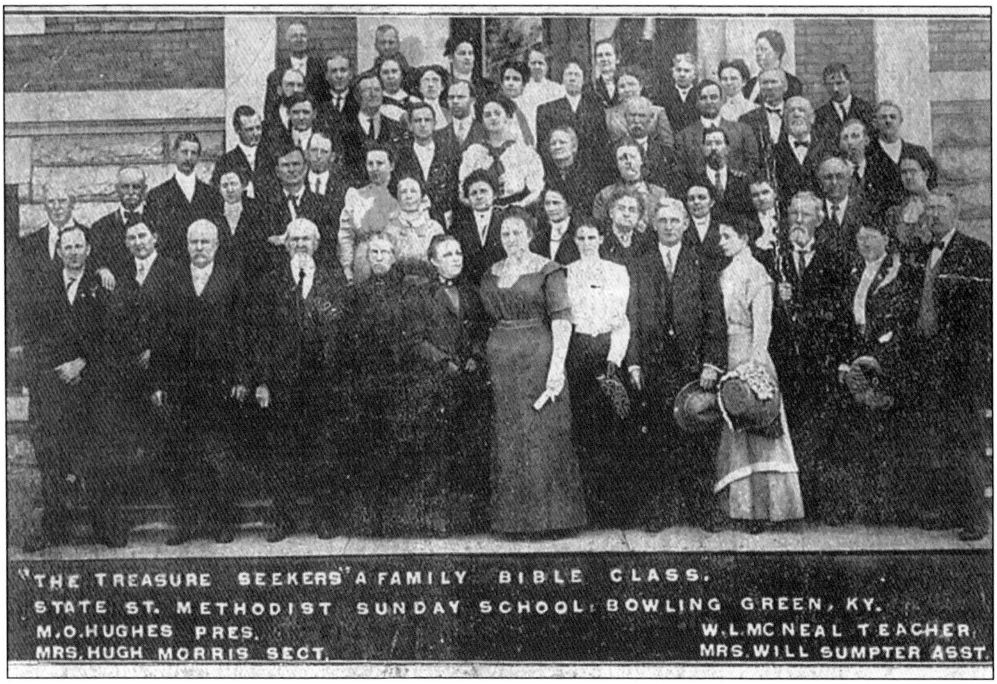

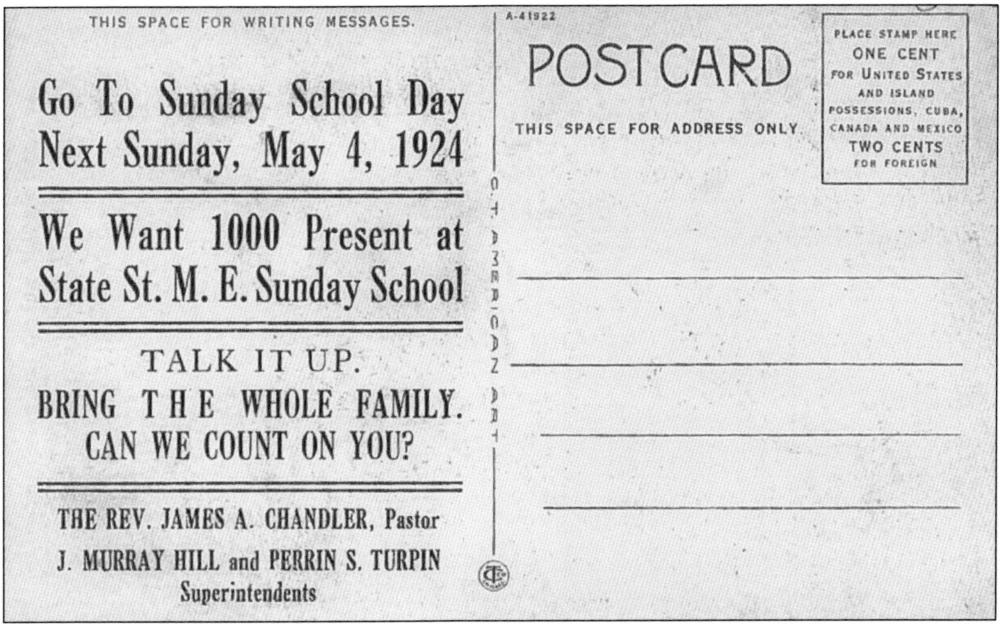

SUNDAY SCHOOL DAY. Sunday Schools or Sabbath Schools were 19th-century creations and, in the beginning, were almost exclusively for children. In the 20th century, the educational program was expanded to include all ages. Here, State Street Methodist Episcopal Church is calling for 1,000 people to attend a Sunday School Day in 1924.

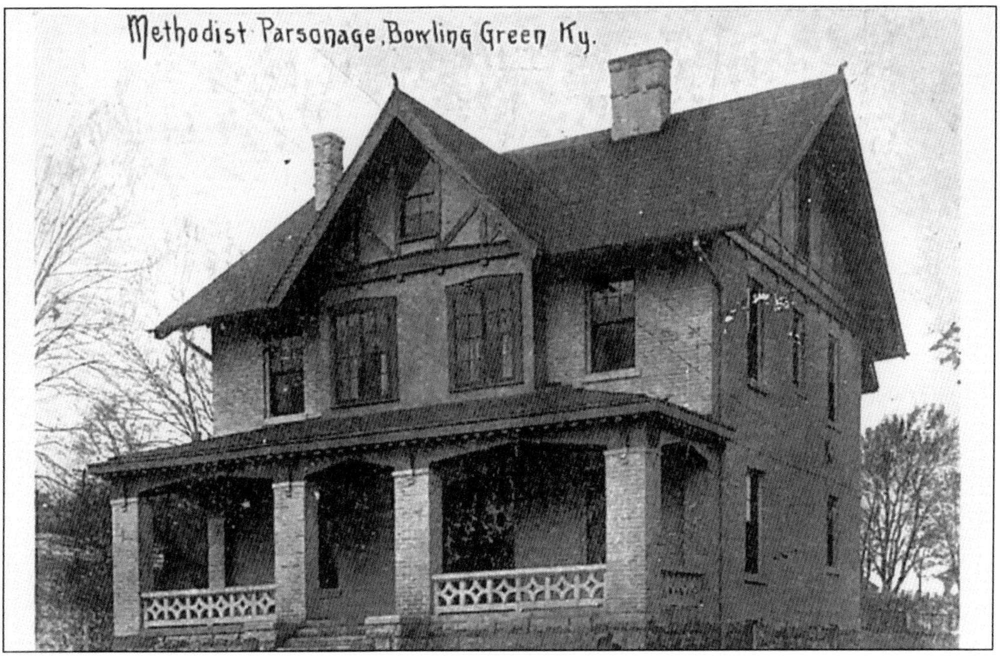

METHODIST PARSONAGE. Postcard views of residences are quite rare. This home was built in 1910 and served until 1950 as the manse for State Street Methodist Church. The focal point of the house is the projecting bay in the centered front gable, which features simulated English timbering. Another nice feature is the stylized porch balustrade of Bowling Green limestone. The house was restored in 2001.

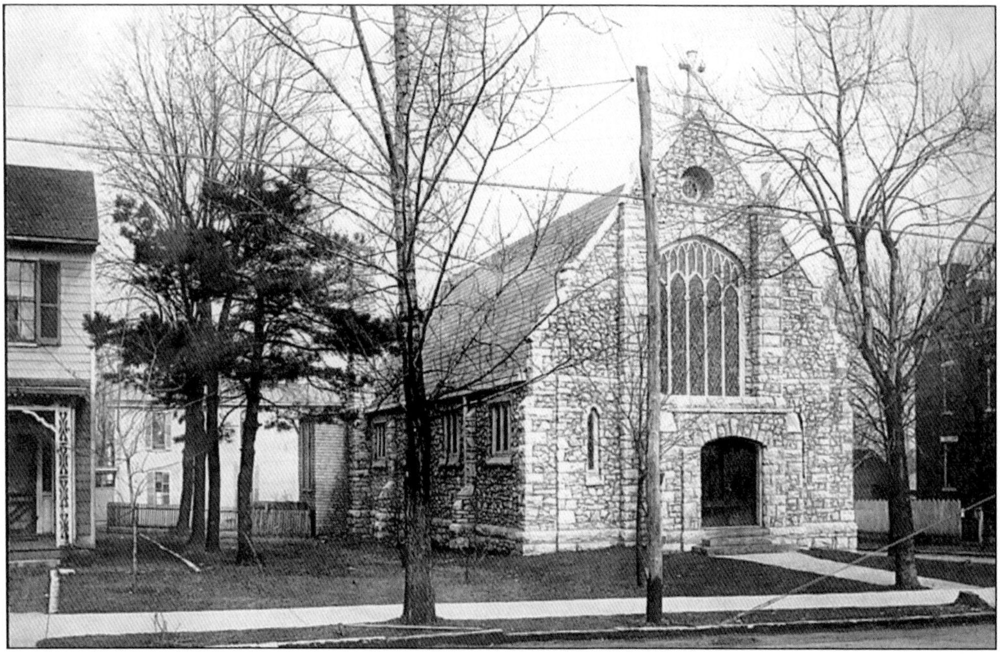

CHRIST EPISCOPAL CHURCH. This church organized in 1844 and constructed its first building on East Main Street. It was dismantled by soldiers during the Civil War. The congregation built again in 1867 on College Street and constructed this building on State Street in 1912 of Warren County limestone. Designed by George Herbert Gray of Louisville, the church is an excellent example of English Gothic architecture. The parish hall, offices, and chapel were added in 1976 and a substantial but sympathetic addition to the sanctuary was made in 1992. The interior postcard dates from *c.* 1920.

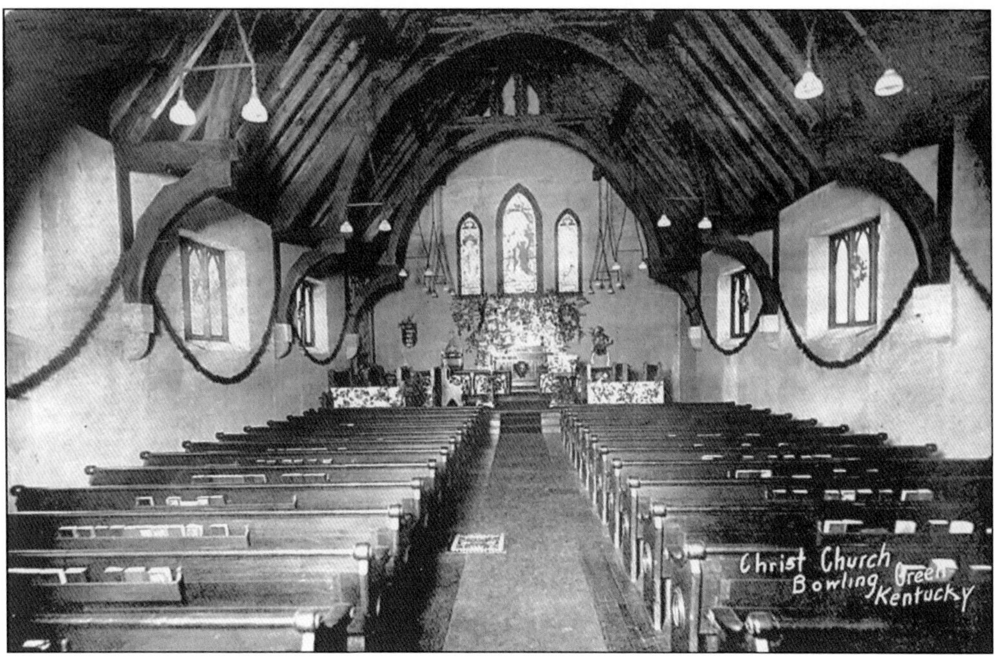

KERR MEMORIAL METHODIST CHURCH. This church was organized in 1890 as the First Methodist Episcopal Church under the benevolent eye of Rev. Daniel Farmer Kerr. The congregation erected this building in 1891 at a cost of $6,000. In 1937, when southern and northern Methodists united, the church voted to change its name to Kerr Memorial Methodist Church in honor of its first pastor.

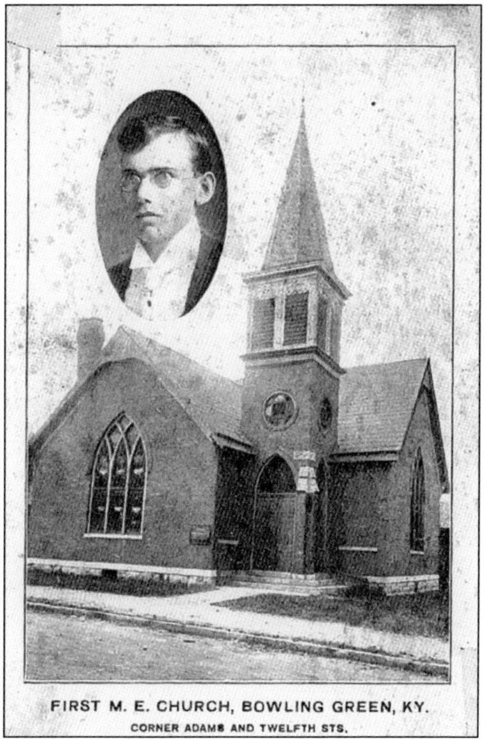

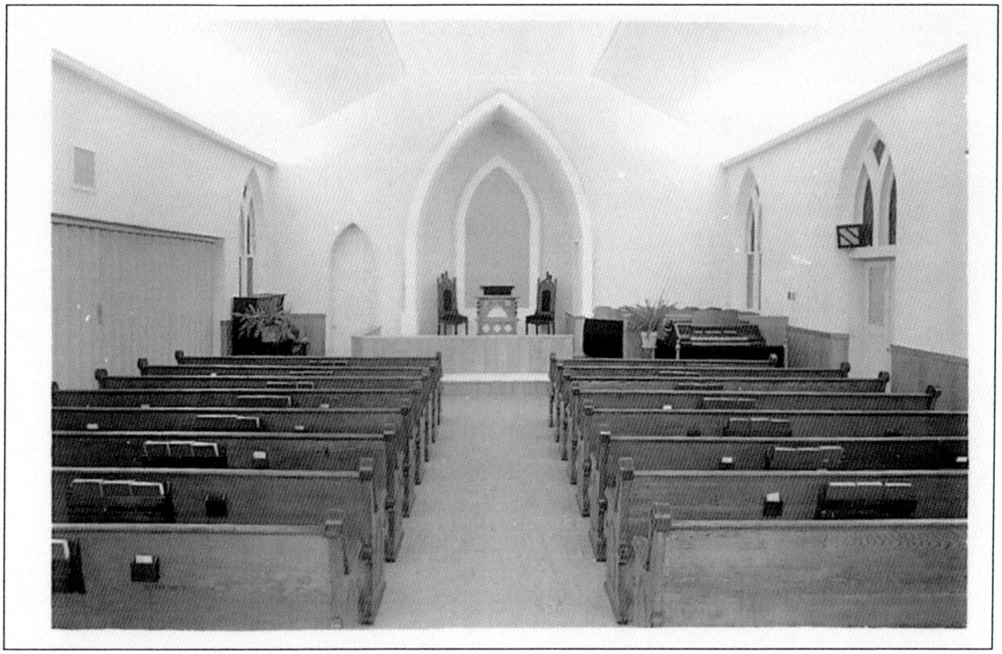

KERR MEMORIAL. The interior of the church is influenced by the exterior's Gothic arched windows. In October 1995, Westside Methodist Church joined Kerr for services while its new building was being constructed. The two churches eventually merged in 1999 as Faith Methodist Church. The old building, at the corner of Adams and Twelfth Streets, was eventually sold and adapted as a child advocacy center.

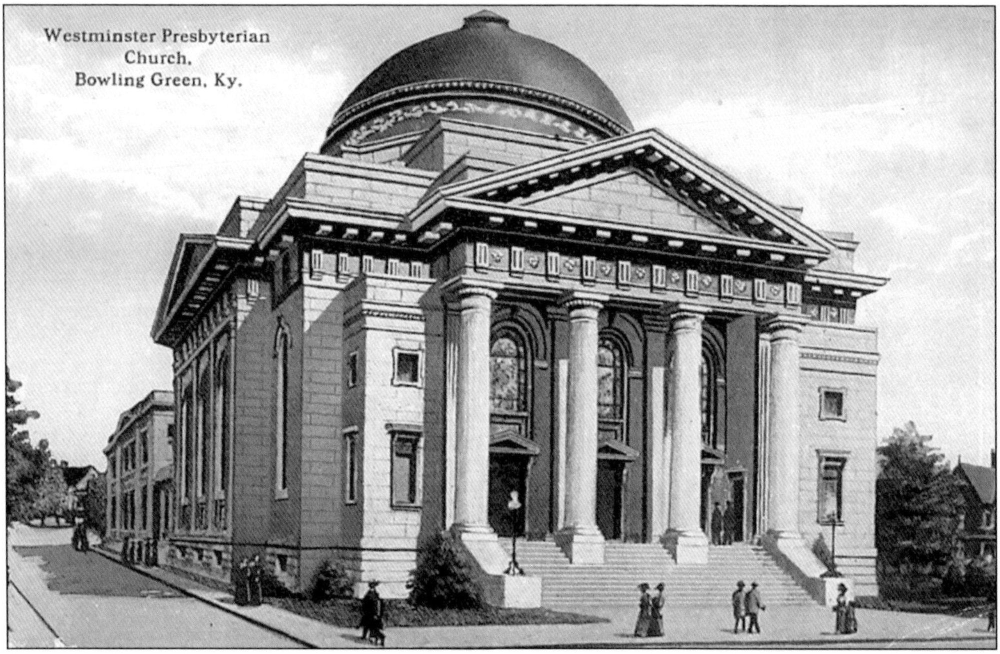

WESTMINSTER PRESBYTERIAN CHURCH. This attractive building was constructed in 1912 for a congregation of the Presbyterian Church USA. The church is a cruciform in massing and boasts a beautiful Roman temple front. The building is clad in Bowling Green limestone and crowned with a cast-iron dome. The church's exquisite stained glass windows were memorial gifts from various congregants.

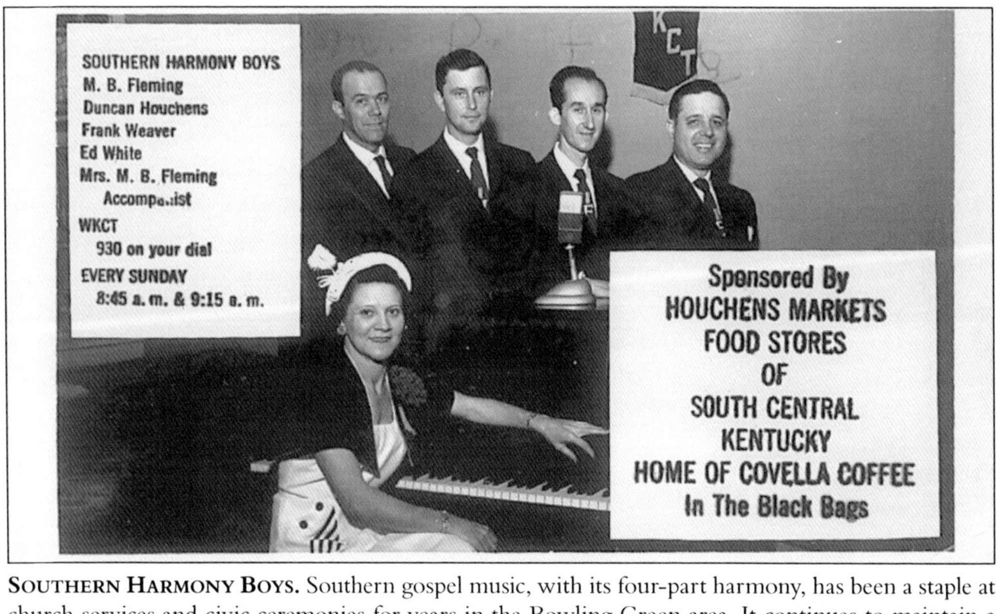

SOUTHERN HARMONY BOYS. Southern gospel music, with its four-part harmony, has been a staple at church services and civic ceremonies for years in the Bowling Green area. It continues to maintain a faithful following as evidenced by the large attendance at "singings" held in rural churches and as fund-raisers. Picture postcards were a popular way of advertising groups such as the Southern Harmony Boys who were heard on local radio station WKCT.

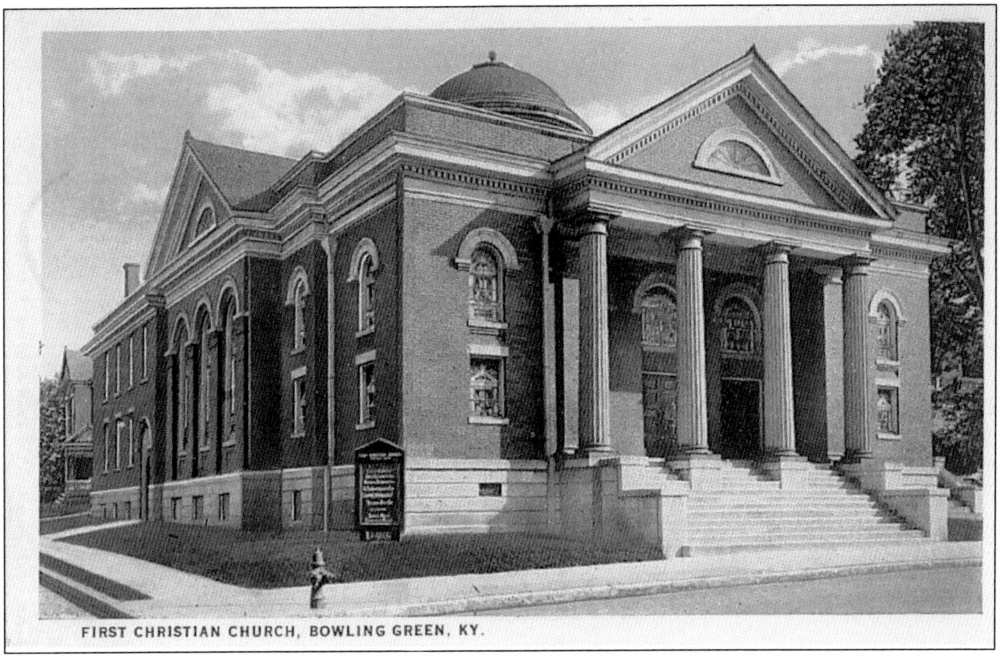

FIRST CHRISTIAN CHURCH. Organized in 1845, the first building of this church, at 716 College Street, is still standing. The top postcard shows the congregation's third building erected in 1913. The Neo-Classical structure was similar to many built at the time, complete with a lovely portico, cruciform plan, and crowned with a dome. The dome began slipping in the 1950s, so the building was razed.

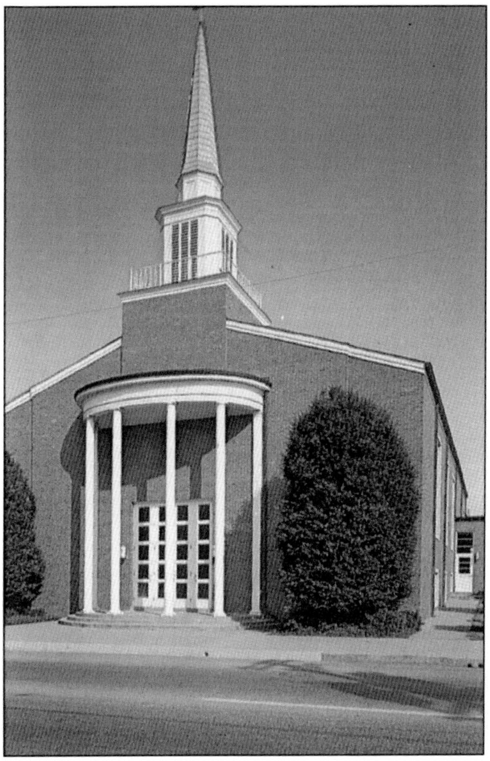

FIRST CHRISTIAN CHURCH. The Disciples of Christ congregation erected this traditional church building in 1959. In 2001 the facade of the structure was dramatically altered with the removal of the steeple to a new bell tower and other exterior and interior alterations.

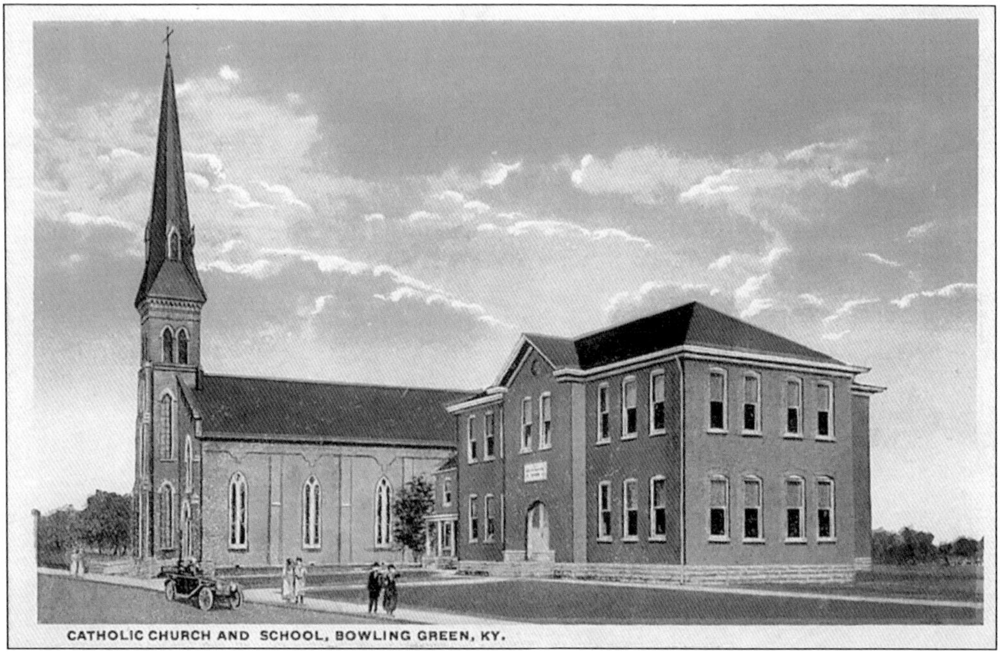

ST. JOSEPH CATHOLIC CHURCH. Rev. Joseph DeVries organized the Catholic Church in Bowling Green in 1858. They built a small frame building the following year, and in 1862 built a brick structure. When it proved too small, the church's rear wall was removed and the sanctuary was enlarged. Its present building was constructed around the smaller building in 1884. Designed by Frank Kister, the new construction resembled the Cologne Cathedral. The sanctuary was completed in 1887 and dedicated two years later. The tower originally soared 142 feet, but a windstorm in 1923 made it necessary to remove the steeple and replace it with a shorter, sturdier one. The building to the right of the church is St. Joseph's School, which began holding classes in 1912.

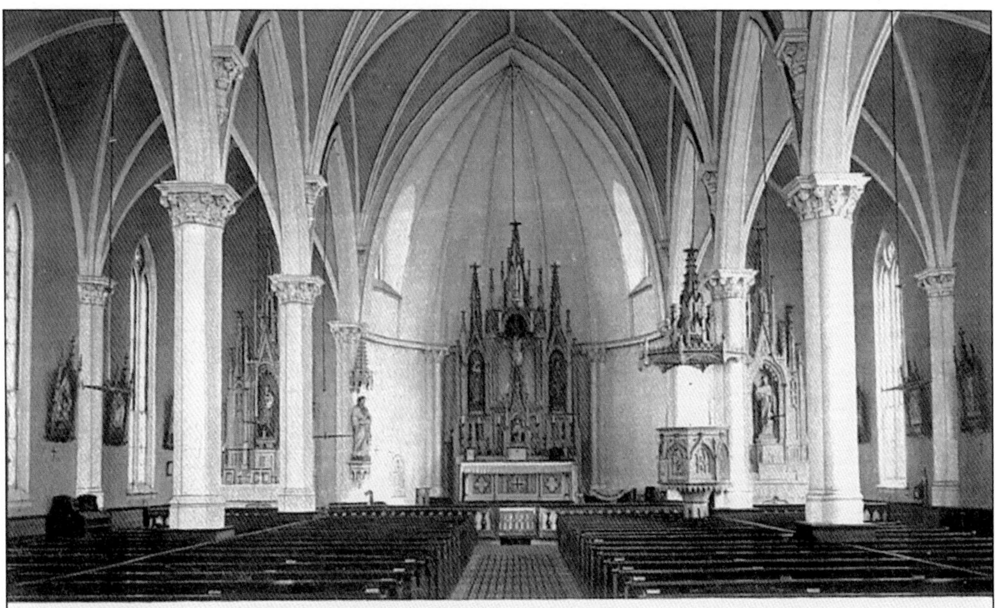

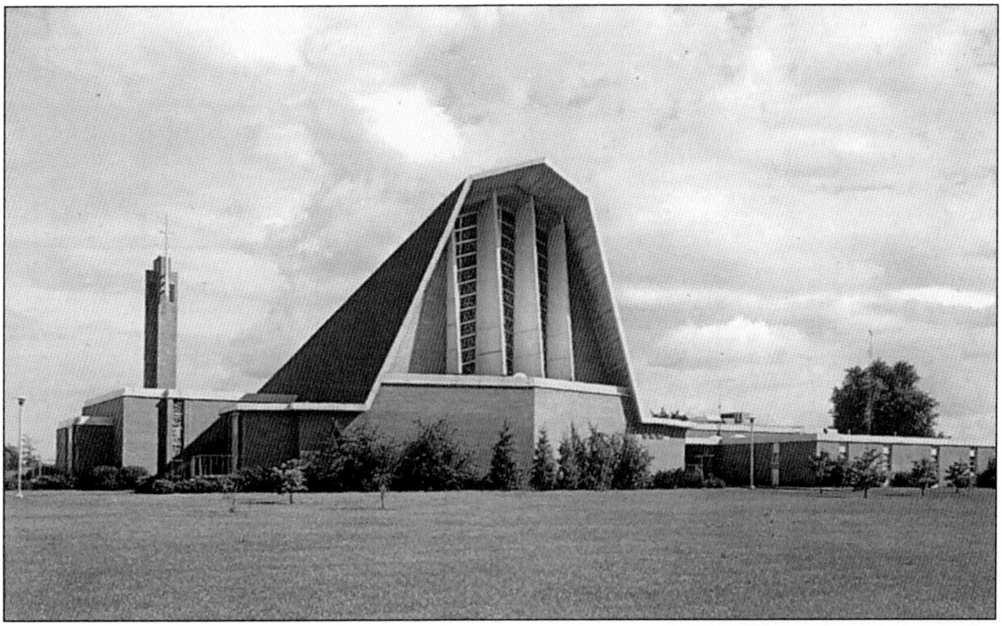

Holy Spirit Catholic Church. This modern church structure was designed by local architect Joseph P. Wilk in 1970 for a Catholic parish that had started in 1967. Wilk also designed the church's modernistic stations of the cross. The complex included the church, parish hall, and rectory. Building costs amounted to $450,000.

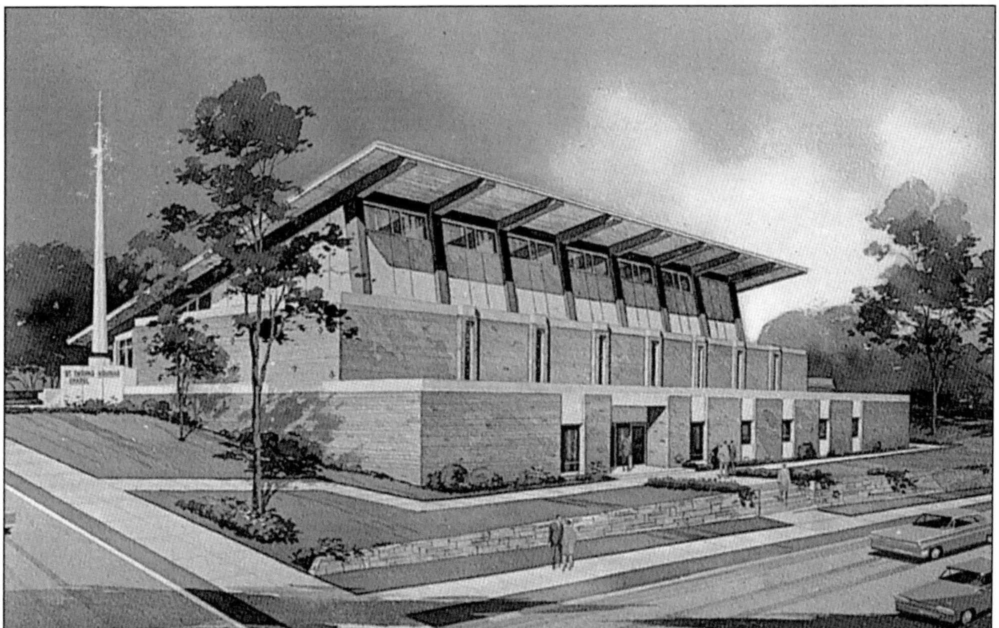

Newman Center. The soaring roof of the Newman Center on College Street was designed by Joseph P. Wilk of Bowling Green. The building houses Lyddane Hall and Saint Thomas Aquinas Chapel. The facility was constructed to minister to students at WKU and was dedicated in October 1968. The steeple toppled in a heavy windstorm in 1990 and was replaced in 2000.

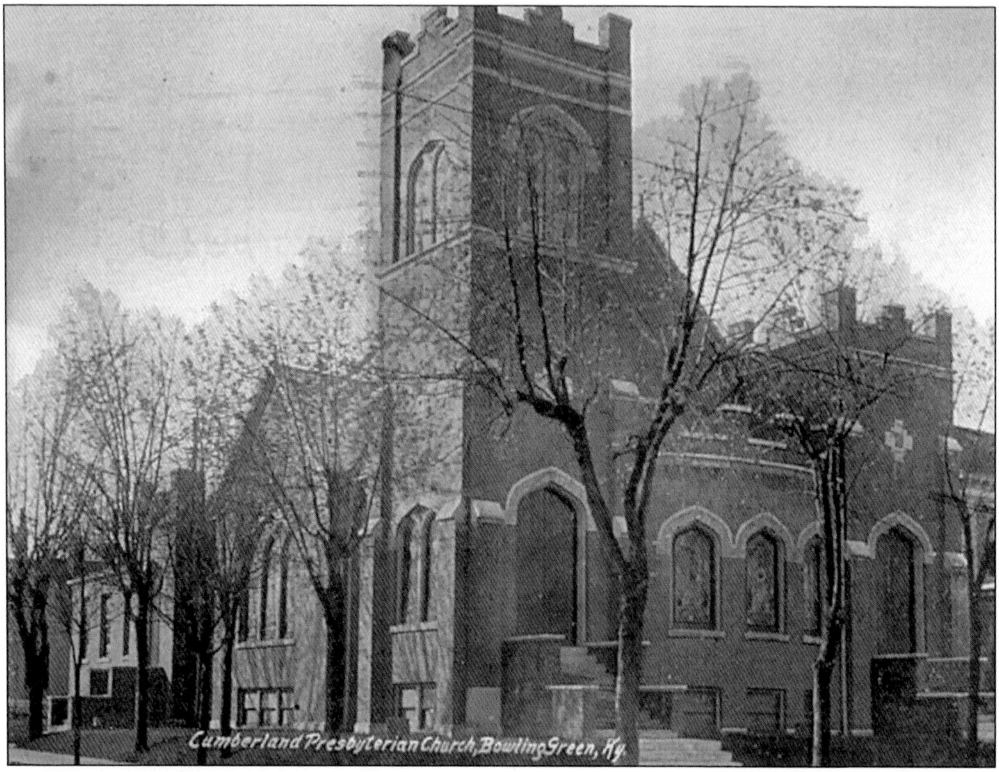

CUMBERLAND PRESBYTERIAN CHURCH. Rev. Jesse Grider organized the Cumberland Presbyterian Church in Bowling Green in 1866. The congregation erected the building pictured here at College and Eleventh Streets in 1909 for $20,000. This building was used until the congregation moved to their new church on Campbell Lane in 1971.

EIGHT SERMONS ON PROPHECY

—At—

Bowling Green, Kentucky

Cumberland Presbyterian Church

College Street at Eleventh

BEGINNING SUNDAY NIGHT, JULY THE 23RD AND CONTINUING EACH NIGHT THROUGH SUNDAY, JULY THE 30TH, PASTOR E. C. COMFORT WILL PREACH THE FOLLOWING SERMONS AT 7:45 P. M. DAILY:

Sunday, July 23—"The Study of Prophecy." Dan. 9:1-23.

Monday, July 24—"The Spirit of Prophecy." Rev. 19:10.

Tuesday, July 25—"The Certainty of Prophecy." 2 Pet. 1:19.

Wednesday, July 26—"The Interpretation of Prophecy." 2 Pet. 1:19-21.

Thursday, July 27—"The Children of Prophecy." Acts 3:25.

Friday, July 23—"The Opposition to Prophecy." Matt. 23:31-34.

Saturday, July 29—"The Counterfeiting of Prophecy." Jer. 23:21.

Sunday, July 30—"The Climax of Prophecy." Dan. 7:13-14, 1 Thess. 4:16-17.

SERMON SERIES. This postcard was used to announce a sermon series delivered by Pastor E.C. Comfort at the Cumberland Presbyterian Church. Comfort was minister of the Gospel Center, a non-denominational congregation later called the Bible Presbyterian Church, from the late-1930s through the late-1940s. Reverend Comfort traveled extensively as an evangelist. In 1947, he was convicted in Bowling Green of contributing to the delinquency of a juvenile.

The Presbyterian Church. The first Presbyterian congregation in Bowling Green organized in 1819. They erected a building in what is now Pioneer Cemetery, but it burned in the early 1830s. Renowned architect Hugh Roland designed the present masonry building with Gothic windows and an elegant steeple; construction began in 1833.

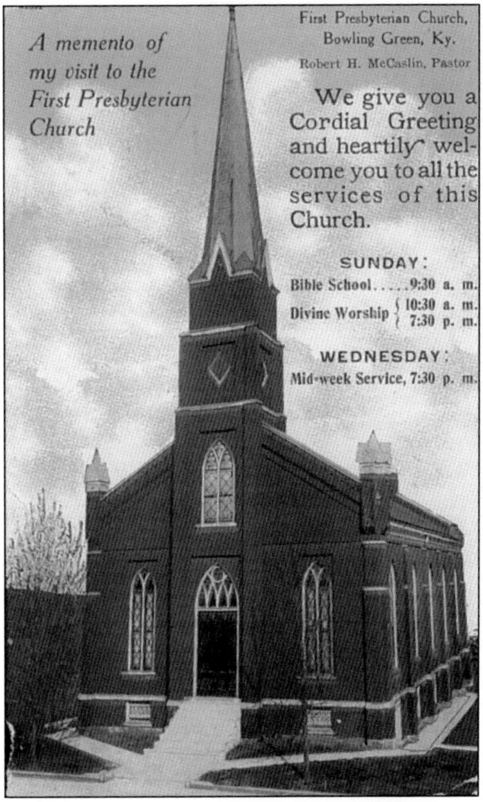

The Presbyterian Church. This church provides wonderful maintenance of its historical structure. A careful interior restoration took place in 2000. When built, the basement was completed first to accommodate the Bowling Green Female Academy. The congregation fully occupied the building in 1837 making this the oldest ecclesiastical structure in the city. It was used during the Civil War as a temporary hospital.

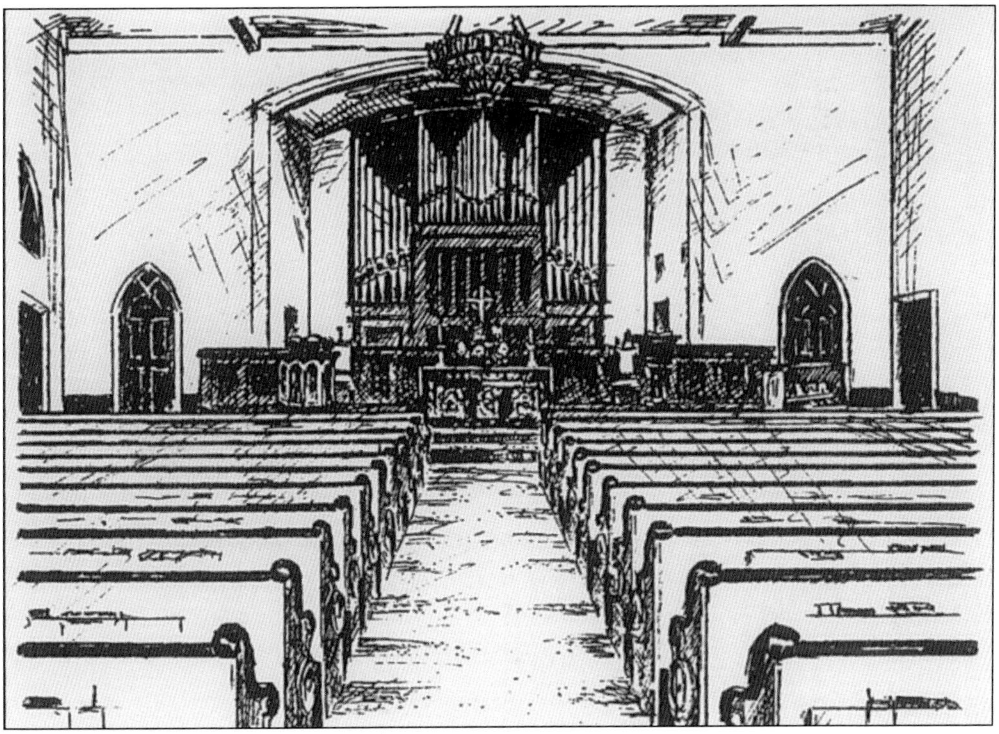

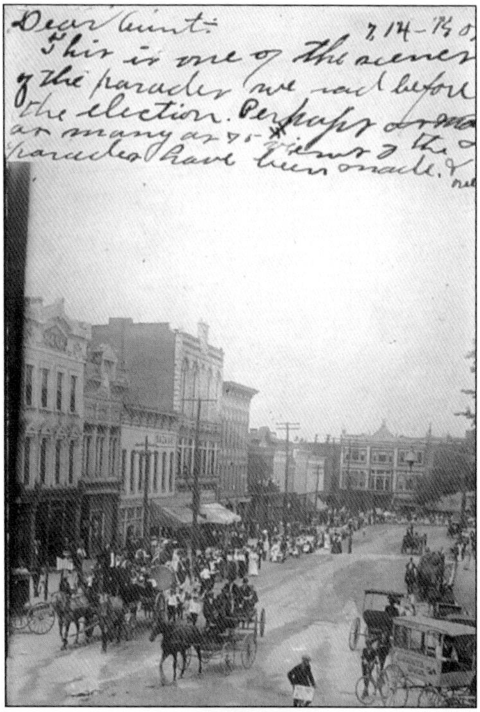

PROHIBITION PARADE. Bowling Green has been through an inordinate number of local option elections. One of the largest occurred in the summer of 1907. This Park Row view shows people preparing for the big dry forces parade on June 6, 1907. A band is assembled on the sidewalk. The card sender indicated that "as many as 75 views of the parade have been made and been put on postcards."

BUGGY BRIGADE. The great 1907 Prohibition Parade included a brigade of decorated baby buggies to tug at the hearts of those watching. Here, several ladies have decorated both their buggies and hats with live flowers and American flags. The second lady from the left is wearing a placard that reads "Please vote for me." Prohibition forces won the election by over 300 votes, but the decision was reversed in an acrimonious 1910 referendum.

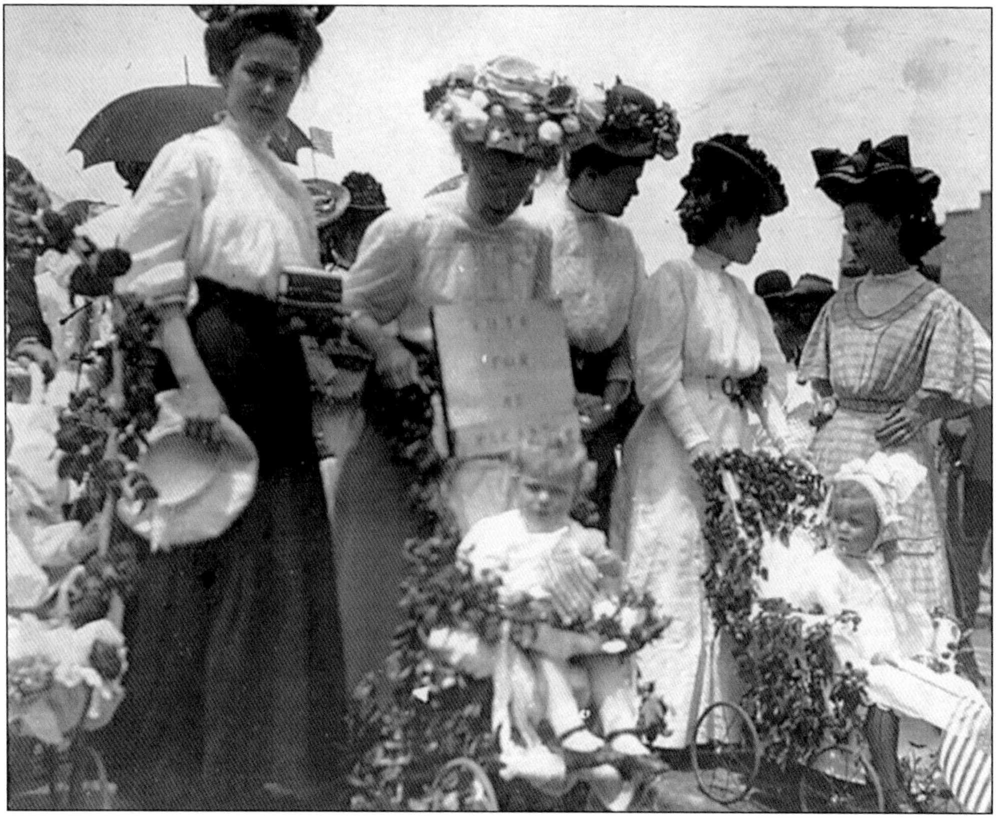

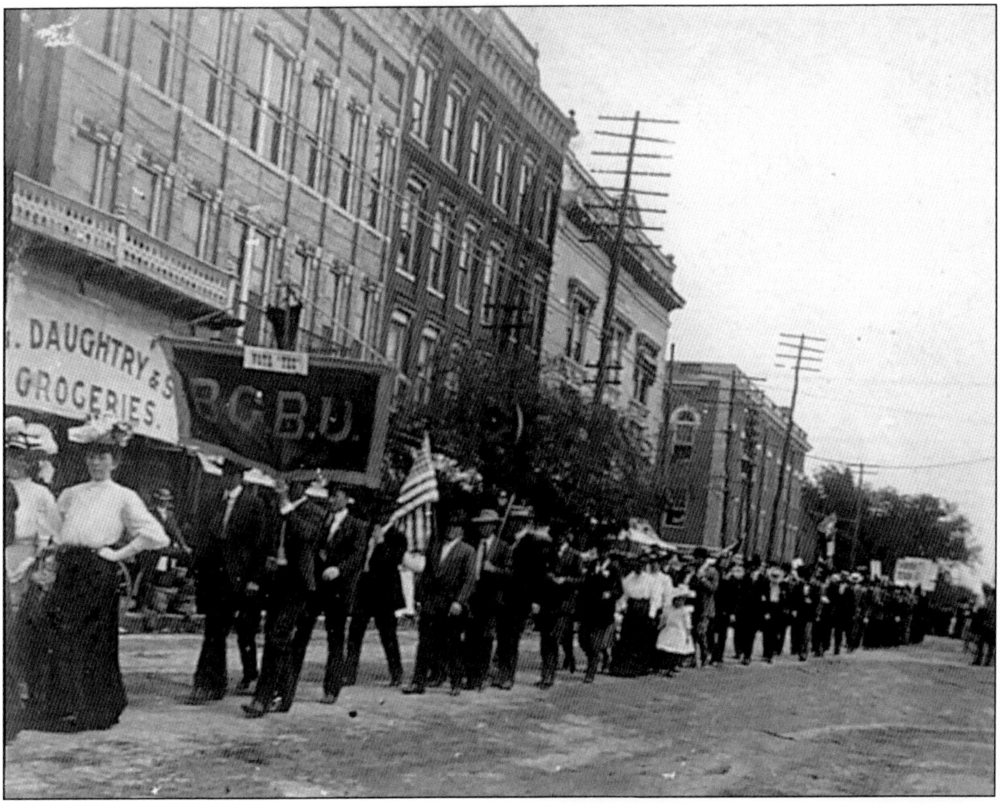

BGBU Delegation. Students from the Bowling Green Business University marched in the 1907 Prohibition Parade behind a large banner. This view was taken on College Street. Notice the awkward looking balcony on the second floor of the Daughtery Grocery at 915 College Street.

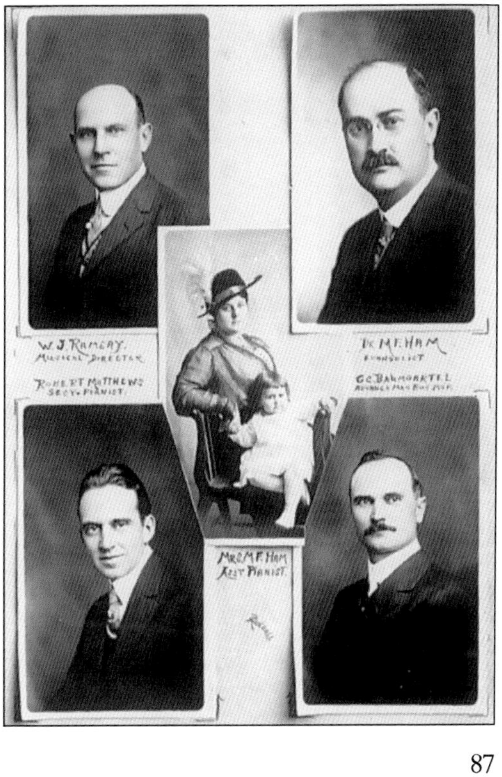

The Ham-Ramsay Party. A deciding factor in the local option election of 1907 was a revival concurrently conducted by Mordecai Ham, an evangelist and Prohibition supporter. Ham is best known as the minister instrumental in converting Billy Graham. A Glasgow, Kentucky correspondent noted that Ham was "conducting a big revival in Bowling Green. He is working hard to save the city. May God Bless his efforts, and victory be ours. Pray for us."

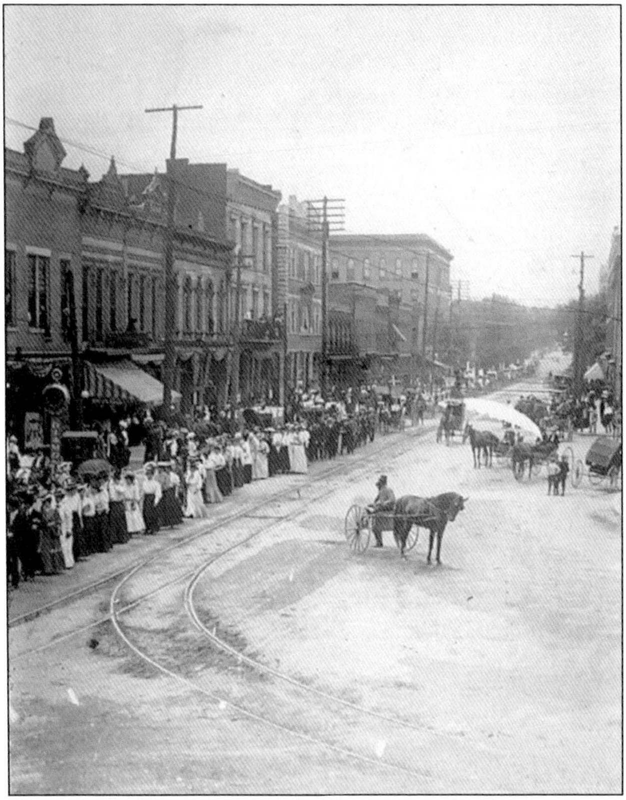

PROHIBITION PARADE. Here you can see the parade participants lined all the way up State Street. Besides documenting the event, the photographer captured details about the buildings along this important commercial avenue. The rails for the city's streetcar system are also clearly seen in this photo.

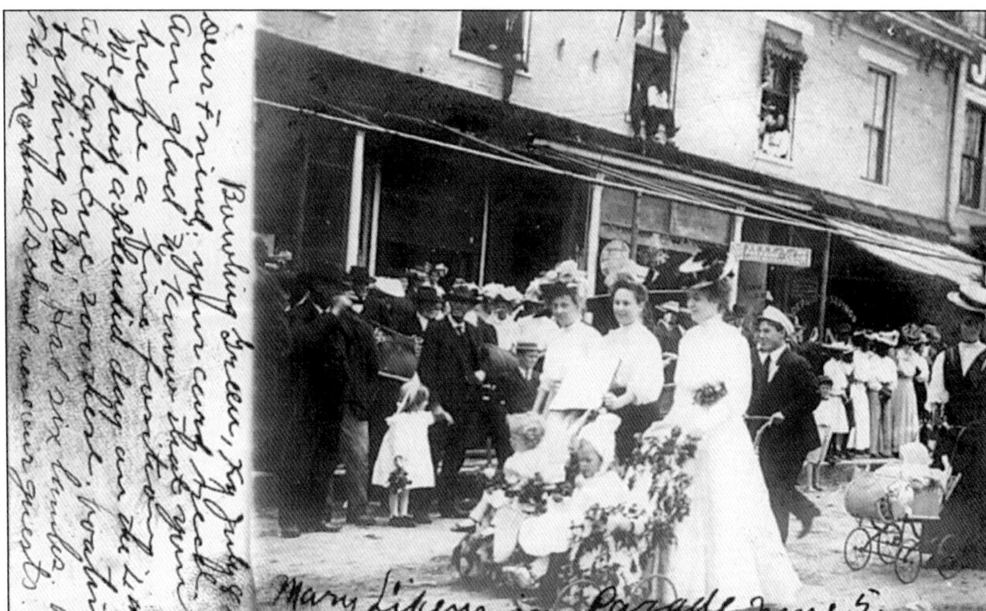

BUGGY BRIGADE. The children in their perambulators are being viewed by a crowd gathered in front of the old Rochester Hotel at the corner of Main and College Streets. Notice the onlookers peering from the windows.

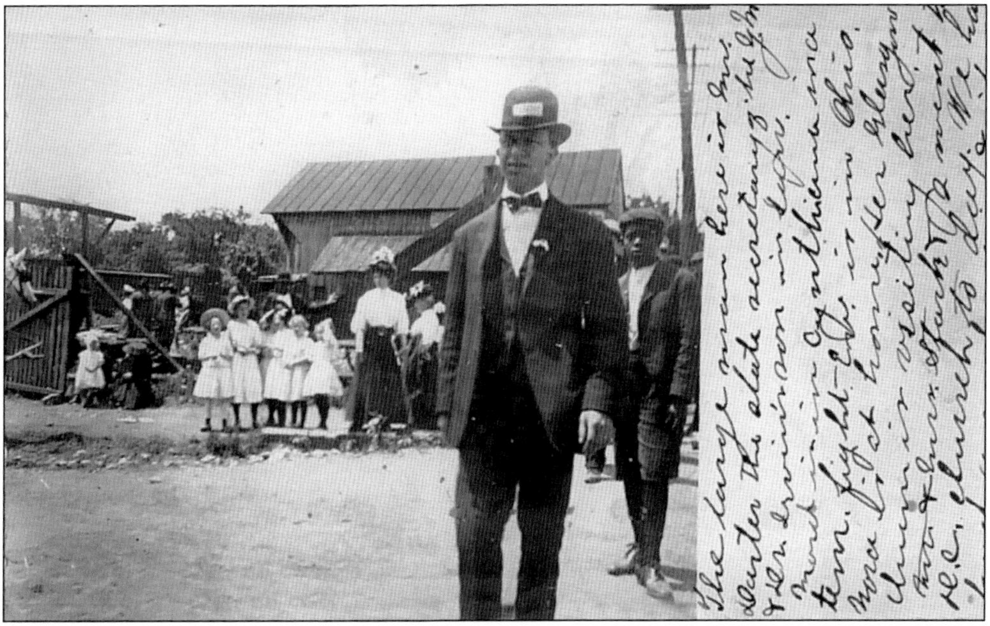

LOUIS DARTER. No event as large as the 1907 Prohibition Parade can take place without good leadership. Louis Darter, pictured prominently here, was the manager of the local YMCA. He took an active role in planning the parade. Darter was a close companion of Edgar Cayce and encouraged him in the development of the still popular game of Pit.

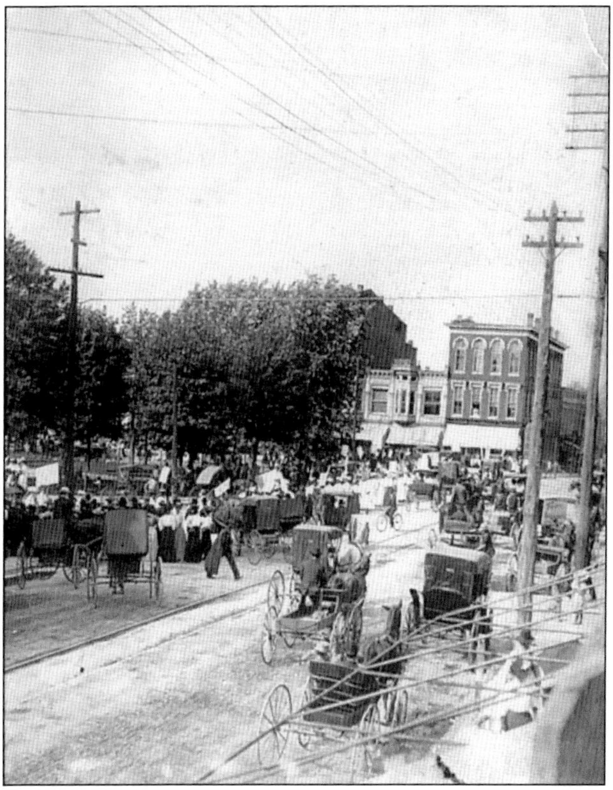

PARADE OBSERVERS. Here you see people on foot, on bicycle, and sitting in buggies watching women in white make their way around Fountain Square Park. This view gives a nice glimpse of the Barr Building and the Ogden Building on Main Street.

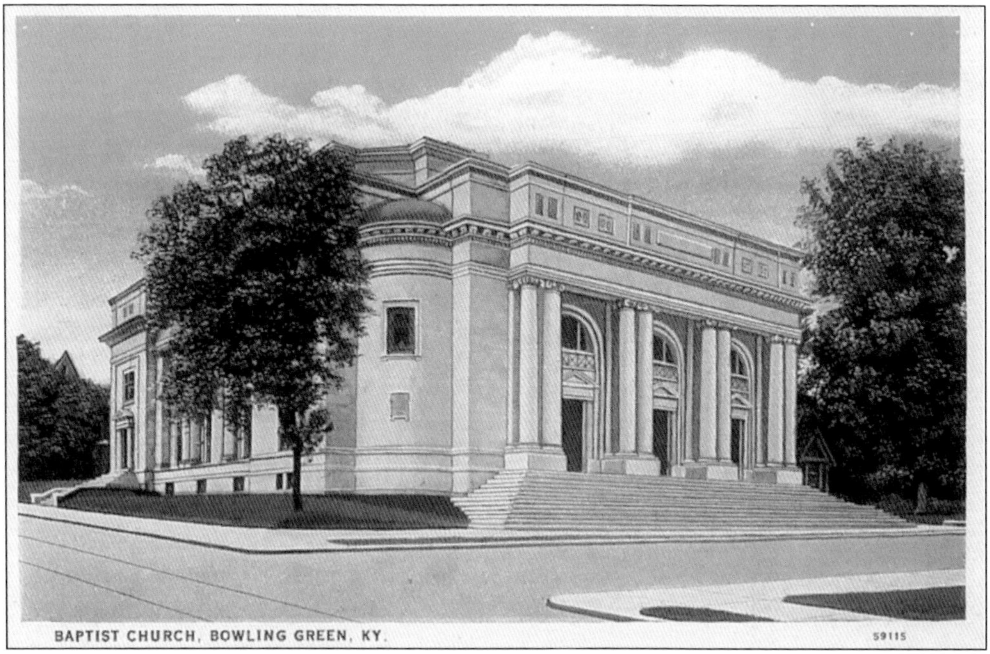

FIRST BAPTIST CHURCH. Baptists organized this church in 1818 and met in a log structure and a later frame building until they erected a commodious two-story brick building on Main Street in 1854. Local architect Creedmore Fleenor designed the church seen here in 1913. It was built for $135,000 and dedicated in 1915. Fleenor's design resembled a Parisian theater he had seen, and it was constructed with Bowling Green limestone, which led to it being called the "White Temple." It burned in 1993, and the church re-built at the same location.

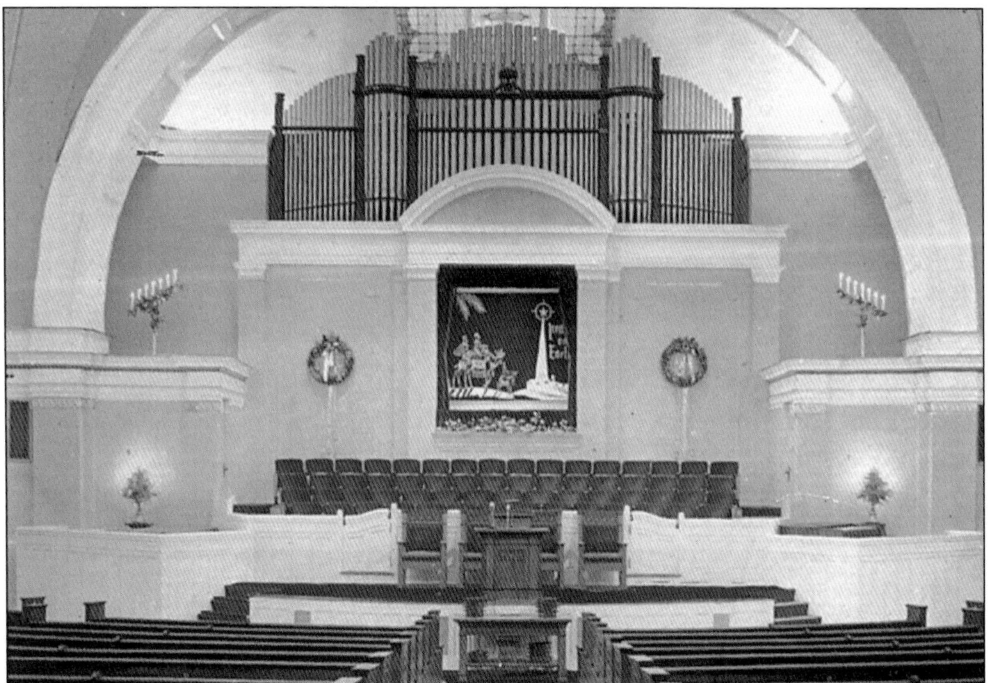

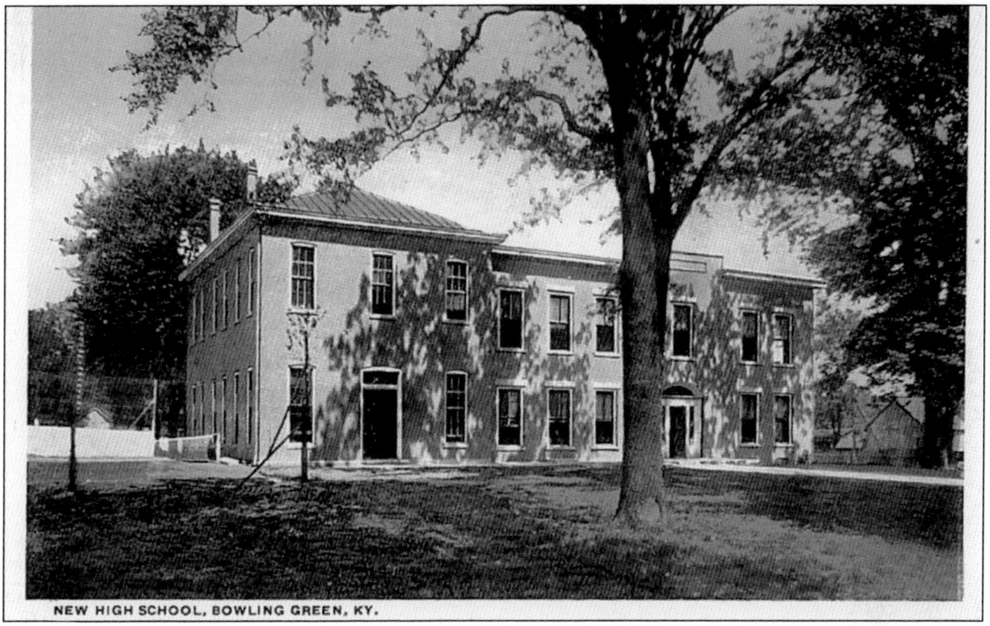

BOWLING GREEN HIGH SCHOOL. This building served as Bowling Green's high school from 1914 until 1923 when the new building at 1141 Center Street was completed. The above building was erected as a residence in the 1850s by John Q. Burnam, a successful businessman and the treasurer for Kentucky's Confederate state government. It became the junior high in 1923 and was razed in the late 1920s when the new junior high was constructed.

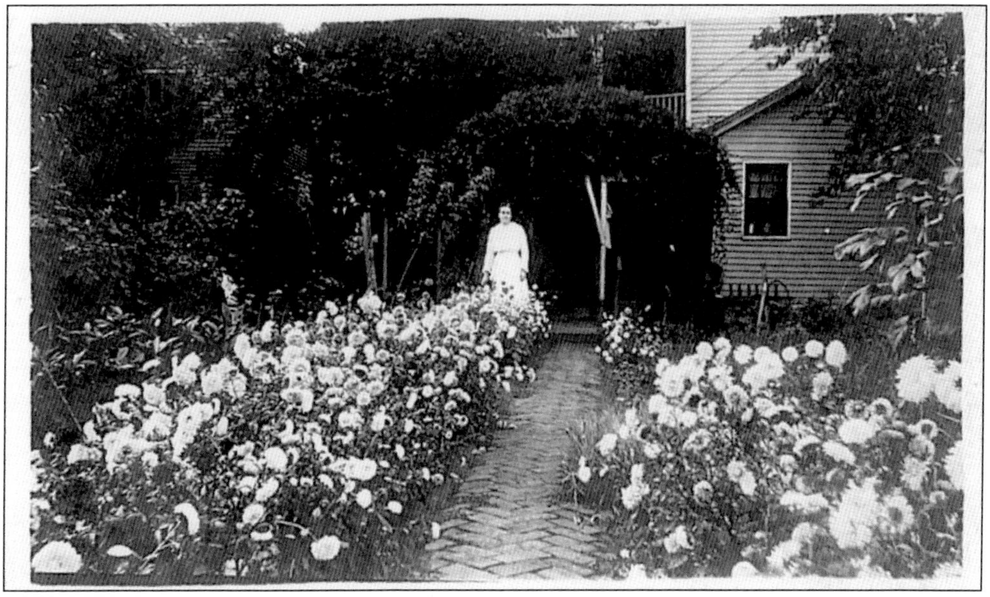

NINA MCGINNIS. Beautiful flowers lined the brick sidewalk in the yard of veteran educator Nina McGinnis at 1055 Adams Street. McGinnis graduated from Potter College in 1897 and began teaching mathematics there the following year. When that school closed in 1909, she began teaching Latin and mathematics at Bowling Green High School. She became principal at the high school in 1911, a position she occupied until her death in 1928.

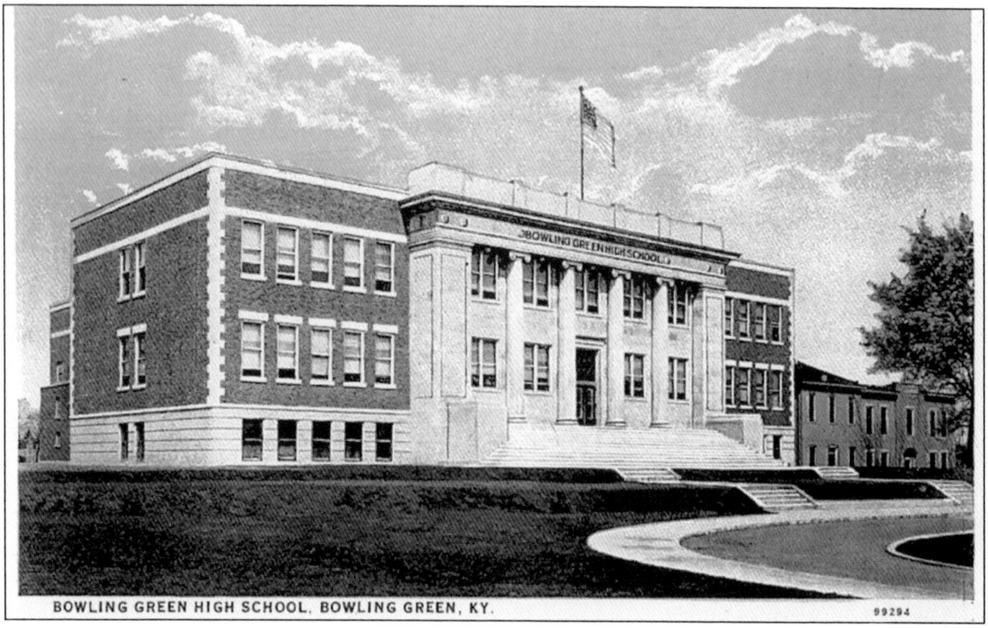

BOWLING GREEN HIGH SCHOOL. This Classical Revival building, designed by Clifford Shopbell and Co. of Evansville, was completed in 1923 at a cost of $100,000. It housed Bowling Green High School until its new complex on Rockingham Avenue was completed in 1970. The Junior High School moved in and remained here until its new facility on Campbell Lane was completed in 2001.

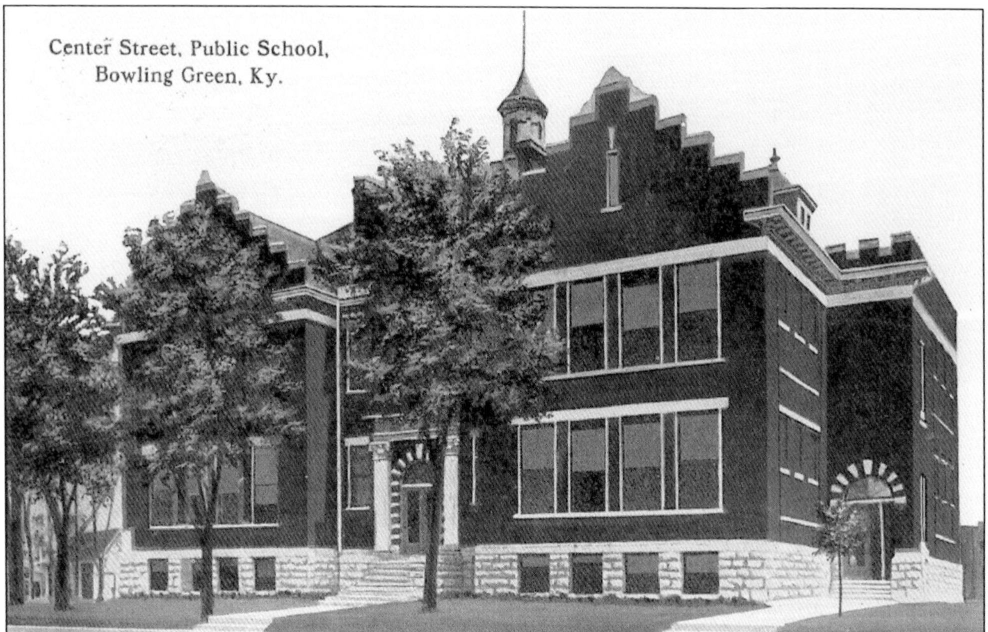

CENTER STREET SCHOOL. This impressive school, erected at the corner of Eighth and Center Streets in 1907, replaced the Green Street School. The two-and-a-half story building was accented with a rough ashlar limestone basement, continuous limestone sills and lintels, variegated door surrounds, unusual corbeled gables, and a pert cupola. The building was razed in 1962.

College Street School. This school was one of Bowling Green's original public school buildings, erected in 1882. It was three stories tall with walls four bricks thick. Former students often recall the building's horrendous circular fire escape. The building, which had restrooms only on the first floor and never had a cafeteria, was razed in 1961, when the new post office was built on the property.

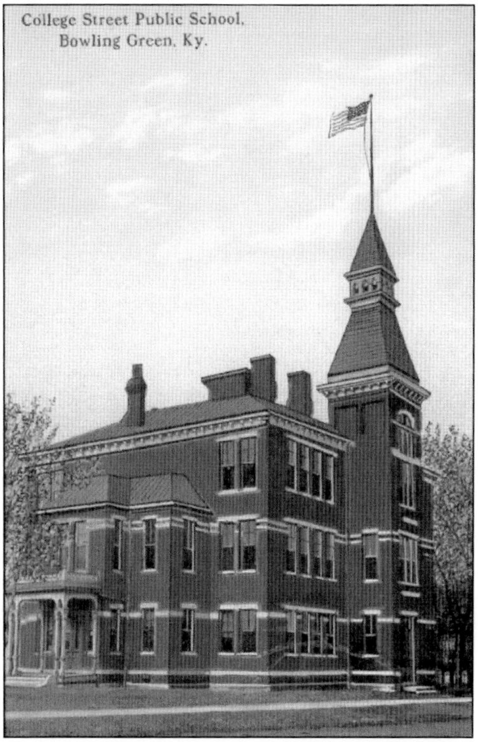

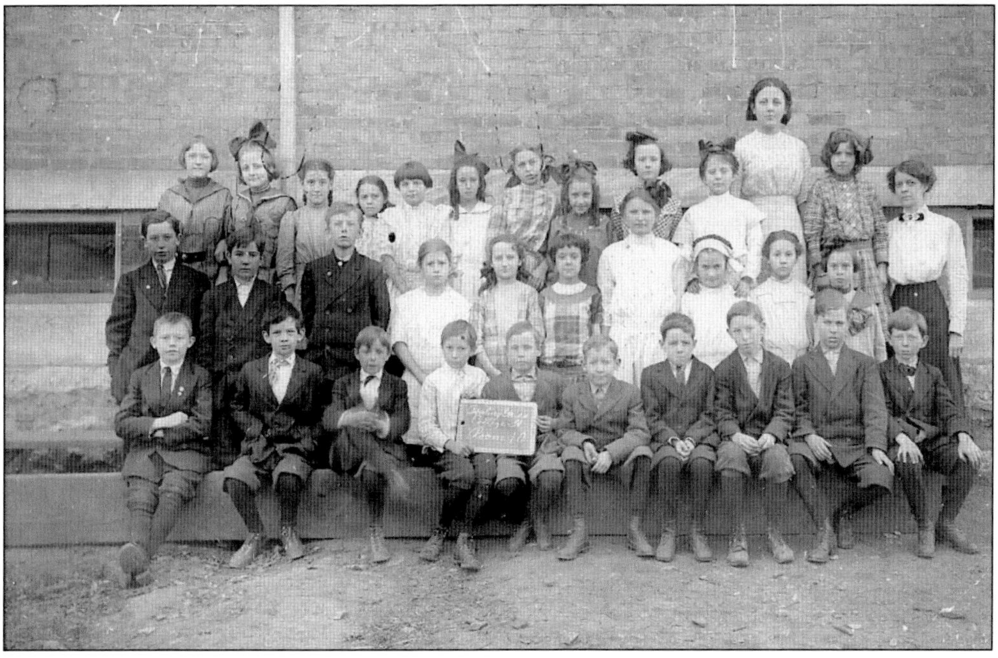

College Street Class. This is Lyda Flenniken's fourth grade class at College Street School in 1913. This was the standard classroom picture of the period with the students lined up by a flat wall of the building. Someone in the center usually held a small slate with the name of the school and the room number on it. Sometimes the slate would contain the teacher's name or the grade.

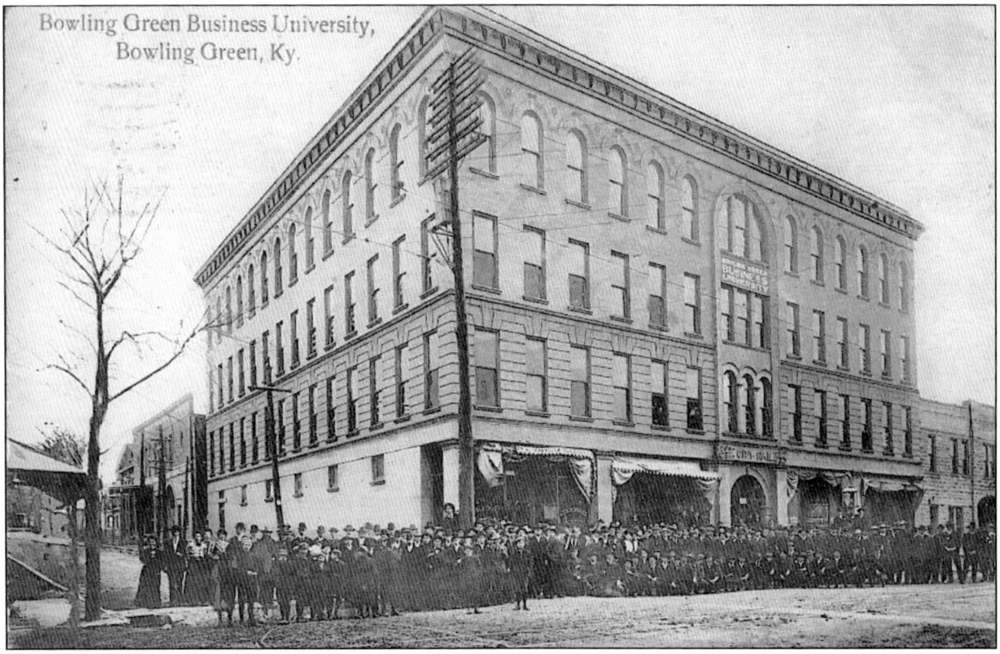

BGBU. The beloved Bowling Green Business University, or the BU as most locals and alumni call it, started as an outgrowth of the Cherry brothers' Southern Normal School. Students were trained in stenography, penmanship, accounting, finance, telegraphy, business law, and business machines. The school once boasted that it was the largest commercial college in the United States. The BU met in several locations, including the pictured (top) McCormack Building downtown before the erection of its permanent home in 1901. Designed by local architect Creedmore Fleenor, the Center Street building (below) was sometimes referred to as "the castle" due to its castellated parapets. Edgar Cayce also included a small inset photo of Henry H. Cherry for this card.

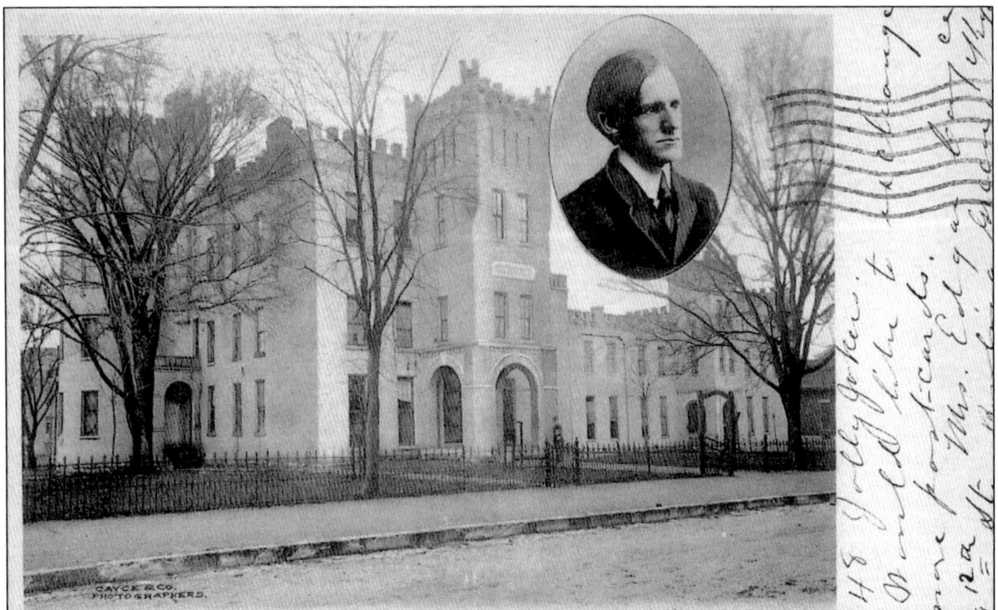

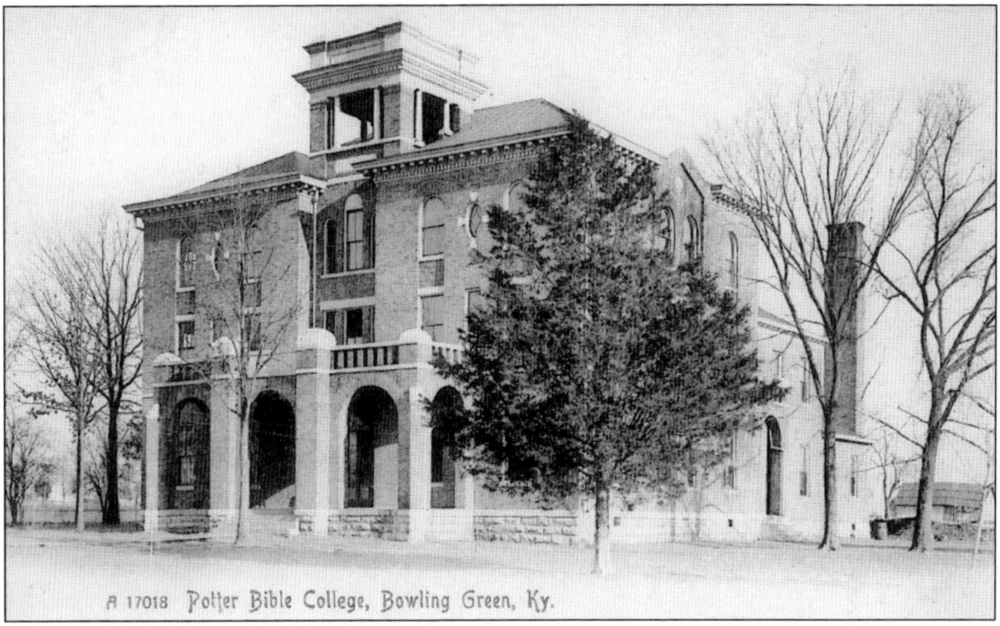

POTTER BIBLE SCHOOL. Clinton and Mary Potter established this school as a memorial to Mrs. Potter's son, Eldon S. Potter. It began operation on September 24, 1901 with 107 students. The main college building, pictured here, was erected for $11,000, but burned in 1941. The school also used the Potter home next door. The school closed in 1912 and two years later became Potter Orphan Home and School, which it remains to this day.

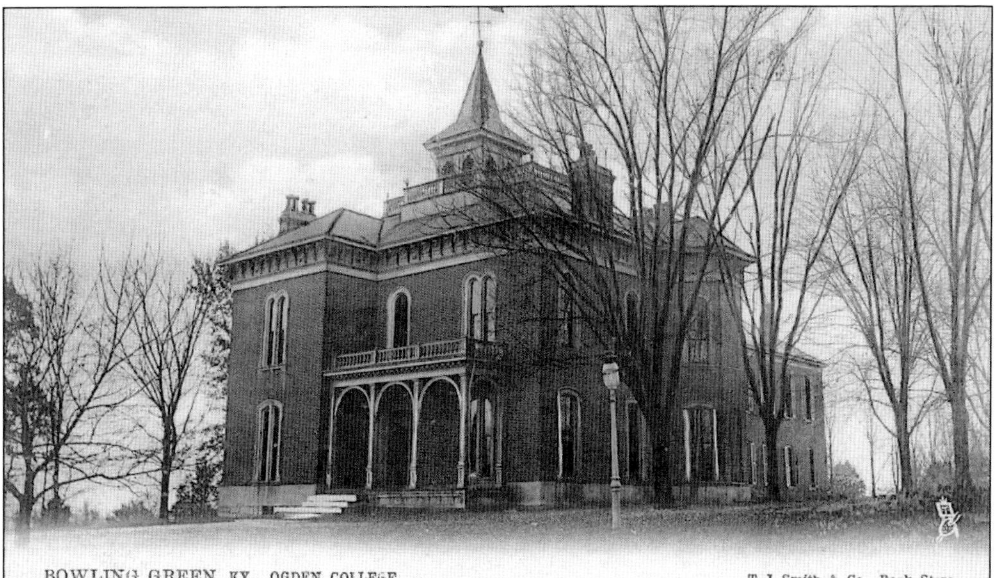

OGDEN COLLEGE. This school was founded in 1877 through the generosity of Robert Wren Ogden of Bowling Green. Its purpose was to provide secondary education for young men from Warren County. It evolved into a degree-granting institution and had an enviable reputation in the region. The building was originally designed as a private residence for Thomas Calvert, but during the construction phase was adapted for educational purposes. Ogden College merged with WKU in 1927.

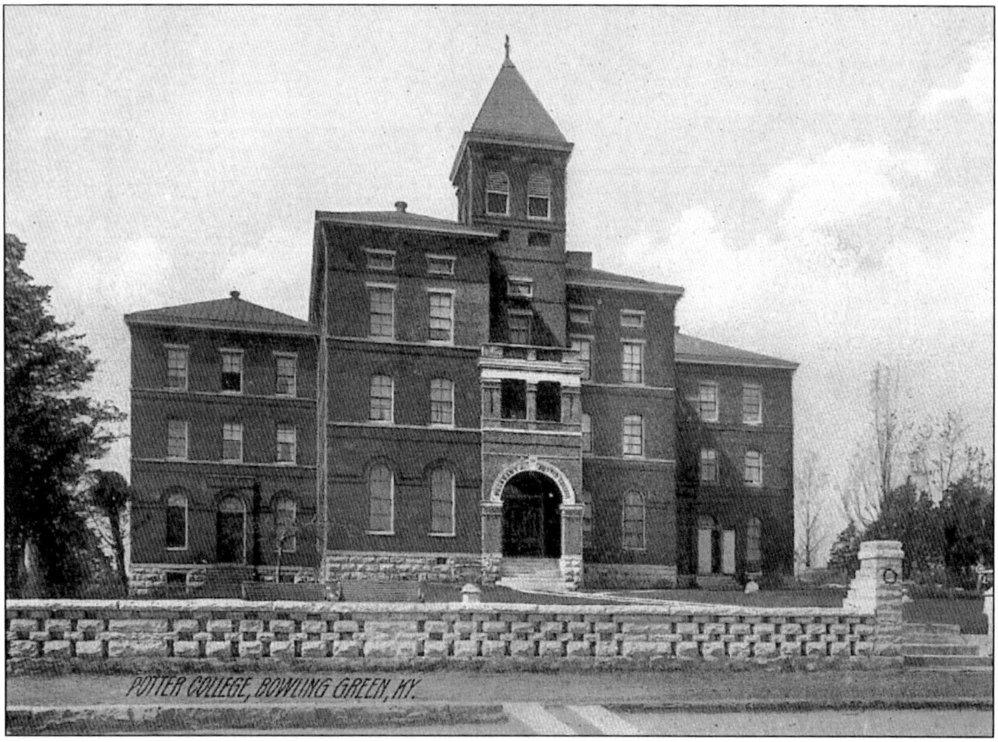

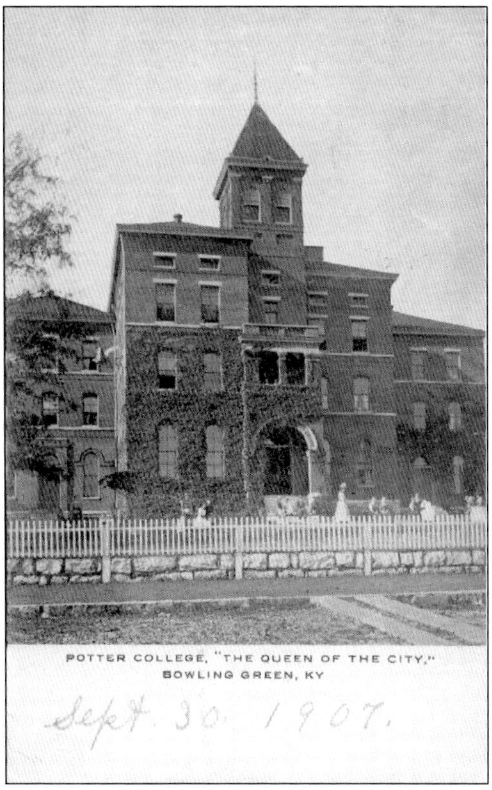

POTTER COLLEGE. Potter opened atop Vinegar Hill on September 9, 1889 with approximately 200 students. In a period of rapid evolution in women's education, Potter College lasted, due in great part to the tenacity of its president B.F. Cabell. The school closed in 1909 and the property was purchased for the new campus of WKU. The attractive building designed by McDonald and McDonald of Louisville was razed in 1937. The top postcard is the newer card, and you can see subtle differences, particularly the lovely lattice stone fence and the cast-iron planters on the lawn. The bottom card from 1907 shows some young belles out enjoying the lawn.

Five

PARKS AND RECREATION

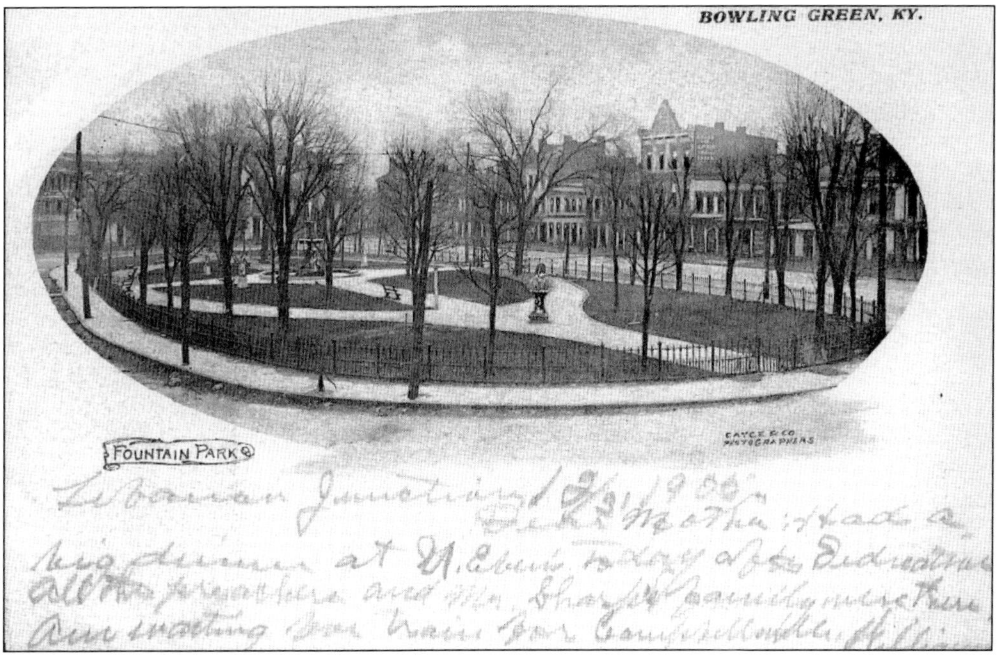

FOUNTAIN SQUARE PARK. The earliest postcards of Bowling Green are of Fountain Square Park. Edgar Cayce, who became one of America's most acclaimed clairvoyants, took the photograph for this postcard in 1905. Bowling Green's second mayor, John Cox Underwood, designed Fountain Square Park in 1870. The park was dedicated in May 1872 by Henry Watterson, editor of the *Louisville Courier-Journal*, who called it a an "enchanting green gem."

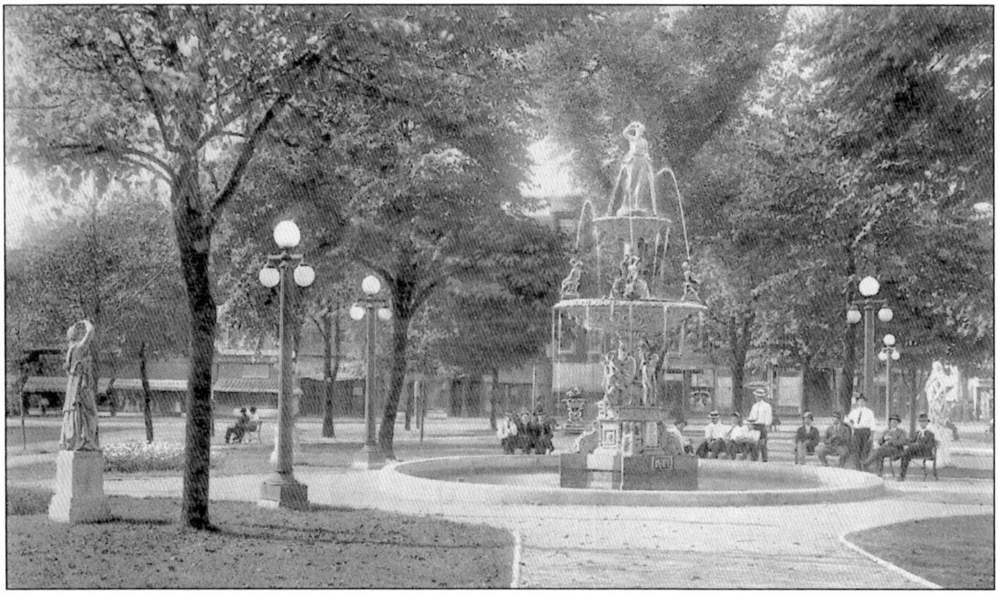

FOUNTAIN. The Hebe fountain is the focal point of Fountain Square Park. The park's first fountain, erected in 1872, was carved of local limestone and survived for less than 10 years. In 1881, the city trustees purchased a 6,000 pound precast fountain from the J.L. Mott Ironworks of New York City for $1,500. Hebe, the Greek goddess of youth, crowns the fountain. The Robinson Iron Works of Alexander City, Alabama, recast the fountain in 1987.

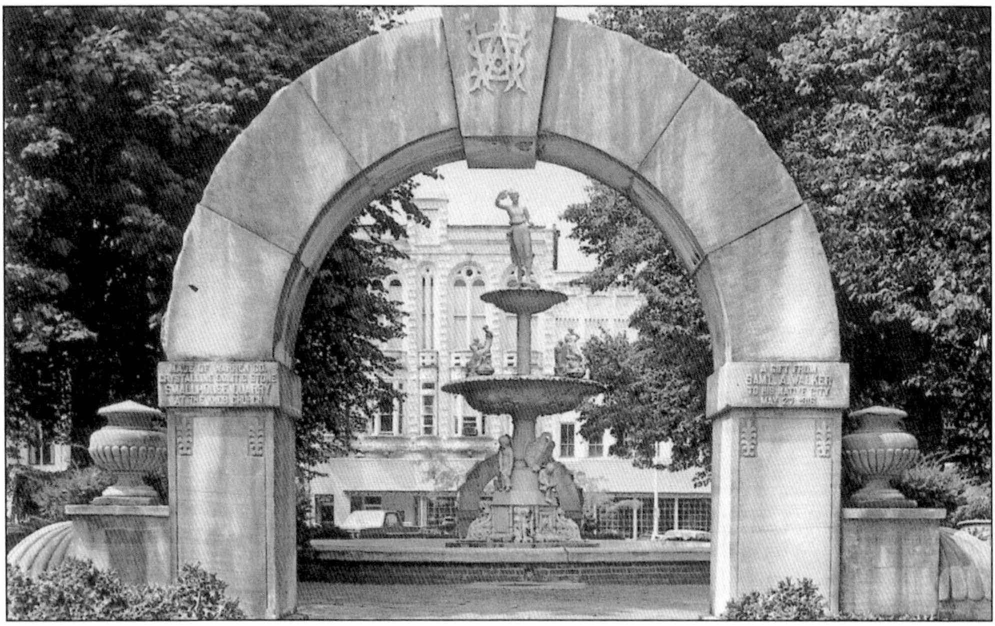

ENTRANCE ARCHES. Samuel A. Walker, a local businessman, donated this beautiful limestone arch to "his native city" in 1916. As noted on the left side, the arch is "made of crystalline oolitic stone from the Smallhouse Quarry at the Knob Church" referring to the Providence Knob Baptist Church, one of the county's oldest congregations. The matching arch directly across the park was donated in honor of the Lampkin brothers.

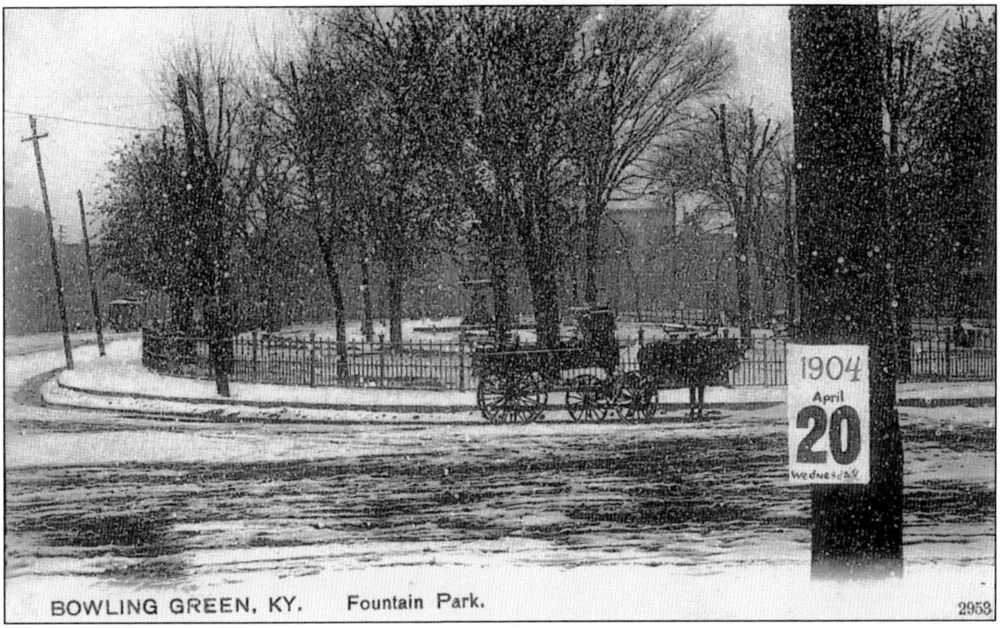

WINTER PARK SCENES. Despite the weather, Fountain Square Park is always a jewel. The park was a welcome respite for the many farmers and families who came to shop or trade in Bowling Green on court days. Here you could eat breakfast, buy clothing, have shoes repaired or shined, buy a bag of popcorn outside and watch a movie inside, buy a piece of farm equipment, purchase a new pair of spectacles, see the doctor or dentist, or just window shop. The top postcard displays the mode of transporting freight in 1904. The old iron fence is featured in both cards. It was erected to protect this enchanting green space from livestock. The fence was removed in 1910 and purportedly installed at Fairview Cemetery, where it remained until sacrificed to the scrap drives of World War II.

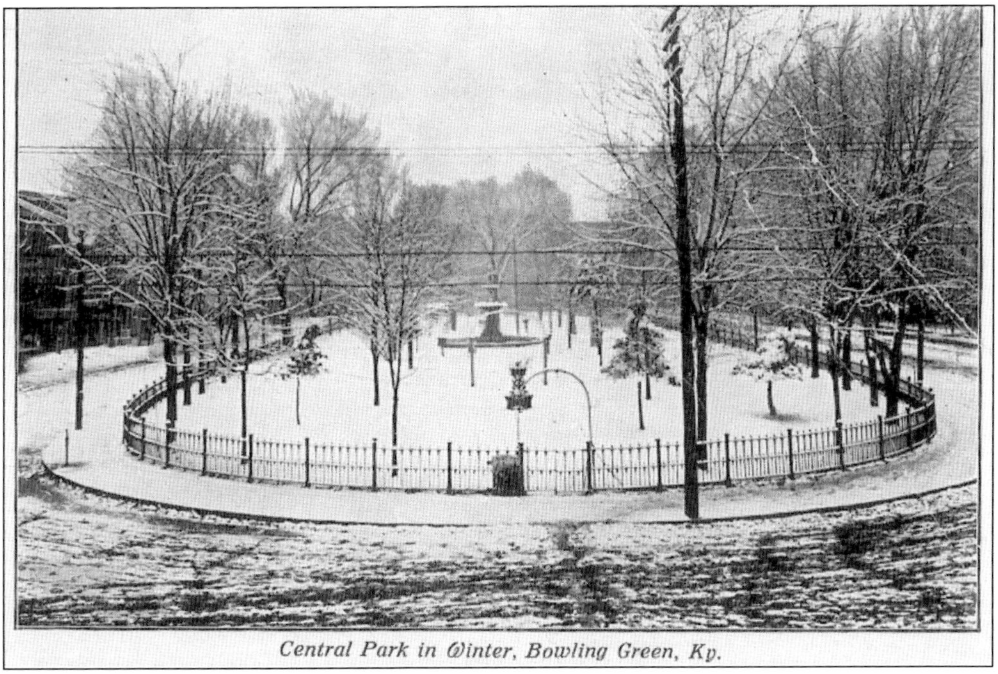

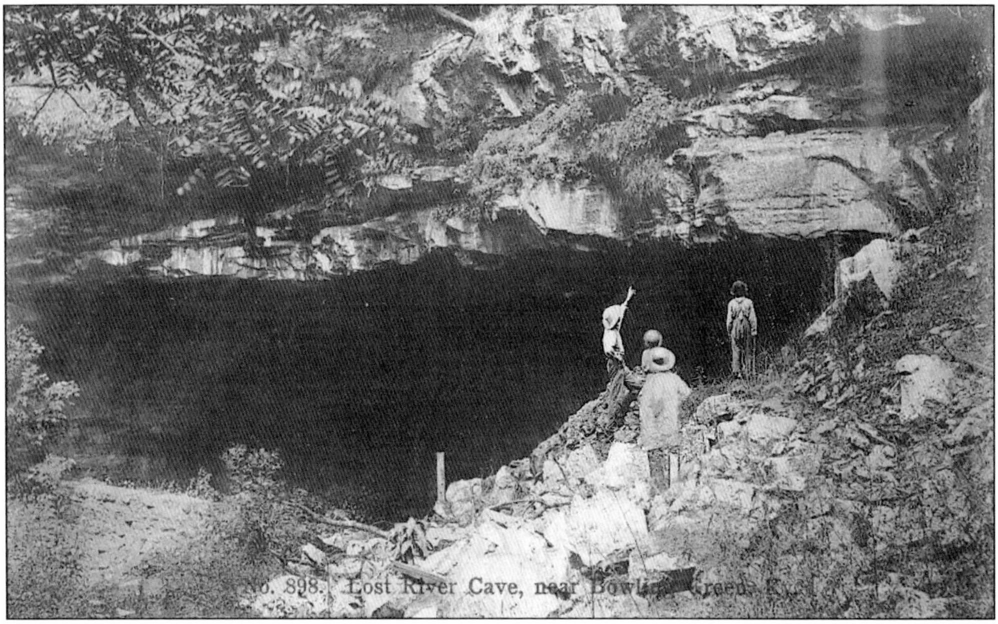

LOST RIVER CAVE AND VALLEY. This cave is perhaps Bowling Green's most unique tourist attraction. The collapse of a cave ceiling that once protected the underground watercourse, created the valley thousands of years ago. The cave's mouth is the second largest east of the Mississippi River. In the early 1930s, an enterprising owner created a subterranean "Nite Club" complete with colored lights, a dance pavilion, and dining facilities. Luminaries, such as Dinah Shore and Francis Craig and his NBC orchestra, once crooned or played in the unusual facility. The naturally moderate temperatures encouraged business, particularly during the summer months. Through a cooperative arrangement with Western Kentucky University, the Friends of Lost River re-opened the cave and valley for foot and boat tours in the early 1990s.

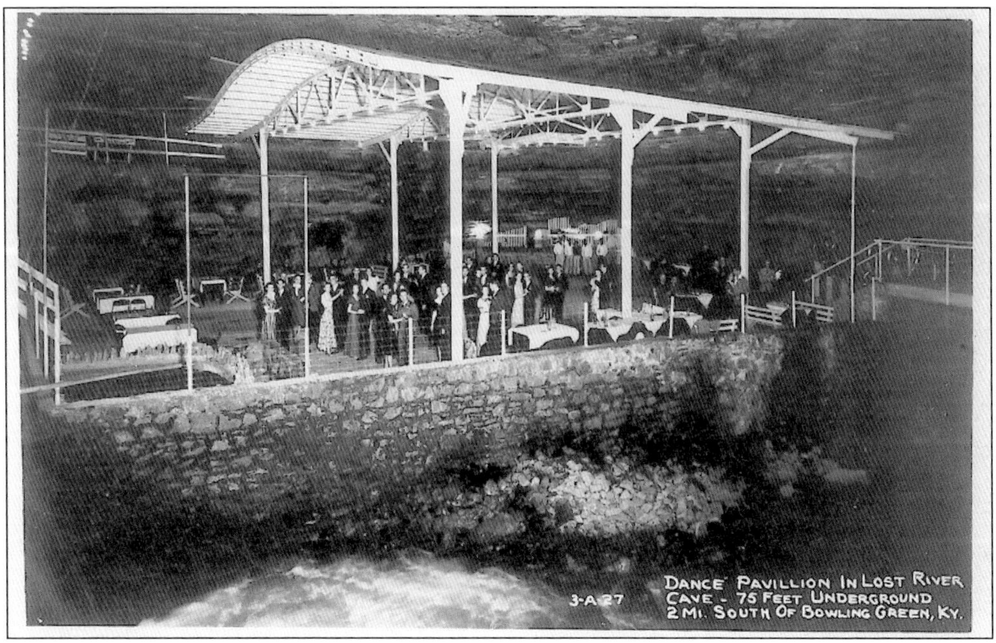

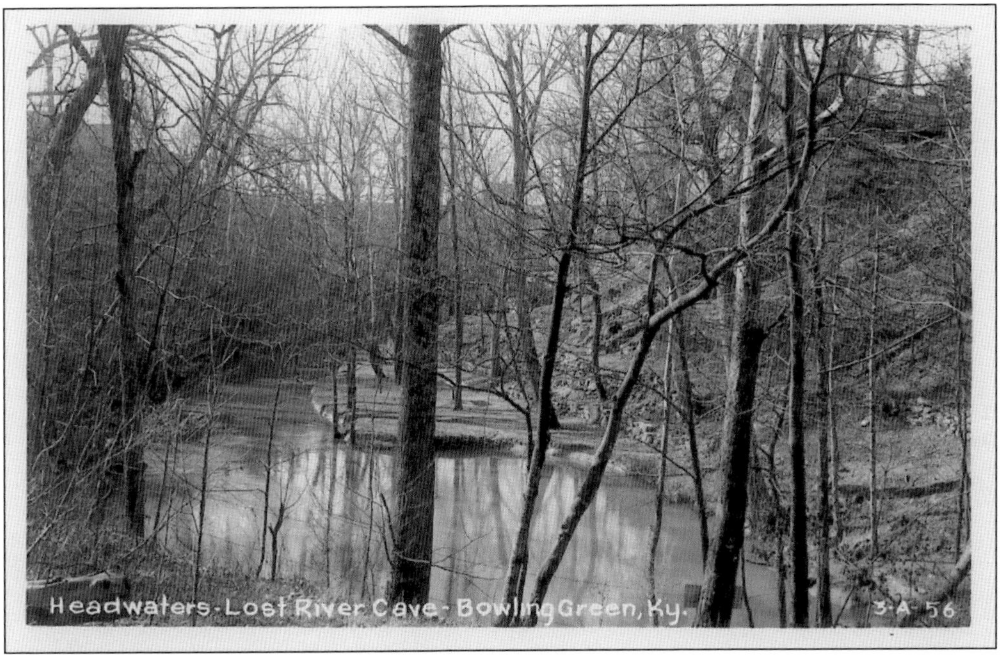

LOST RIVER. The focal point of the Lost River Cave and Valley, located two miles south of downtown Bowling Green, is Lost River. Fed by natural springs, the river meanders for a few hundred feet before entering the cavern. It flows underground for several miles before re-emerging to the surface.

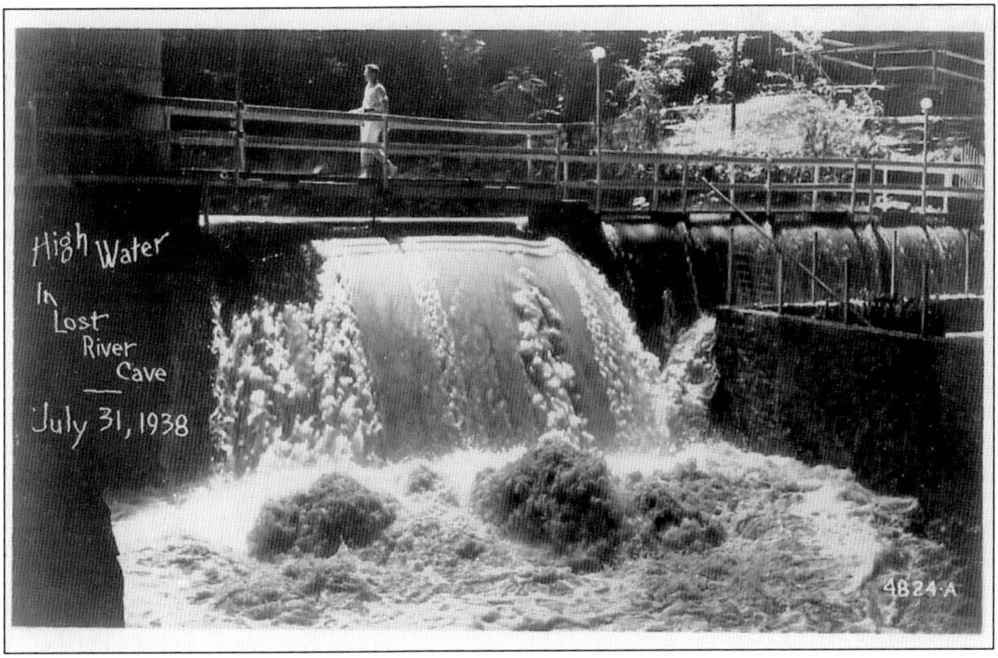

LOST RIVER DAM. The river has been dammed for well over 150 years, first for a gristmill and later for hydro-electricity production. The power plant provided enough electricity to supply all the cave's activities plus tourist cabins and the owner's home. The valley still occasionally floods after heavy rains. *Ripley's Believe It or Not* once pronounced Lost River the world's shortest river.

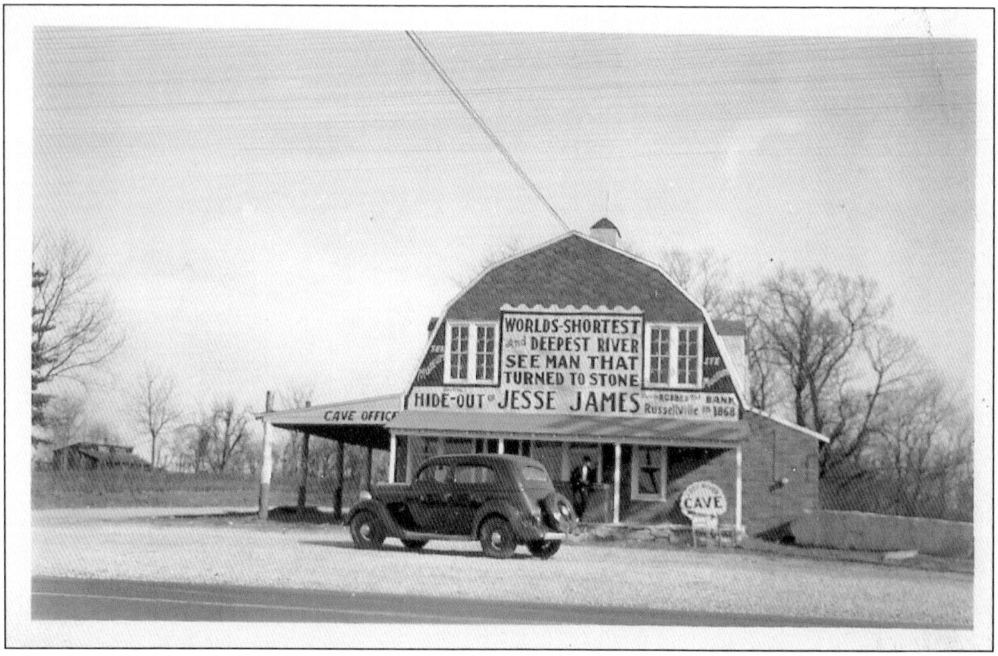

Lost River Reception Center. This gambrel-roofed building was built directly above the cave on 31-W (Nashville Road), which was the site of the 1874 grist mill. Signage blared out the cave's attractions, including the claims that the cave was purportedly used by Jesse James after a bank robbery in Russellville, that the river was the country's shortest and deepest, and that a man had been found in the cave who had been turned to stone. Some of these claims still remain rather dubious, but they attracted the curious such as the duo in the lower postcard. The reception center burned in 1990.

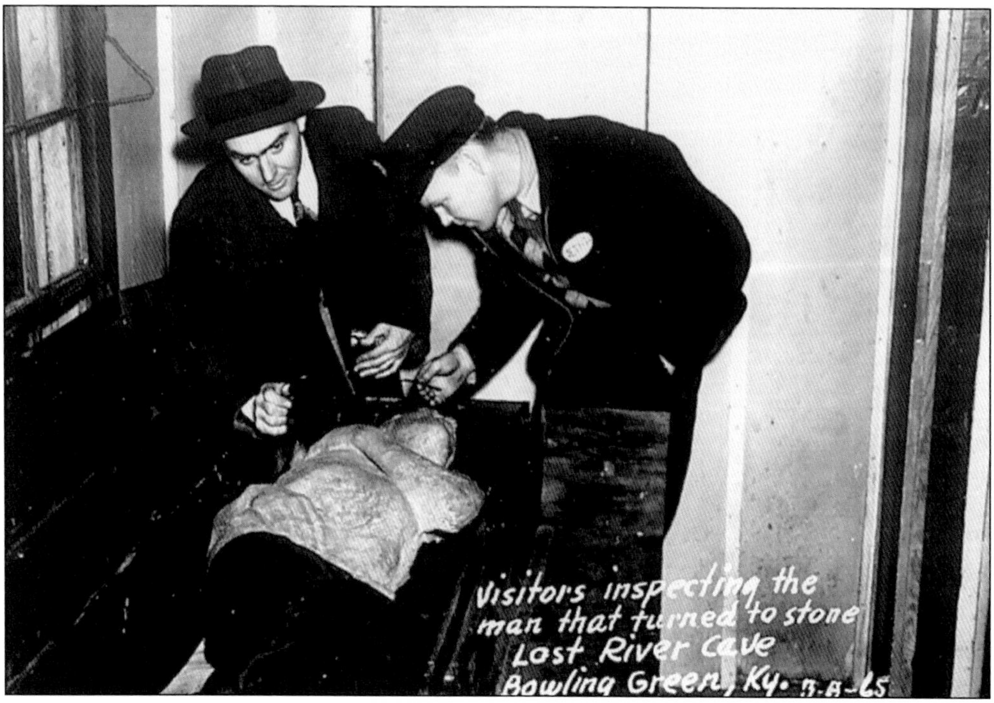

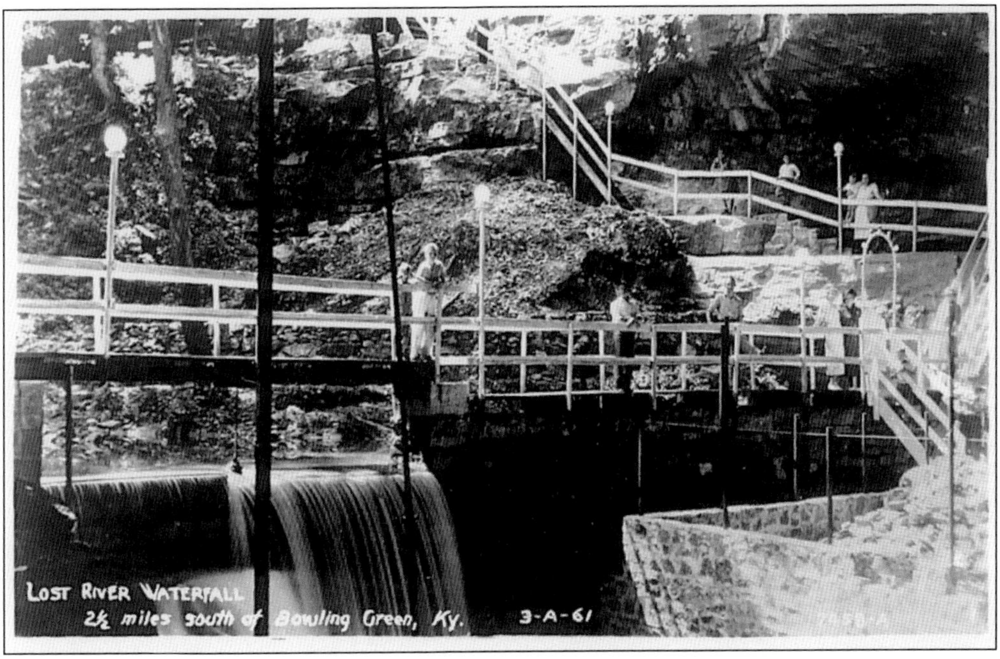

LOST RIVER. As with many popular tourist attractions, Lost River has inspired quite a bit of folklore. One story related that when a young woman looked into the depths of Lost River, she would see the face of her true love. From strolls in the valley to dancing in the cool underground nightclub on a sultry summer evening, romance definitely found a niche at Lost River.

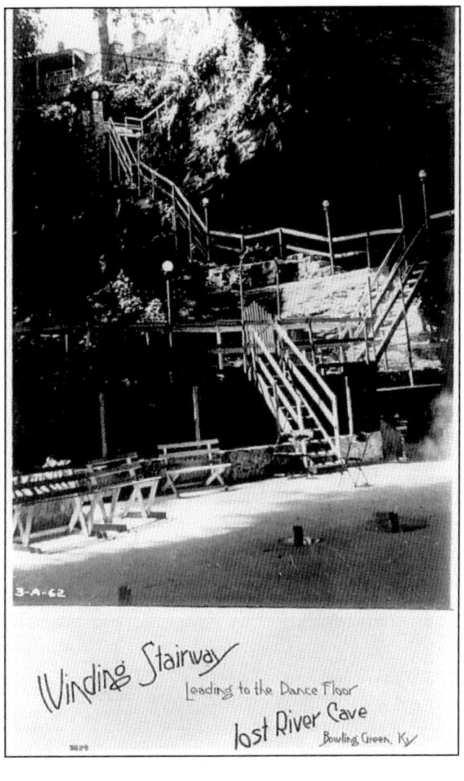

WINDING STAIRCASE. Historically, the descent to the mouth of Lost River Cave was down a rather precipitous set of frame stairways. The stairway is not presently used. Visitors today descend down a series of switchbacks removed from the road. Hikers are encouraged to explore the beautiful and historic cave valley before and after their walking or boating tour of the cave.

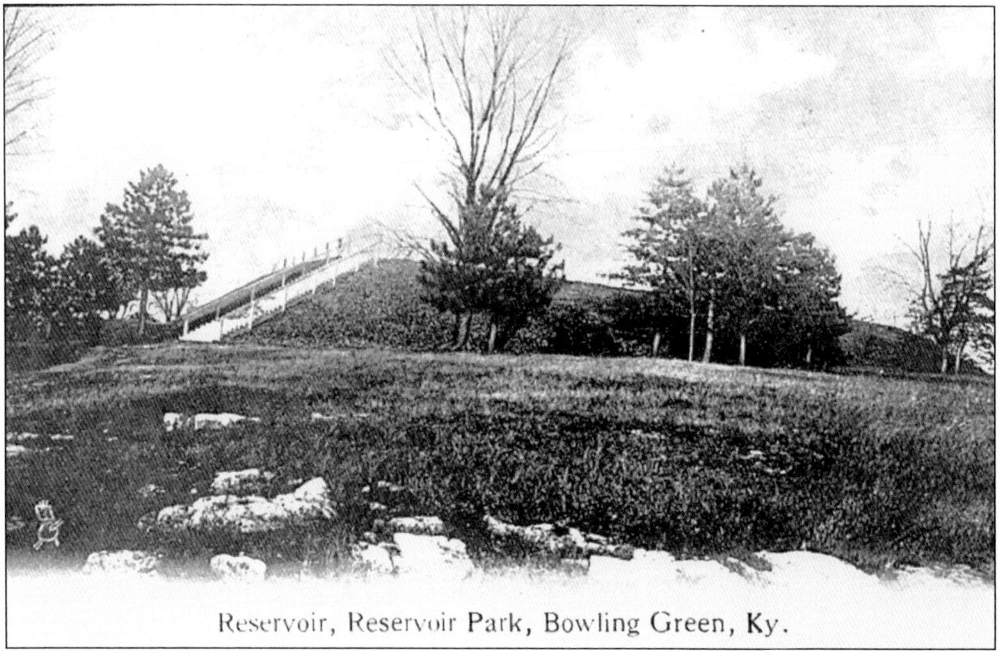

RESERVOIR PARK. This park was named for the man-made reservoir that once topped the hill and provided the city with water. The system was developed in 1868 by Charles Hermany of the Louisville Waterworks. Water was piped into the reservoir from a pump house on the Barren River; gravity created the flow necessary to get water downtown. This system was abandoned when the present water plant was constructed in the late 1920s. A small iron fence surrounded the reservoir to keep animals out. In the bottom postcard several young men observe the water being piped into the reservoir.

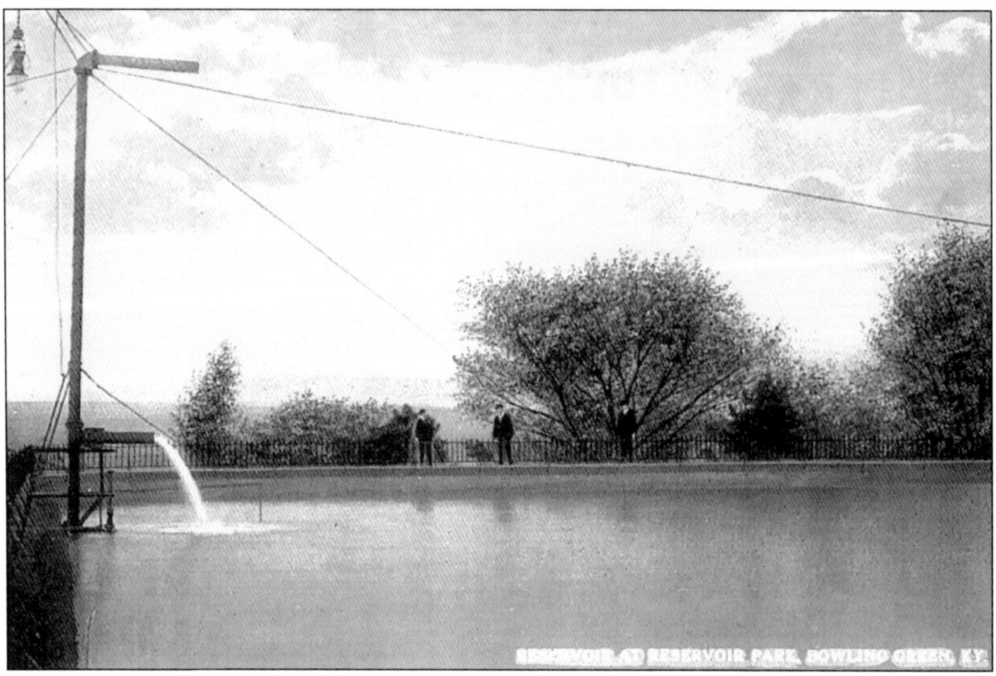

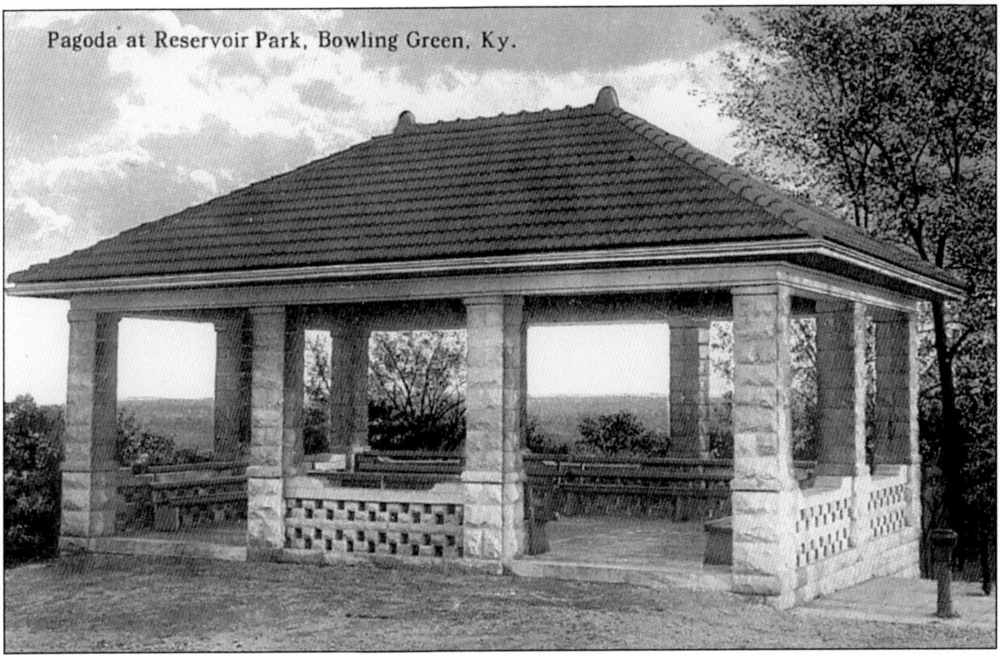

PAGODA. City fathers had this lovely open-air shelter built on the eastern periphery of Reservoir Park in 1911. It was part of a building program at the park that year that included a wading pool, swings, and tennis courts. The pagoda, (so named for the love of all things Oriental at the time) built of native limestone and capped with a lovely red tile roof, was referred to as "a favorite picnic resort."

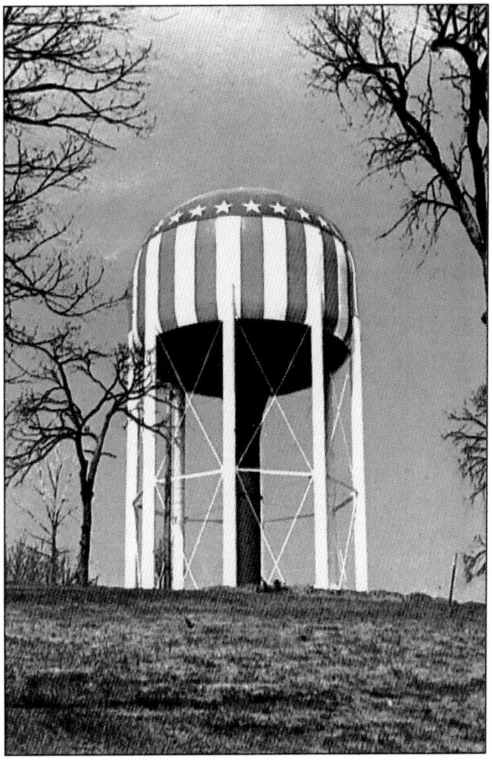

WATER TOWER. This structure is called "the nation's most patriotic water tank." Located atop Reservoir Hill, the tower "is visible from miles around the city." The tower was erected in 1969 by the Water, Sewer, and Sanitation Commission. Some members expressed reservations about the brightly-colored red, white, and blue scheme proposed by Mayor R.D. Graham, but it soon became a Bowling Green trademark. The R.D. Cole Manufacturing Co. painted the tower for $1,500.

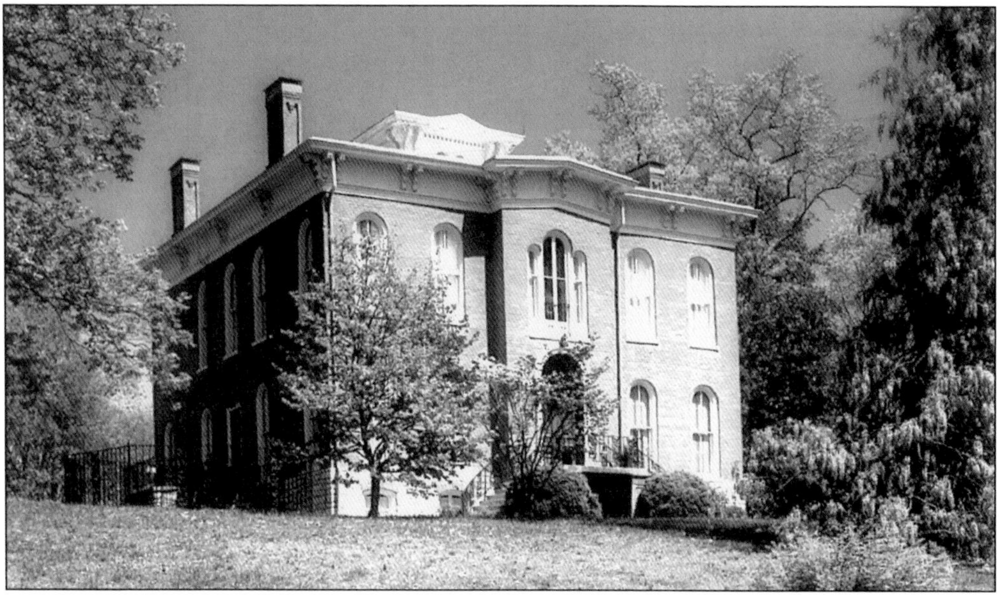

Riverview at Hobson Grove. Atwood Gaines and Juliette (Van Meter) Hobson began this stately country home in 1857 according to the plans of D.J. Williams, the architect for the Warren County Courthouse. When the Civil War started, only the basement walls were completed. Troops used the shell for ammunition storage. Completed in 1872, the house is a splendid example of Italianate architecture with its arched windows, wide bracketed eaves, and crowning cupola. A Hobson family member lived in the home until the early 1950s. The house went through extensive restoration in the early 1970s and opened as a historical house museum in 1972. Guided tours make the house come alive with stories about its past occupants and the beautiful ceiling murals, walnut staircase, "running" water, and period furnishings.

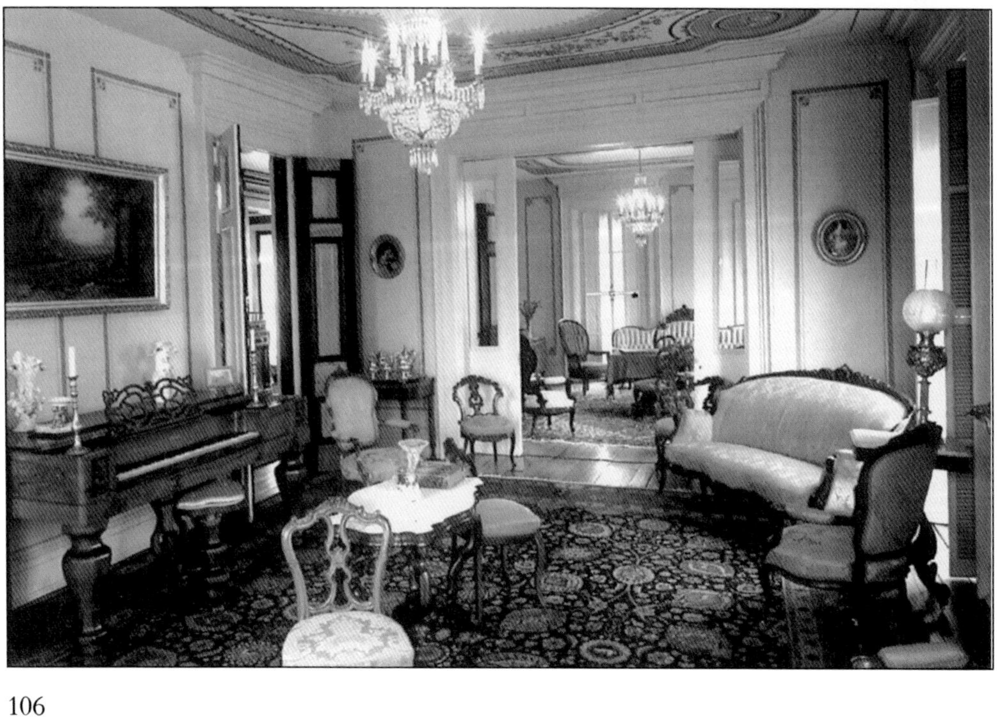

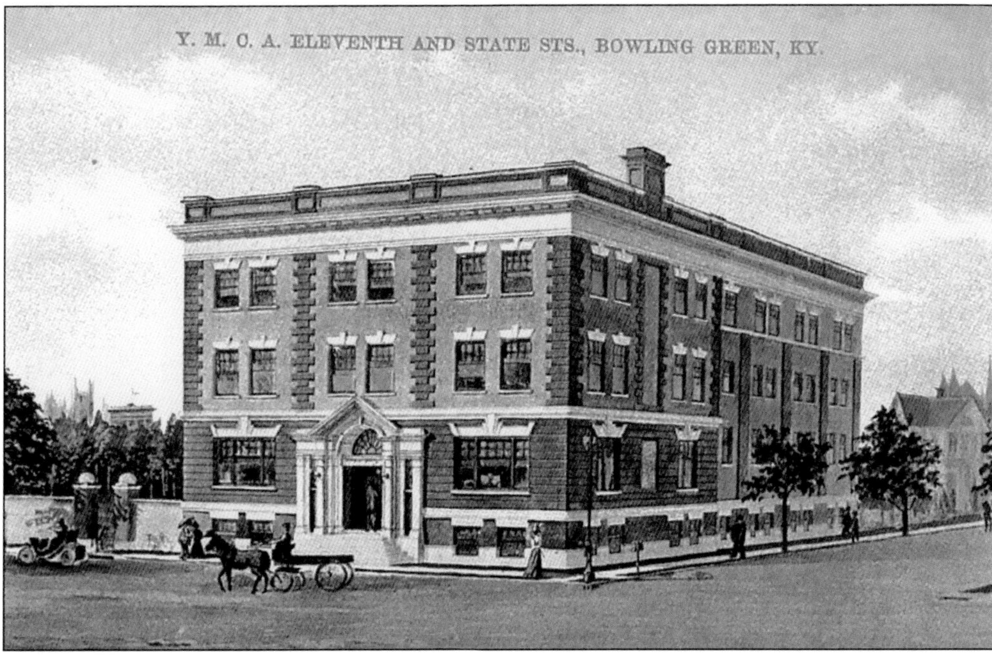

YMCA. Ground was broken for Bowling Green's first YMCA in the summer of 1908. The four-story building, designed by H.H. Hussey of Lansing, Michigan, was built at a cost of $29,000 at the corner of State and Eleventh Streets. It housed assembly and game rooms, a gymnasium, bowling alleys, a pool, and 22 bedrooms that were "not luxurious, but homelike for the young man away from home." The Y was sold in 1931, and the building went through extensive remodeling to become the Park City Hotel. The hotel advertised "reasonable rates [and] no charge for children under 14 when with parents." A fire in 1985 prompted the building's demolition.

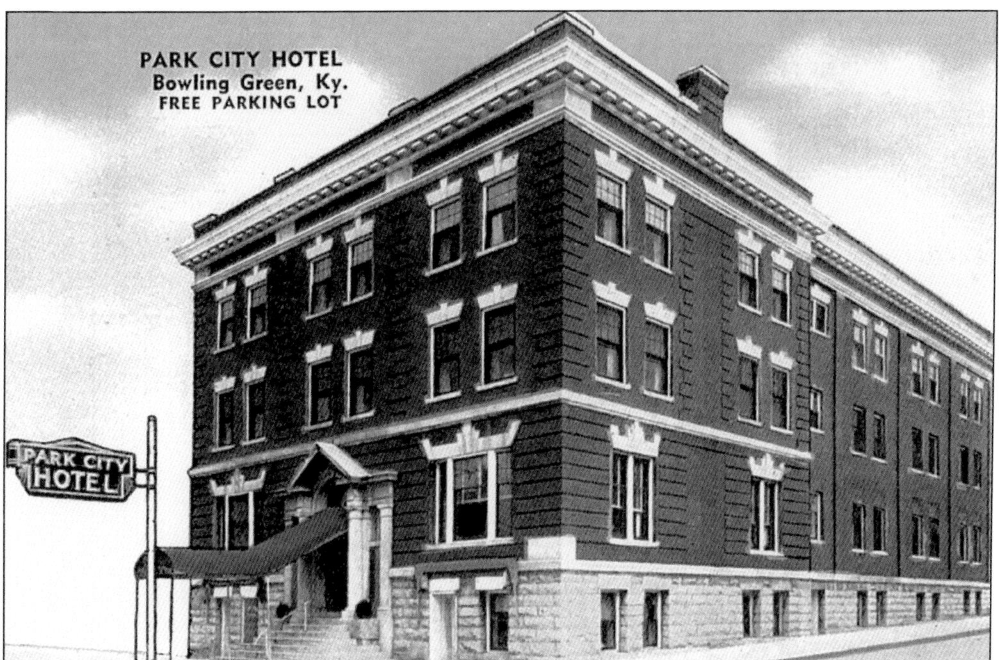

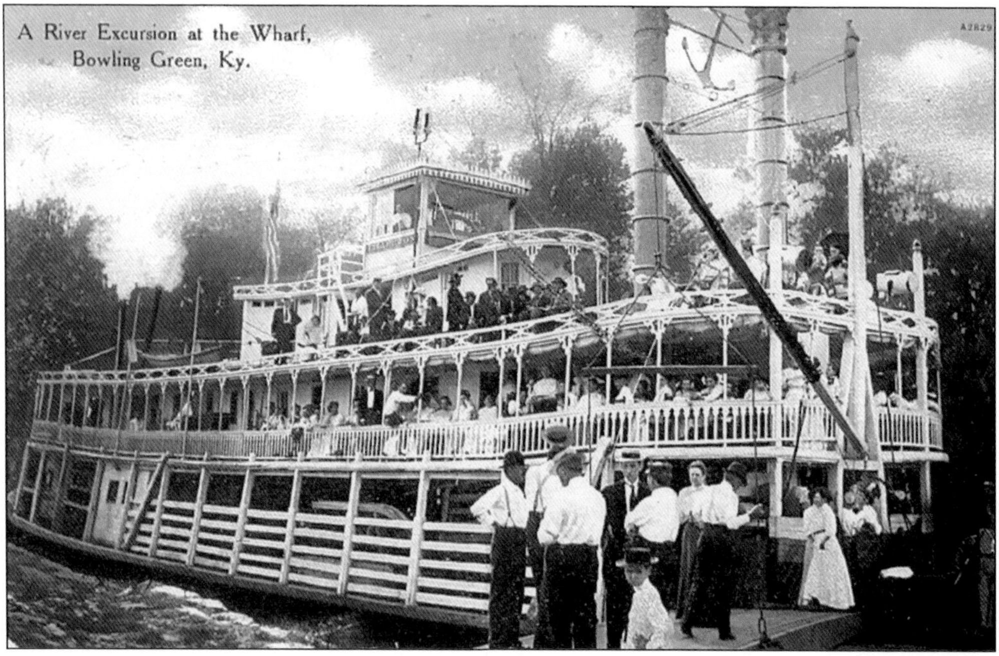

EXCURSION BOAT. A common local entertainment was to rent a paddle wheeler and hire a band for an evening of dancing on the river. Steamboats were also rented for excursions to popular resorts such as Massey Springs and for day trips to Mammoth Cave. These trips were sometimes arranged by local social clubs, WKU, or the Business University. As was typical in the era, the lower deck was used almost exclusively for freight.

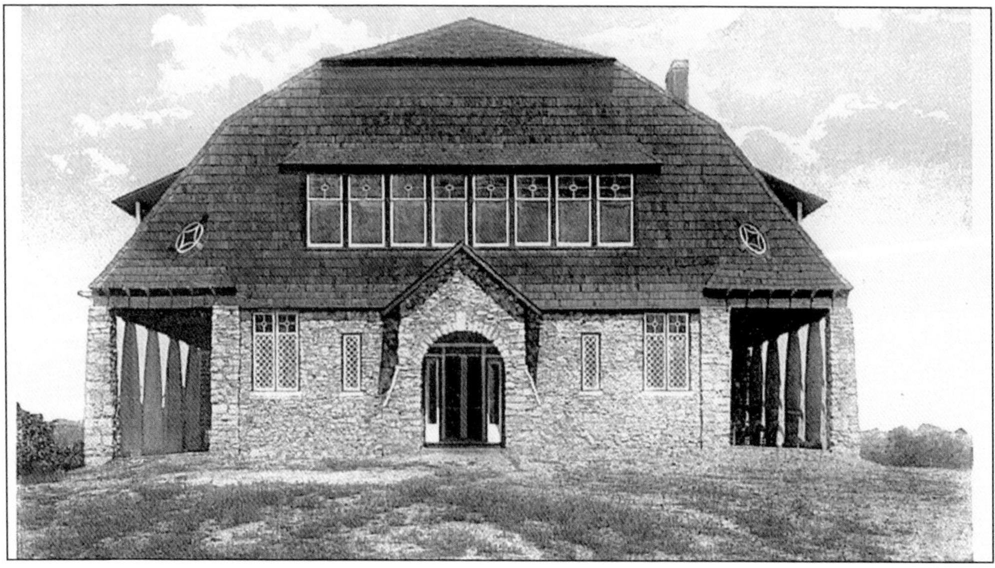

BOWLING GREEN COUNTRY CLUB. Architect Creedmore Fleenor designed this behemoth facility for the Country Club in 1912. The colonnade on the right faced the Richardsville Road (Hwy 185), and the columns on the left faced the Barren River. The 43-acre club site featured a magnificent view of the distant hills, a nine-hole golf course, trapshooting pits, tennis courts, and a swimming place on the river. It burned in October 1929.

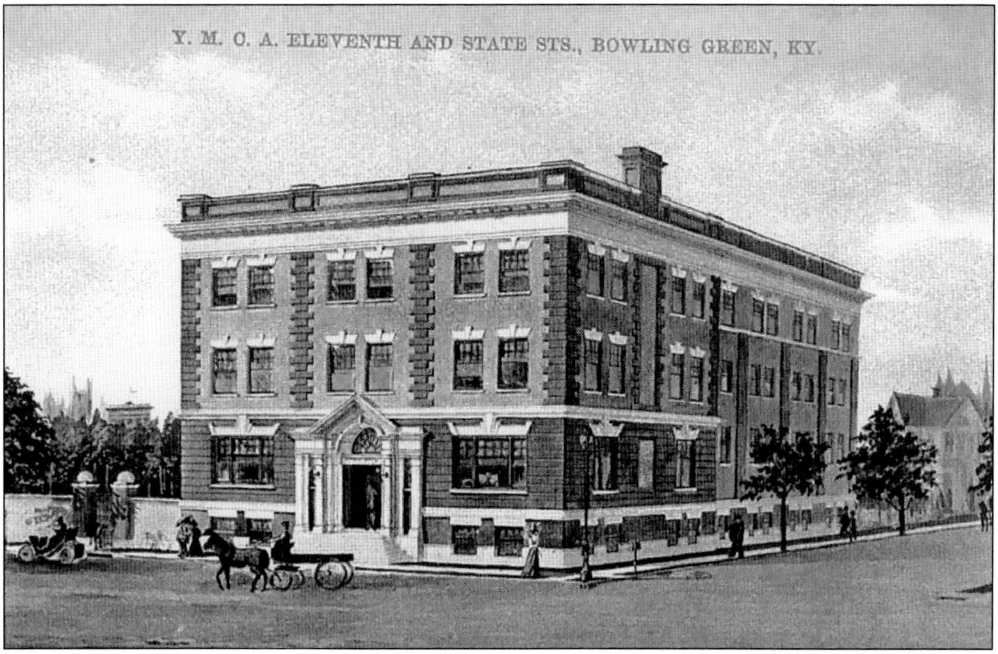

YMCA. Ground was broken for Bowling Green's first YMCA in the summer of 1908. The four-story building, designed by H.H. Hussey of Lansing, Michigan, was built at a cost of $29,000 at the corner of State and Eleventh Streets. It housed assembly and game rooms, a gymnasium, bowling alleys, a pool, and 22 bedrooms that were "not luxurious, but homelike for the young man away from home." The Y was sold in 1931, and the building went through extensive remodeling to become the Park City Hotel. The hotel advertised "reasonable rates [and] no charge for children under 14 when with parents." A fire in 1985 prompted the building's demolition.

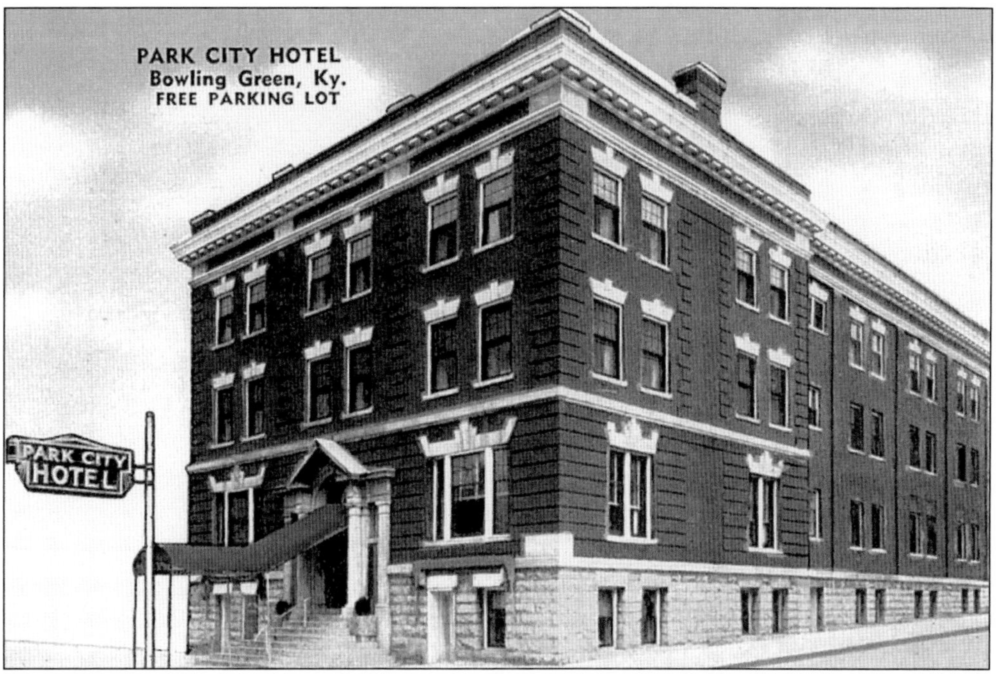

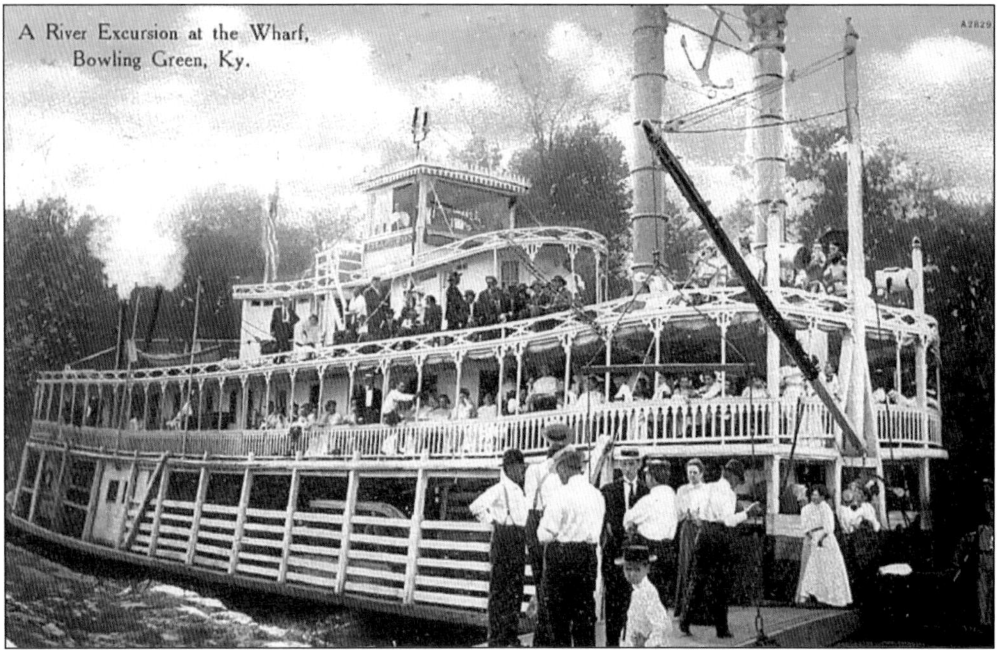

EXCURSION BOAT. A common local entertainment was to rent a paddle wheeler and hire a band for an evening of dancing on the river. Steamboats were also rented for excursions to popular resorts such as Massey Springs and for day trips to Mammoth Cave. These trips were sometimes arranged by local social clubs, WKU, or the Business University. As was typical in the era, the lower deck was used almost exclusively for freight.

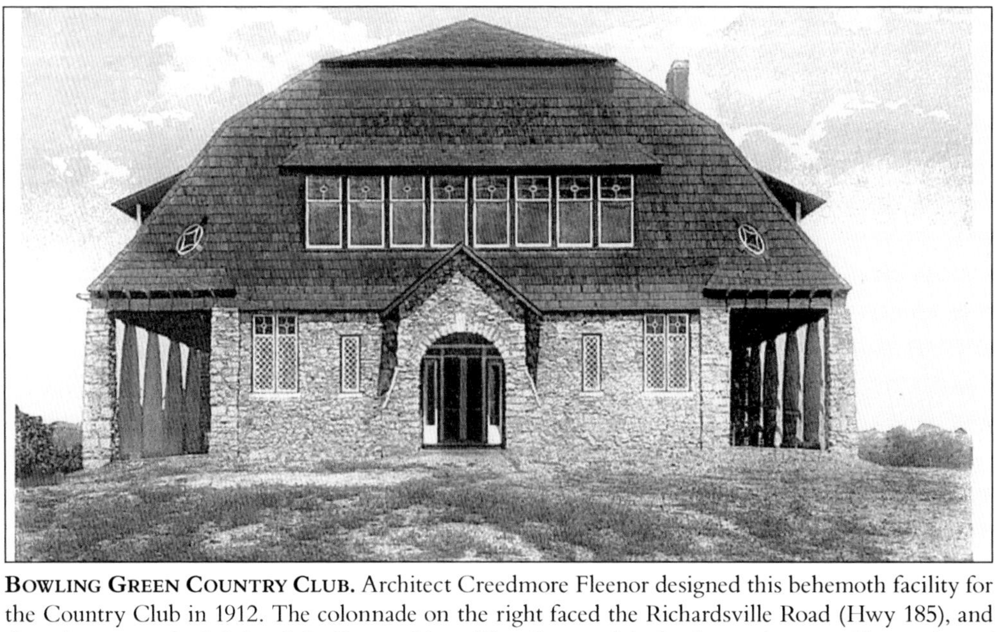

BOWLING GREEN COUNTRY CLUB. Architect Creedmore Fleenor designed this behemoth facility for the Country Club in 1912. The colonnade on the right faced the Richardsville Road (Hwy 185), and the columns on the left faced the Barren River. The 43-acre club site featured a magnificent view of the distant hills, a nine-hole golf course, trapshooting pits, tennis courts, and a swimming place on the river. It burned in October 1929.

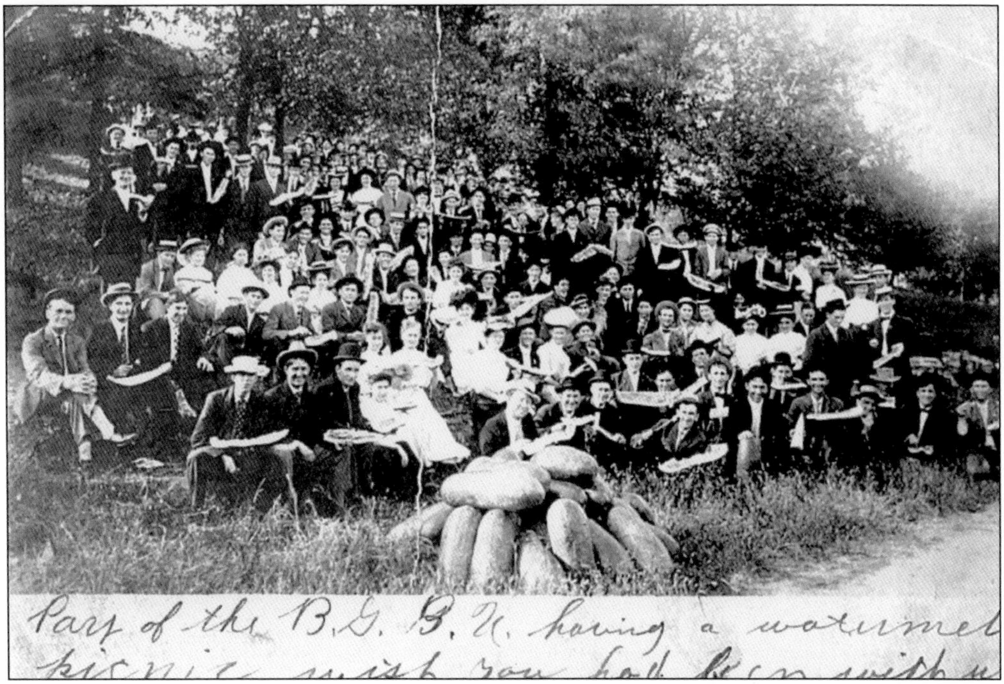

BGBU Picnic. Few things are better on a hot summer evening than a cold watermelon. The Bowling Green Business University sponsored a variety of events during the year, including chestnut hunts, outings to Mammoth Cave, plays, a huge debate with Ogden College, and picnics. This 1907 postcard documents a "watermelon picnic."

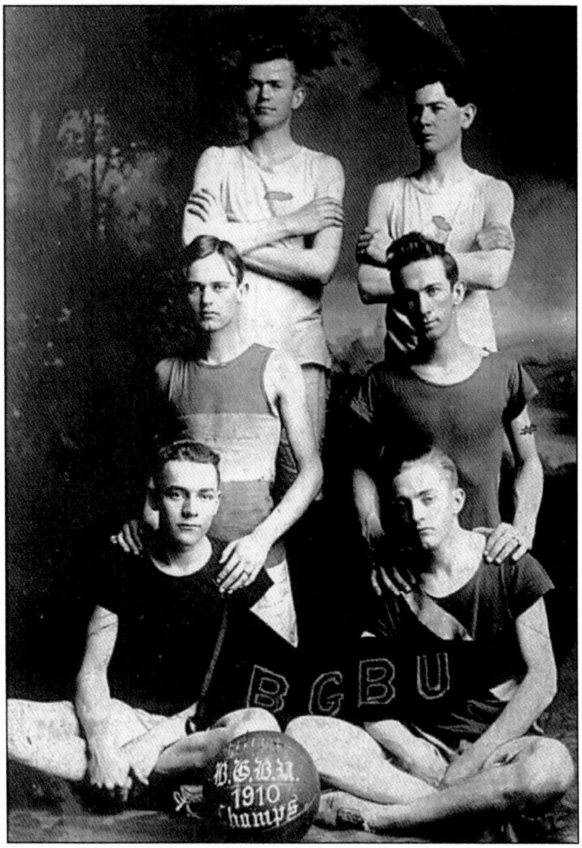

BGBU Basketball Team. This is a rare postcard of the 1910 Bowling Green Business University basketball team. It is rare because the only organized basketball teams documented from the BGBU were in the years 1910 and 1911. This athletic sextet was particularly good. The school newspaper noted, "this crack team holds the championship of Bowling Green." The game winning ball in this postcard confirms that status. Games were often played at the YMCA.

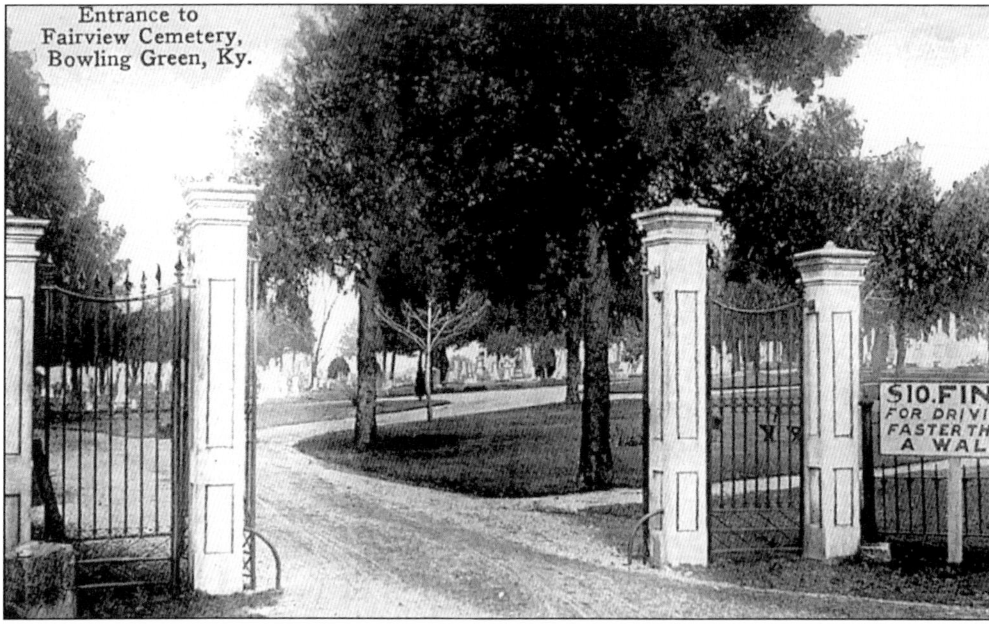

FAIRVIEW CEMETERY. Pioneer Cemetery near downtown Bowling Green filled up during the Civil War. The city had purchased property, northeast of town "near the river," from Thomas C. Calvert in 1862 for a new burial ground. The land was suitable because of its location outside the city, and because the selection committee "found no rock within five feet of the surface." Its park-like surroundings encouraged visitors.

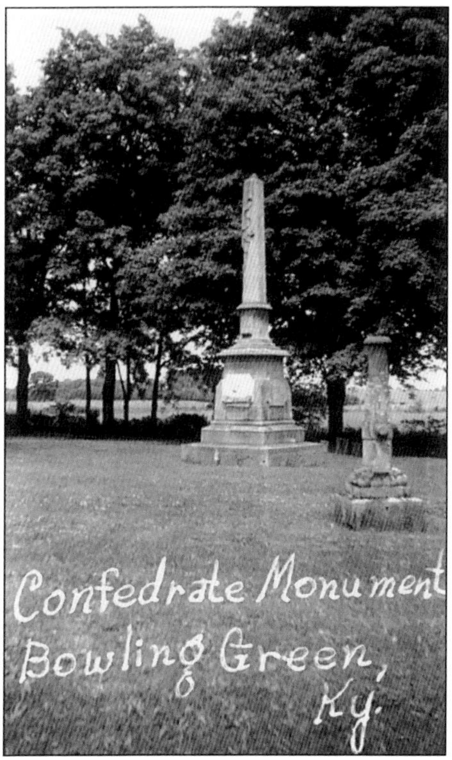

CONFEDERATE MONUMENT. In May 1876, the Confederate Monument was dedicated in the cemetery before a crowd of 12,000. The draped obelisk is carved from local limestone. A marble base relief entitled "The Confederate Soldier Returning Home" is attached to the base's front panel. The circular mounds that emanate from the monument represent the graves of an estimated 312 Confederate soldiers that were disinterred and moved to this site.

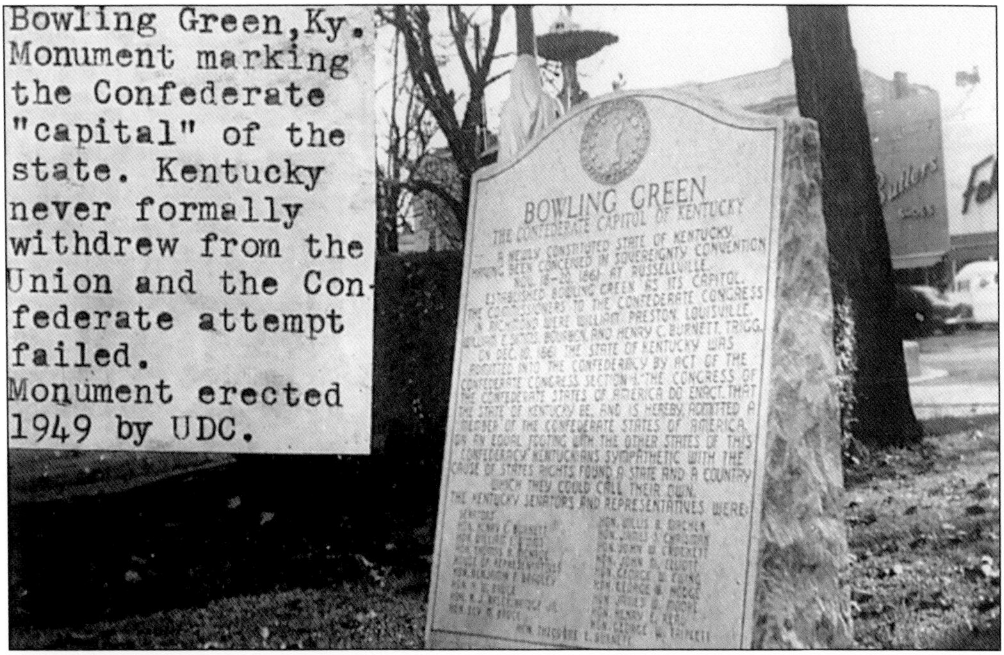

CONFEDERATE MARKER. In 1949, the United Daughters of the Confederacy erected this marker in Fountain Square Park to commemorate the fact that the November 1861 Sovereignty Convention, held in Russellville, selected Bowling Green as Kentucky's Confederate capital. Kentucky never officially seceded from the United States, but a skeleton Confederate government did exist at Bowling Green for a brief period.

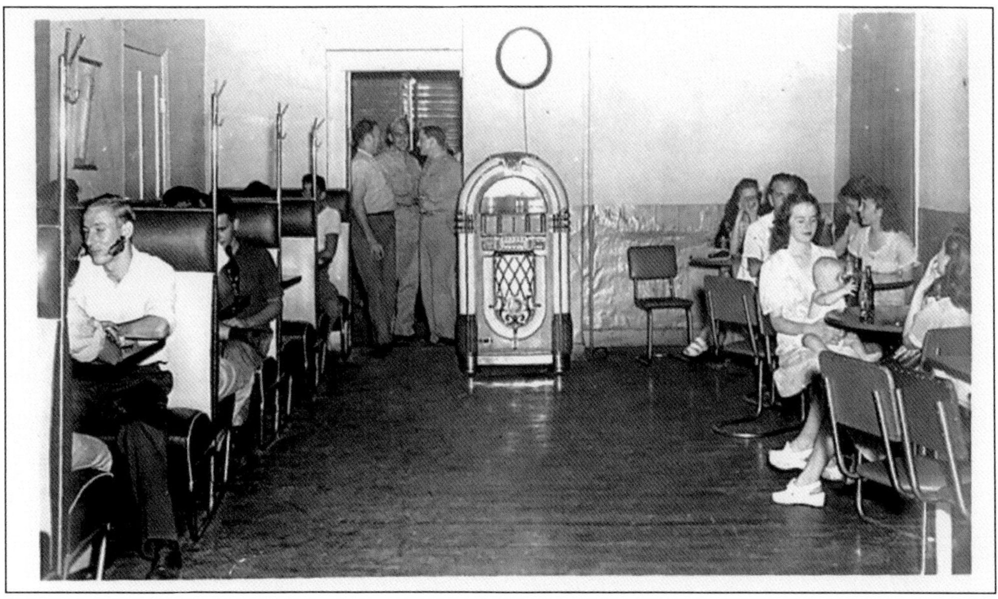

VETERANS OF FOREIGN WARS LOUNGE. When the Bowling Green Country Club was building their new complex in the early 1960s, the VFW purchased the club's old facility on Richardsville Road. Here they set up a comfortable lounge area complete with booths and a jukebox. The VFW was organized here as Post 1298 and is named for Lt. Harold R. Cornwell.

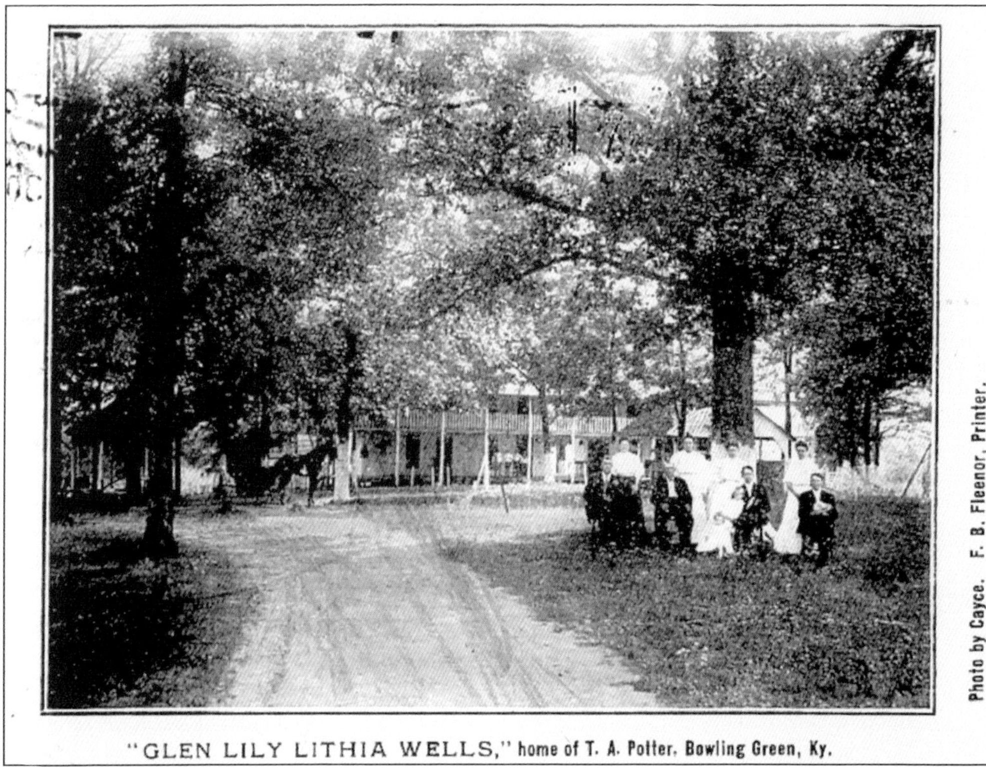

GLEN LILY LITIHIA WELLS. Spas and springs were popular recreational areas during the 19th and early 20th century. People came to these facilities to partake of the curative waters and to remove themselves from congested towns and cities filled with dust and foul smells. Located on the Glen Lily Pike, this operation also sold bottled water for 50¢ a gallon. Its ads claimed the water was "Nature's Remedy for Biliousness and Stomach Trouble."

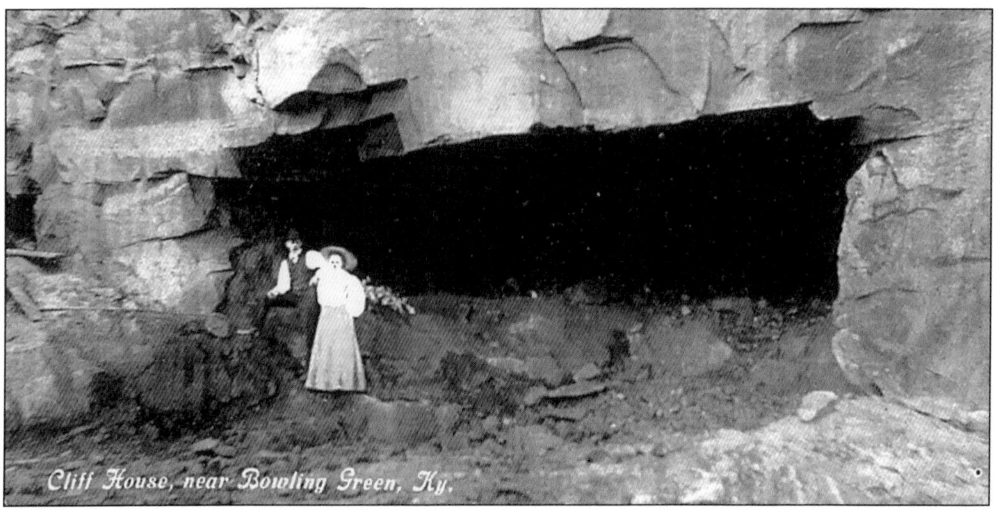

CLIFF HOUSE. Not a common occurrence in south central Kentucky, cliff houses were used by Native Americans and early settlers for shelter. Most of these structures in the Warren County area appear near rivers and have hosted numerous fishing parties over the years.

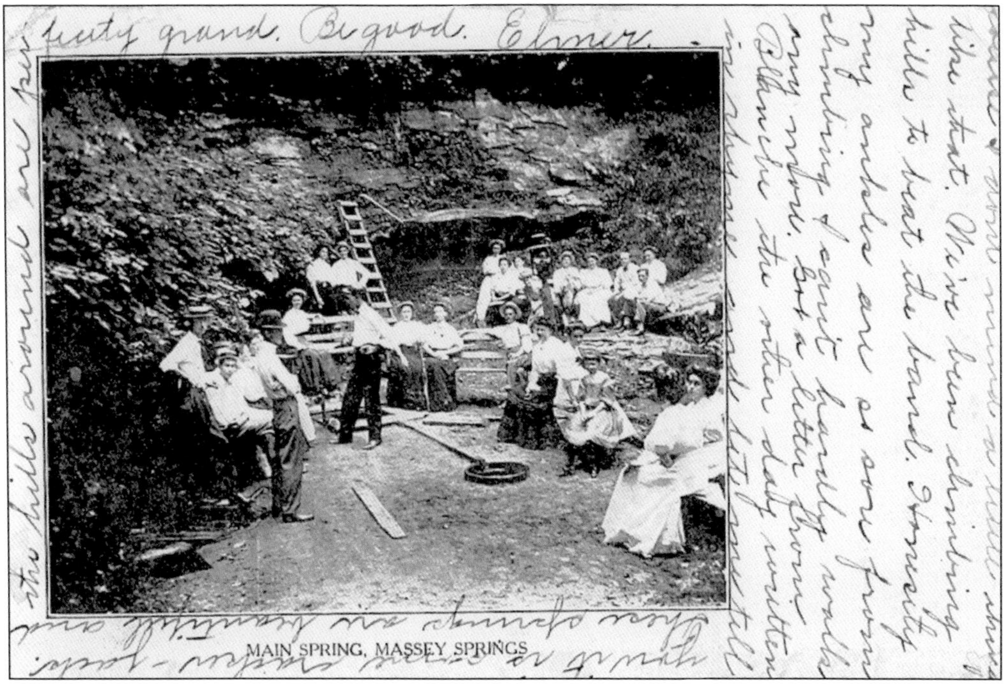

MASSEY SPRINGS. This mineral springs was located 14 miles from Bowling Green on the Green River, near Honakers Ferry. It opened in the late 19th century and was a popular summer resort until 1914 for guests from Louisville, Evansville, and Owensboro. Most people reached the springs by boat because the resort had its own landing. The spring waters were said to have curative powers, particularly the alum water which purportedly cured cuts and sores.

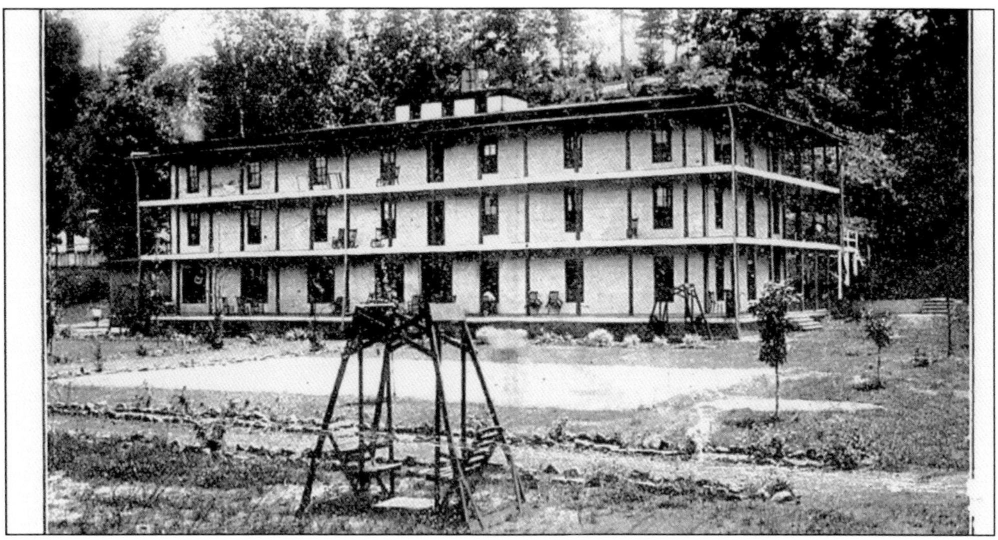

MASSEY SPRINGS HOTEL. After disembarking from a steamboat, visitors to Massey Springs had their effects delivered to this 40-room hotel. This severe-looking structure built by George F. Cole replaced an earlier log hotel. The hotel is similar to other resort structures built around the country, with all doors opening onto porches. The grounds were smartly landscaped for moonlight strolls. Guests were also encouraged to hike around the surrounding hillsides.

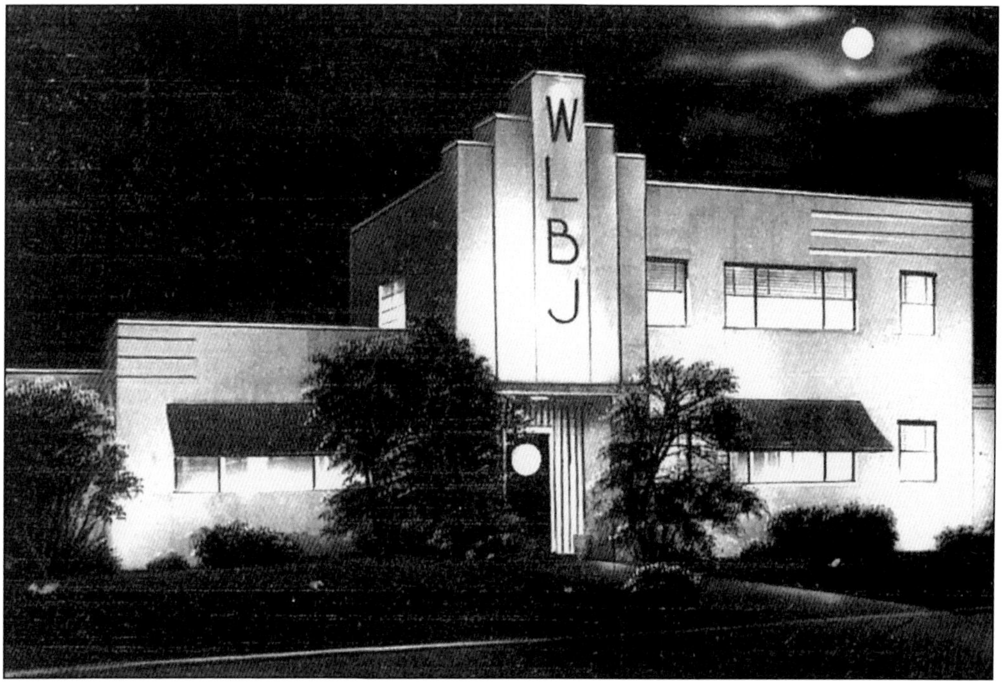

WLBJ. The art moderne WLBJ station was designed by James M. Ingram and located at the intersection of Lehman and Fairview Avenues on property that once housed the grandstands for the Warren County Fair. A top portion of the former station can still be distinguished above a funeral home that now occupies the property. Local broadcasts began in June 1940. Before that listeners tuned into out-of-town stations. The station moved in 1961. Its call letters were the initials of its first owner, L.B. Jenkins. Joe Hamilton, pictured below, was one of Bowling Green's first radio personalities with his "Get Up and Grin" show airing in the late 1940s. WLBJ signed off the air permanently in December 1991.

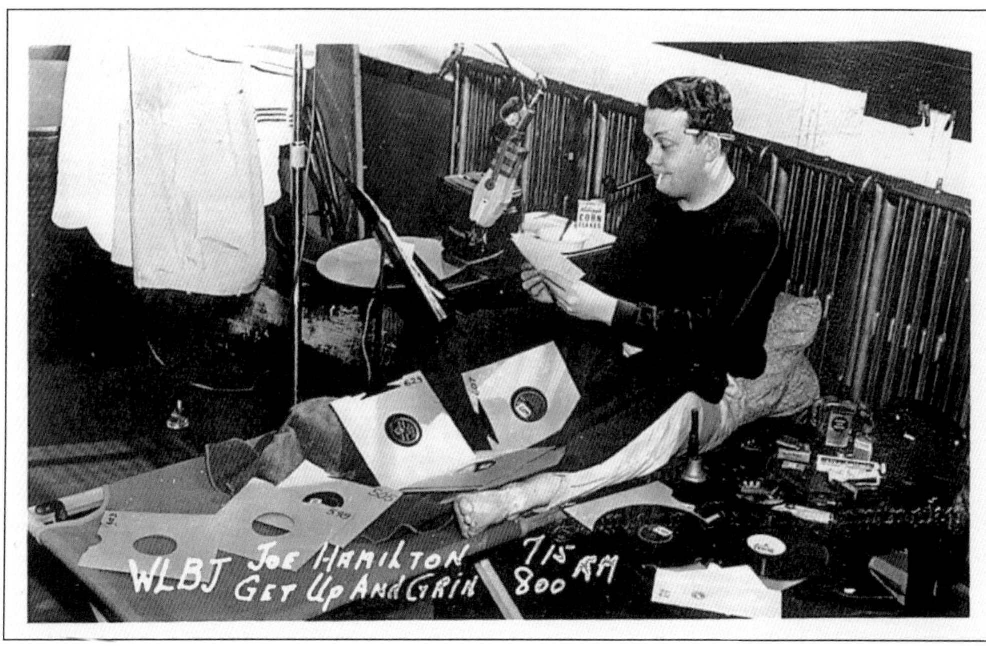

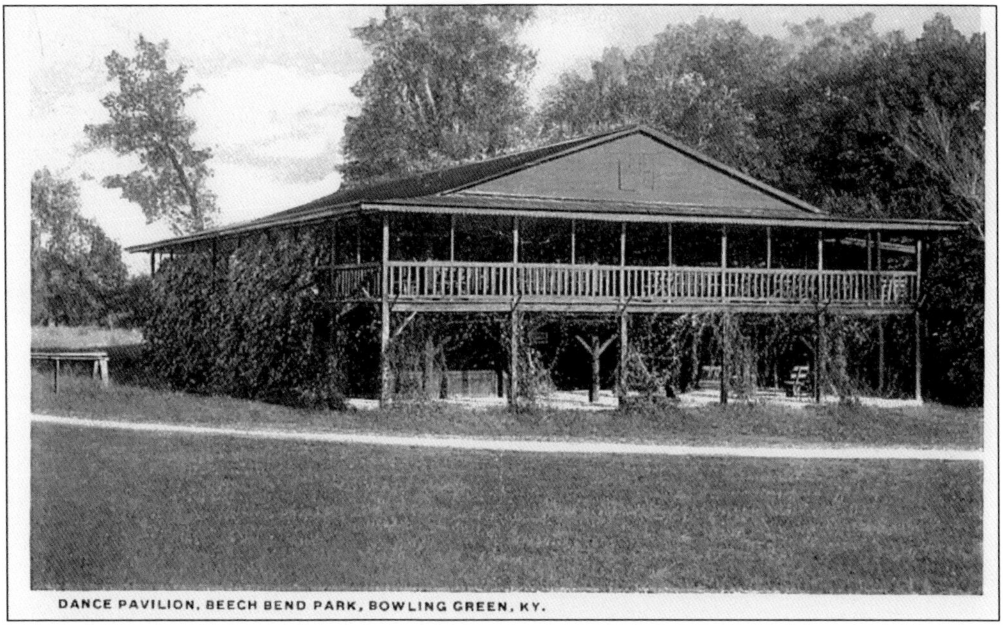

Beech Bend Pavilion. Curren Brashear and his two sisters named their home for the beech trees in a bend of the Barren River. They opened this large pavilion facility in 1907 for dancing and skating. The operation became known for its good food and sylvan setting. The site was used for many "Fair Hops," Warren County's premier annual social event. The Brashears sold the property to Charlie Garvin in 1942.

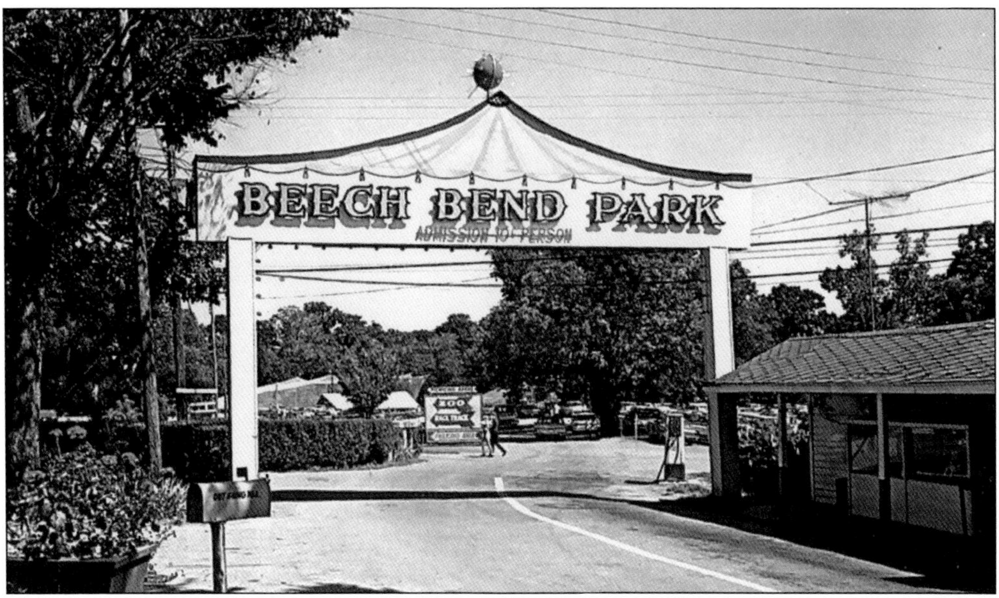

Beech Bend Entrance. This lighted "big top" sign was the beginning point of fun and relaxation for thousands of people daily. The sign stated that the admission price was 10¢, but that only admitted visitors to the park; rides were an additional charge. Beech Bend was a highly recognized amusement park nationwide. With the recent introduction of new rides and its proximity to the race track, Beech Bend is experiencing a revival.

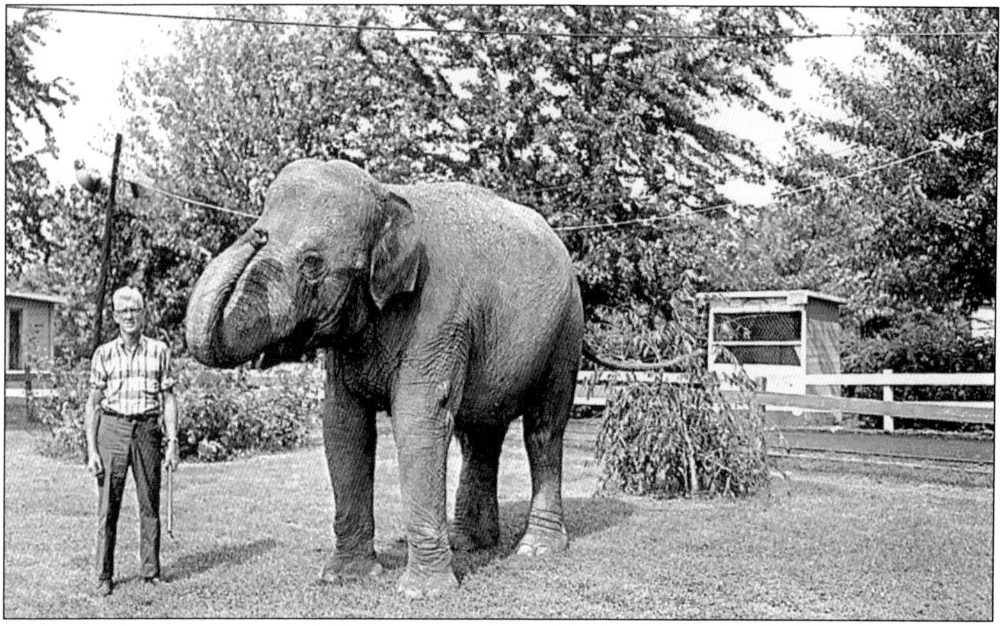

Beech Bend Zoo. One of the most popular attractions at Beech Bend was a large menagerie that included Blondie the elephant, pictured here with owner Charlie Garvin. The zoo featured deer, bear, lions, anteaters, llamas, zebra, ostriches, and other exotic animals. There was no charge to visit the animals and advertising claimed that "animals in the zoo are carefully chosen for their beauty and individuality."

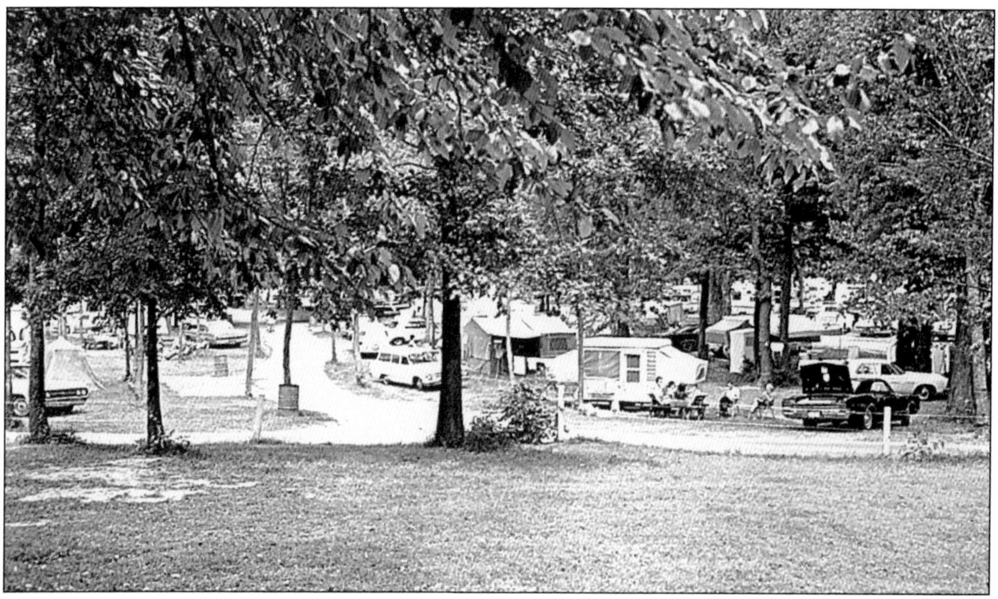

Beech Bend Camping. Facilities for camping near the river made Beech Bend both economical and refreshing. The park featured over 3,000 camping sites, making it one of the largest campgrounds in the country. David Garvin, son of owner Charlie Garvin, noticed the need for outfitting and maintaining the growing number of campers and recreational vehicles that Americans enjoyed. This led to the founding of Camping World, one of the country's largest recreational outfitters.

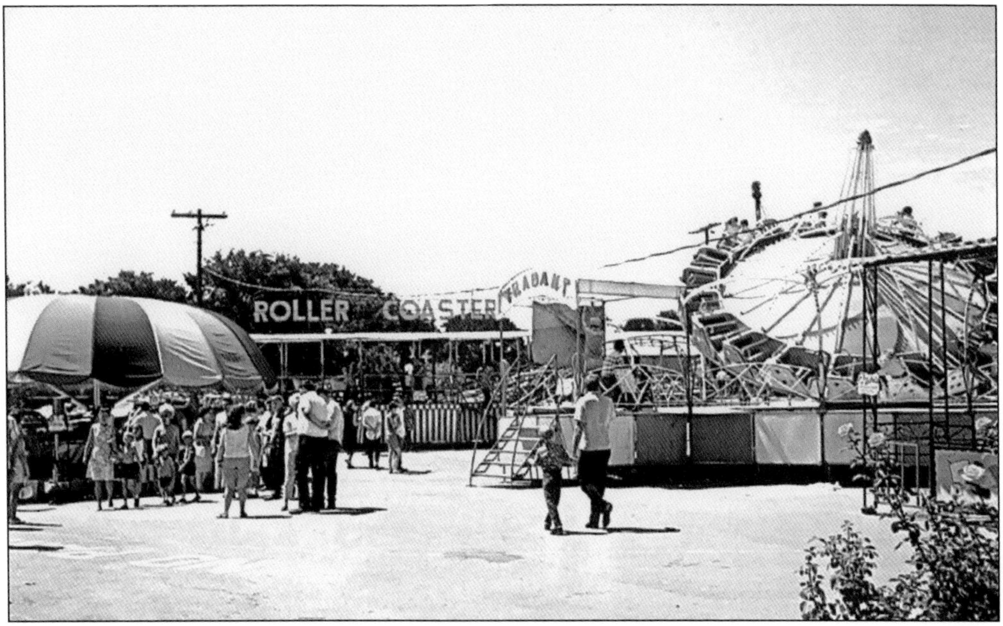

Beech Bend Midway. Tourists from across the country visited Beech Bend for respite and a little thrill on one of its 30 featured rides, including go-carts, the Moon Rocket, the Matterhorn, the Voyage ala Lune, Bayron Kurve, roller coasters, or the Ferris wheel. Visitors could also go swimming, ride horses, play miniature golf, travel on miniature trains, or simply lose a few dollars at the midway's games of chance.

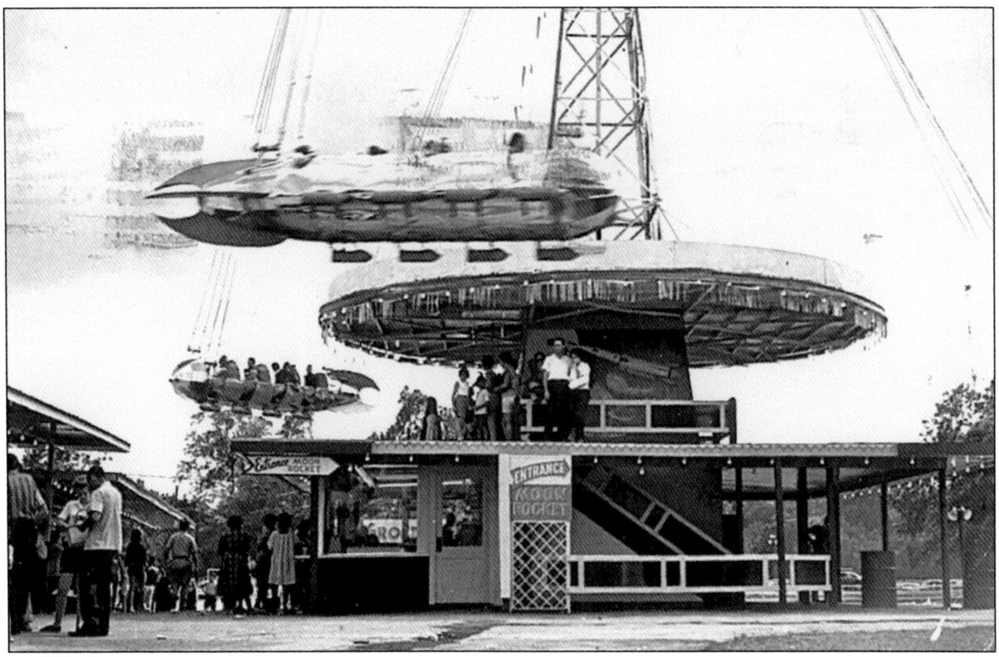

The Rocket. This and Beech Bend's other rides wowed the sender of this card. She says, "This is a place you would have to see to believe! Sort of a Disneyland . . . Boys having big time. Gone to drag racing tonight."

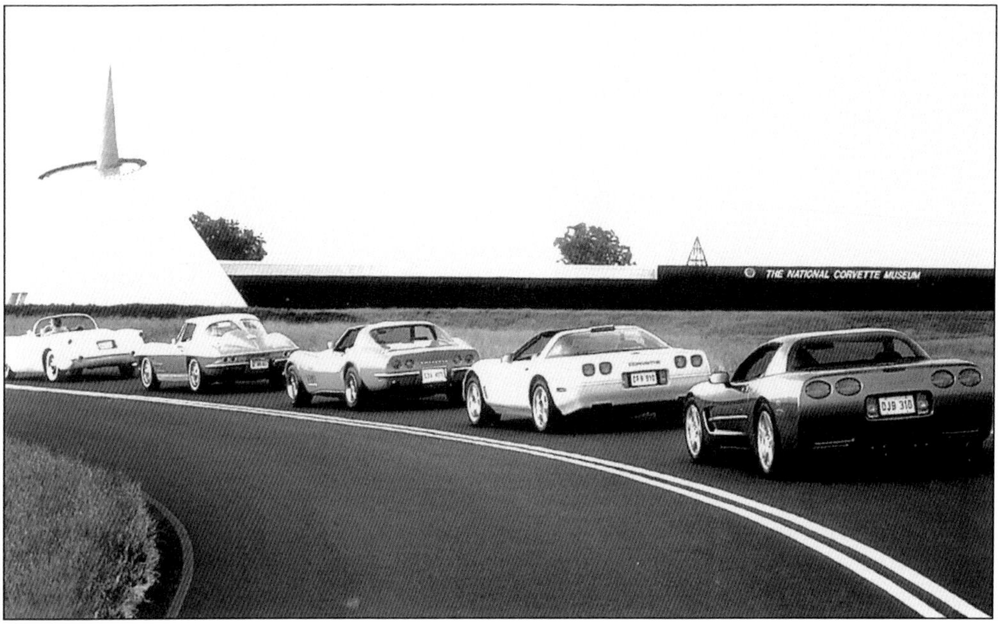

NATIONAL CORVETTE MUSEUM. On September 2, 1994, the 68,000-square-foot Corvette Museum, located off Interstate 65, opened its doors to sports car enthusiasts. The museum welcomes over 150,000 visitors a year for exciting programming and a spectacular exhibition of vintage Corvettes. Bowling Green is also home to the annual Corvette Homecoming.

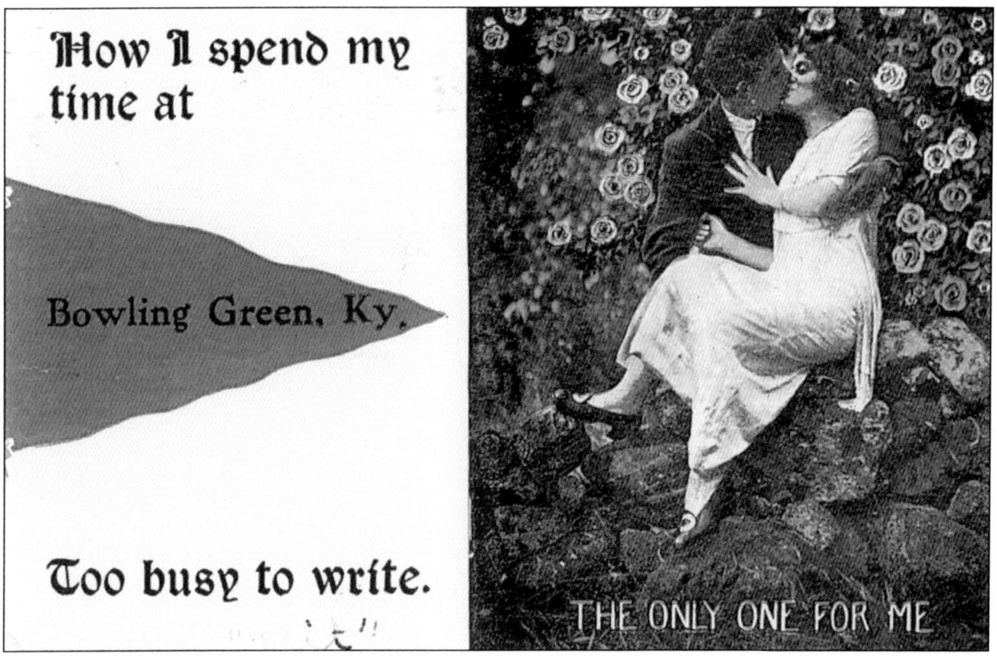

NOVELTY CARDS. Some people might call romance recreational, particularly those early 20th-century coquettes known as flirts. A standard of the postcard trade in the early part of the 20th century, the novelty card used a cartoon character or stock photography with the community's name prominently displayed. Here a couple is romantically entangled in some serious smooching.

Six

Warren County

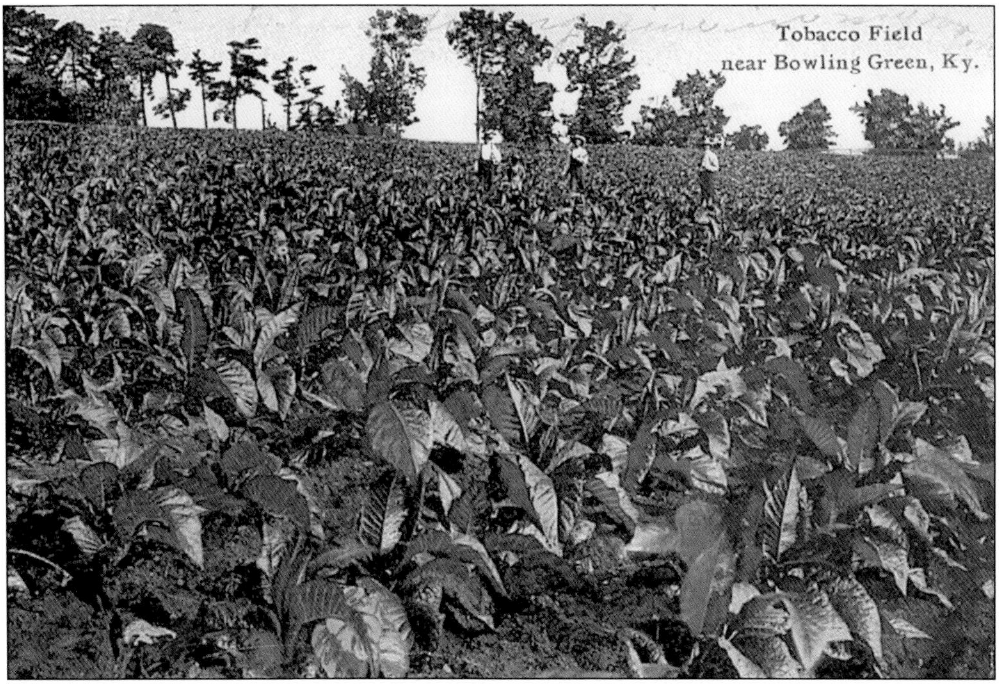

Tobacco Field. Despite recent events that have threatened tobacco culture, small fields across Warren County are still planted each May and harvested in late summer or early fall, hung for dry curing, processed, and taken to auctions in the late fall. Burley tobacco is cultivated in Warren County as opposed to the black tobacco grown in western Kentucky.

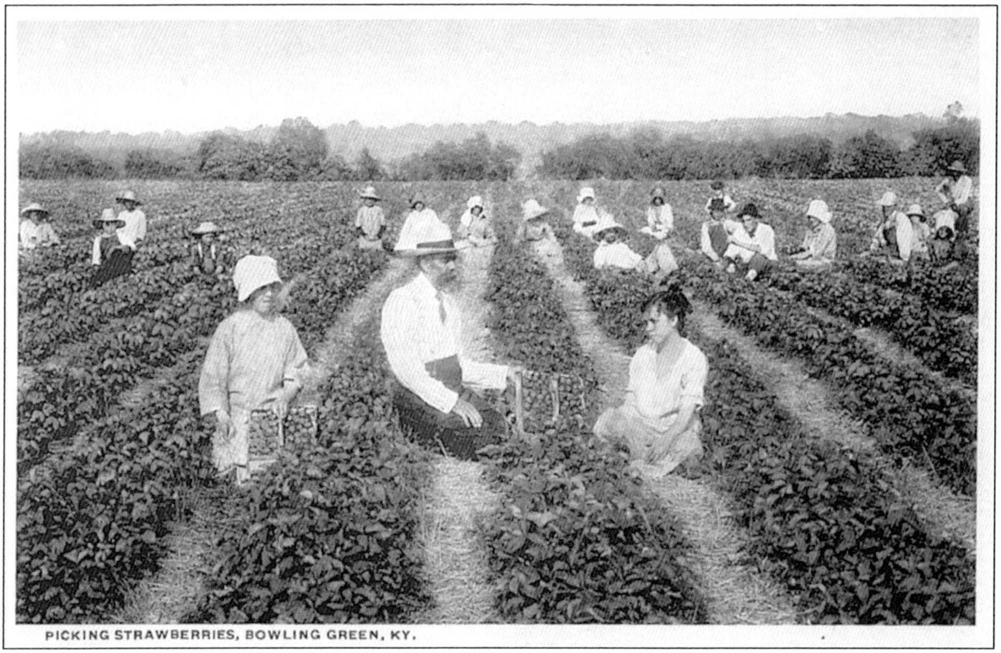

STRAWBERRIES. The cultivation of strawberries began in earnest here after 1880, although even the earliest pioneers mention the wild strawberries native to the area. Several cooperatives were established here, and one Bowling Green radio station once aired a jingle that the city was the strawberry capital of the world. Harvesting strawberries fell conveniently after the planting of tobacco, which allowed farmers to have two cash crops. Harvesting the crop was back breaking work, and it was often relegated to women or children as witnessed in the top postcard. The attractive display in the bottom postcards is of Aroma berries, the most popular strawberry grown in this area. The sender noted on the back: "Every Aroma is a prize winner. This table is just as I found it during a busy hour. Not a berry was posed."

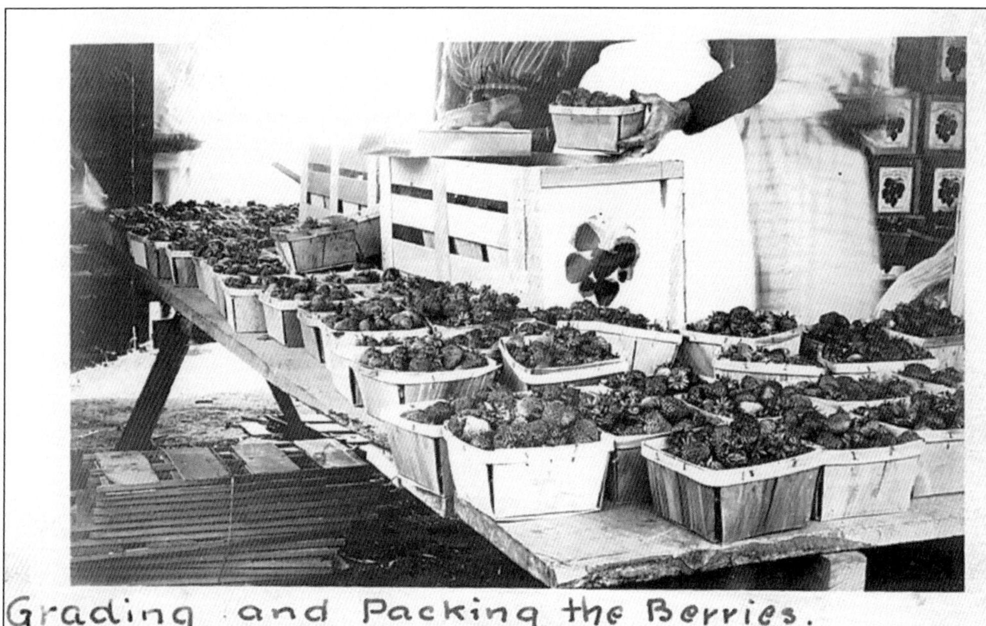

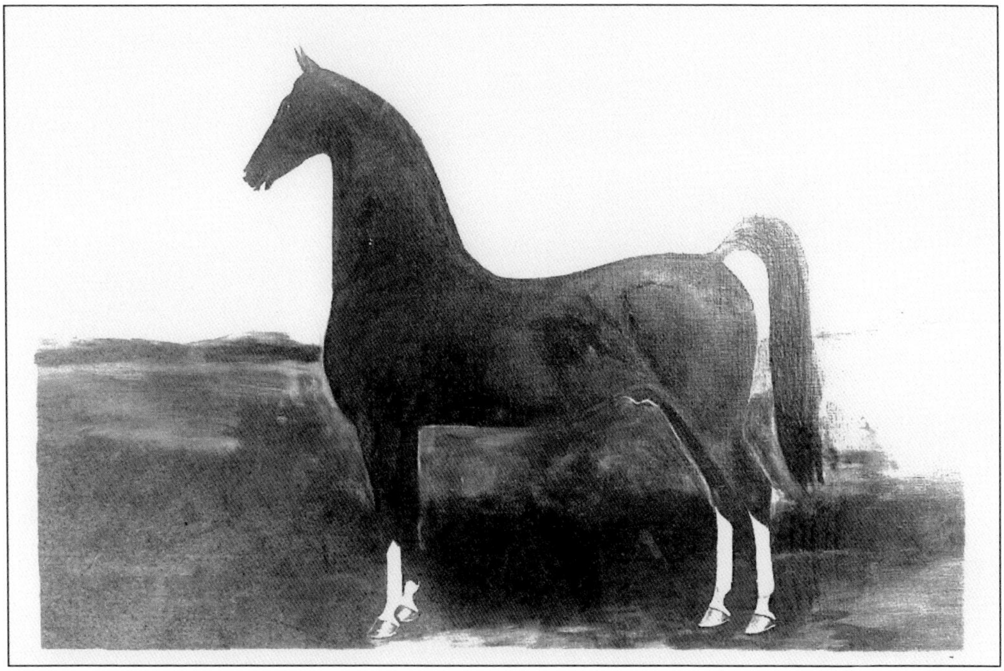

HORSES. Although the Bluegrass is the Kentucky section best known for equine culture, Warren County has produced many fine horses for racing and breeding purposes. Pictured here are "Guided for Love" (top) and "Sunflower". The "Sunflower" card is actually a clever advertisement for Pres. W. Ray's Pink Powders, a concoction that was "unequaled for keeping horses in constant working condition." Warren County and adjoining Simpson County are best known for their mules, which they supplied in great numbers during the Spanish-American War and World War I.

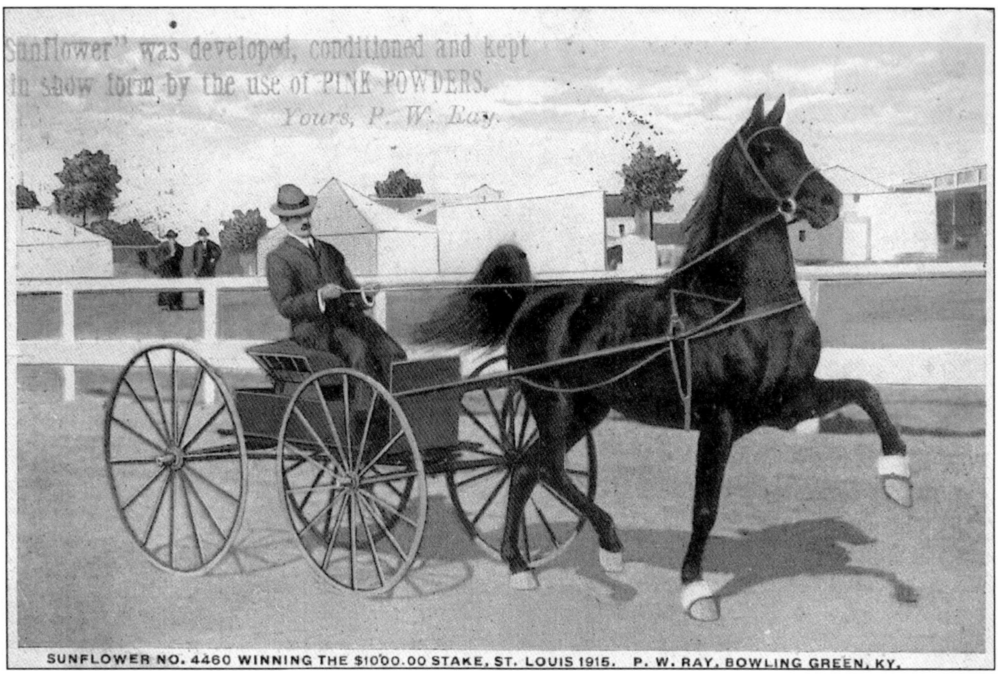

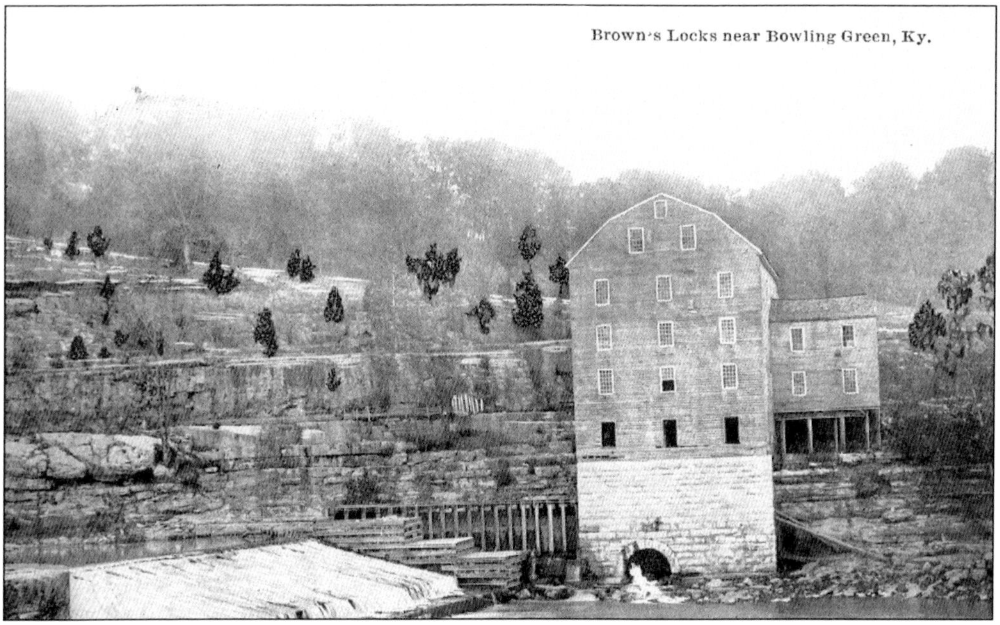

BROWN'S LOCK MILL. The Green and Barren Rivers were made navigable when a series of locks and dams were completed in the mid-1840s. Barren River Lock and Dam No. 1, built at Greencastle, were sometimes referred to as Brown's Lock because of the large four-story mill built there by Capt. William Brown. The mill's construction date on the west bank is unknown, but it could have been built as early as 1850. It attracted customers from Warren, Butler, and Edmonson Counties. Remains of the limestone foundation can still be seen today. Brown's tombstone in Mt. Zion Church cemetery reads: "Brown's Lock named in his honor. A great man!" The bottom card shows the massive Lock No. 1 completed in 1845 by James Ford and Thomas Stephens Sr.

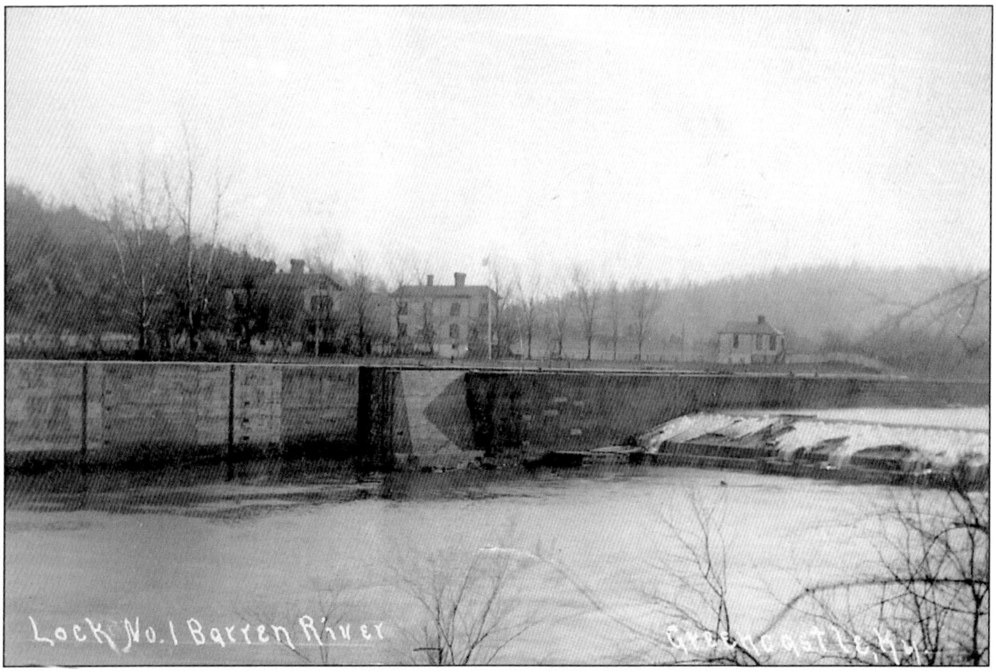

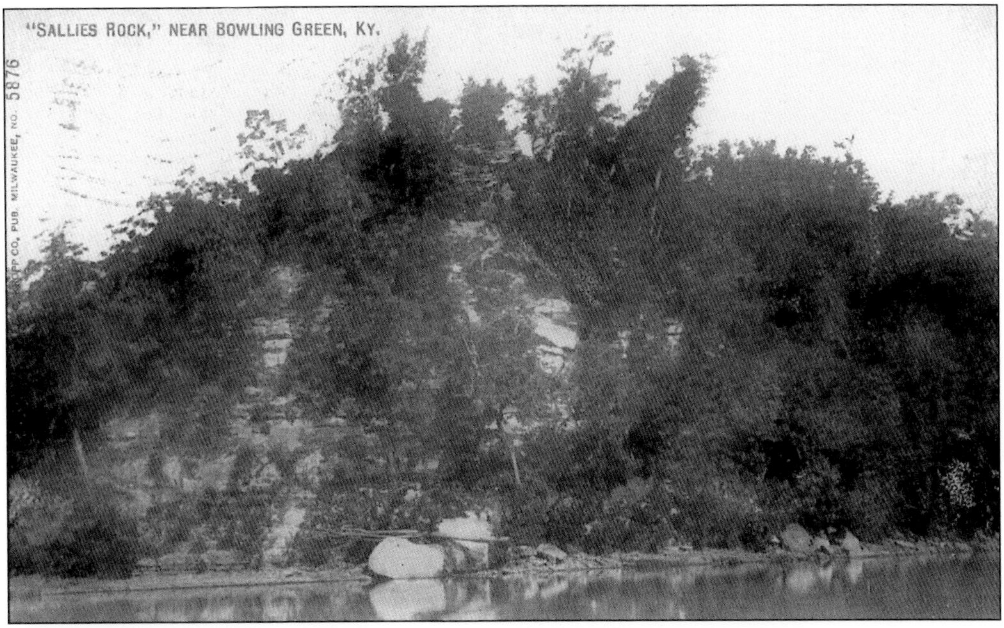

SALLIE'S ROCK. Near the confluence of the Gasper and Barren Rivers, a large rock leaned precipitously away from the bluff. It was named for Sally [Sallie] Beck who stationed herself 198 feet above water level and beckoned to passengers and crews of passing steamboats using a megaphone. Boat crews often returned her greetings with a shrill whistle blast. The rock fell into the river in 1910.

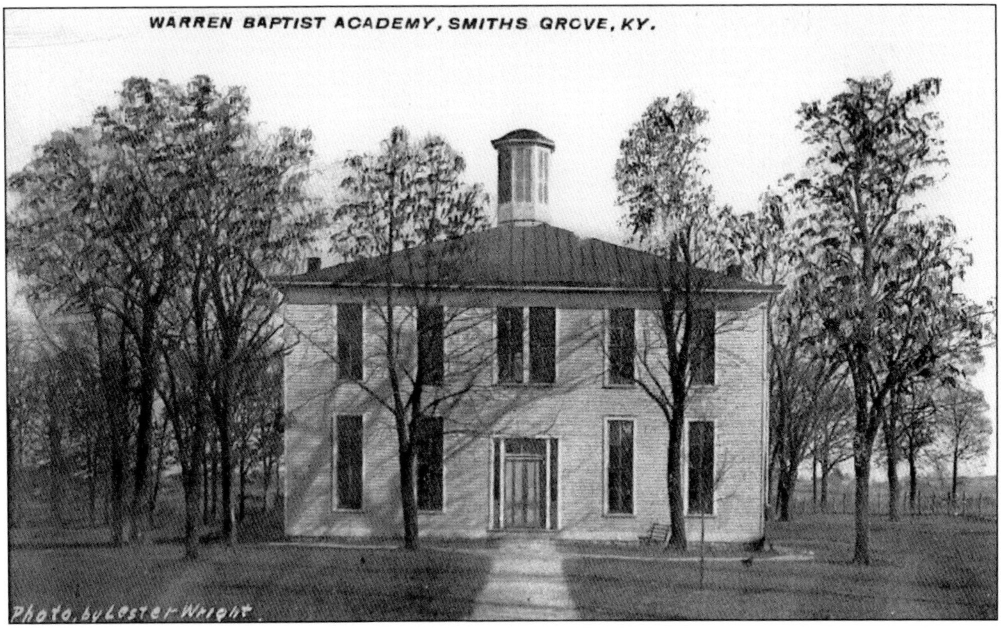

WARREN BAPTIST ACADEMY. This Smiths Grove structure was the main building for four separate schools: Smiths Grove College, 1870s–1900; Vanderbilt Training School, 1900–1910; Warren Baptist Academy, 1910–1916; and Smiths Grove or North Warren High School, 1916–1940s. The Baptist Academy was supported by the Warren Association of Baptists and provided the equivalent of a high school education.

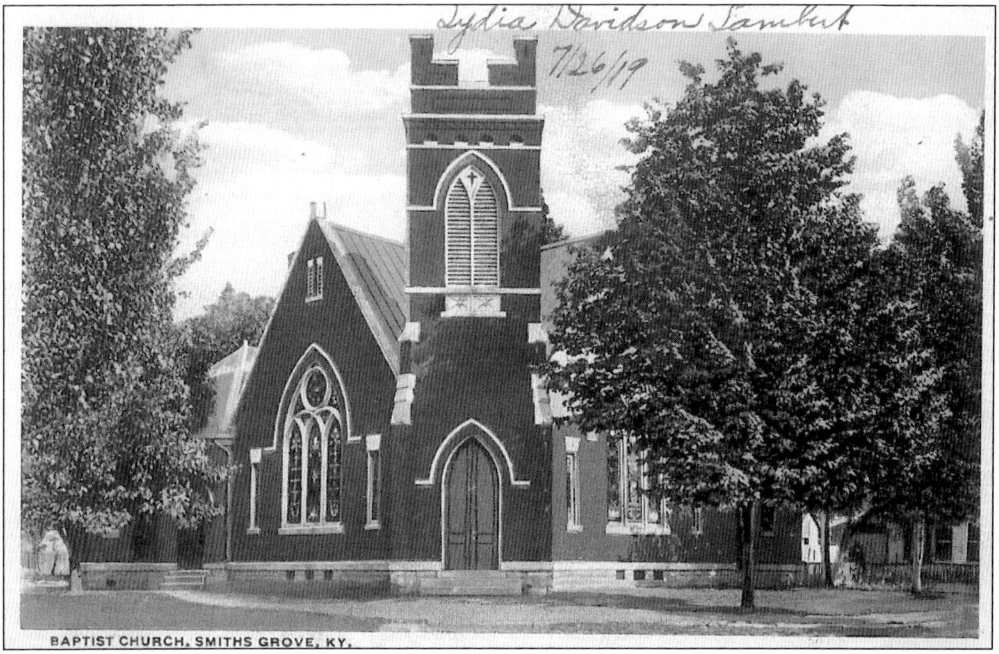

SMITHS GROVE BAPTIST CHURCH. Constituted in 1812, this church is one of the oldest congregations in the county. Creedmore Fleenor designed this architectural gem in 1898. The building is Gothic Revival in styling and boasts 32 stained glass windows. The functioning bell tower features limestone detailing, a castellated roofline, and buttressed corners. The building's artistic effect is enhanced by the beautiful standing metal seam roof with copper finials.

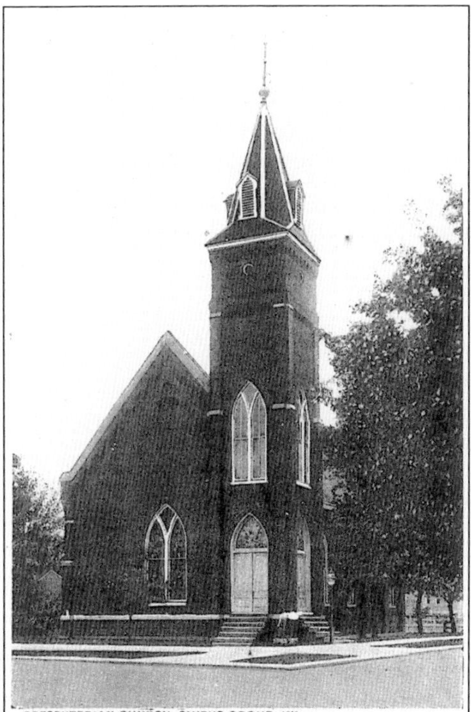

SMITHS GROVE PRESBYTERIAN CHURCH. Presbyterians organized this church as Shiloh Cumberland Presbyterian Church in 1834. They built a log house just north of Smiths Grove. The church moved to town in 1871 and built a "union" house with the local Baptist congregation. In 1889 they constructed this building for $5,900. In 1940, the steeple was removed to discourage the pigeons, which were "disruptive to the church service."

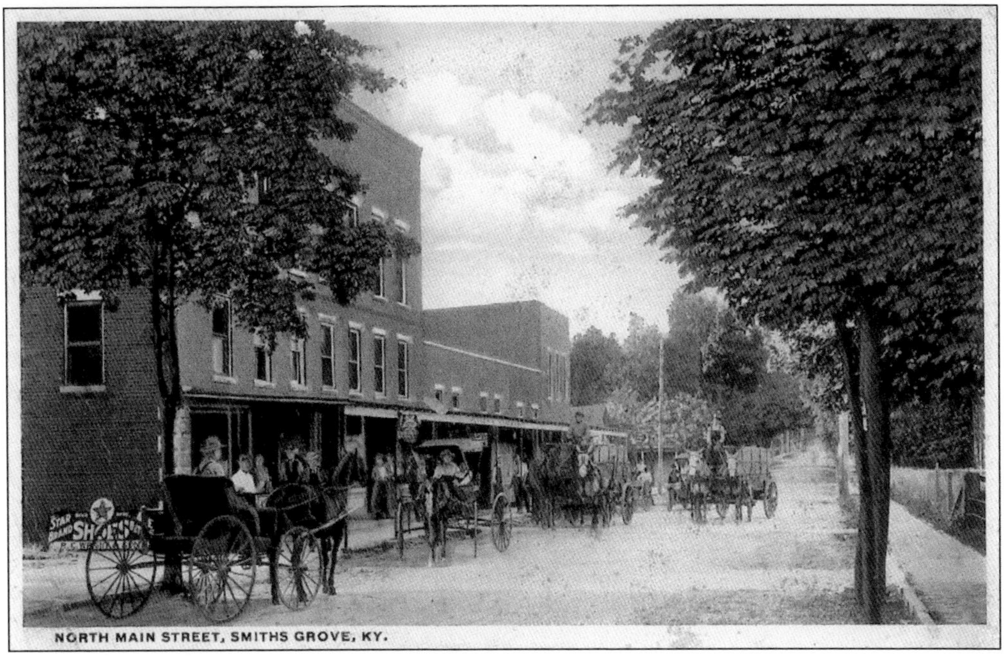

SMITHS GROVE BUSINESS DISTRICT. North Main Street was the hub of business activity in the northern Warren County community of Smiths Grove. The town was incorporated in 1871, but a post office was established there as early as 1829. These masonry commercial buildings still stand and now contain antique stores. With quaint shops and lovely Victorian homes, Smiths Grove has much to offer visitors willing to drive the short one mile off Interstate 65.

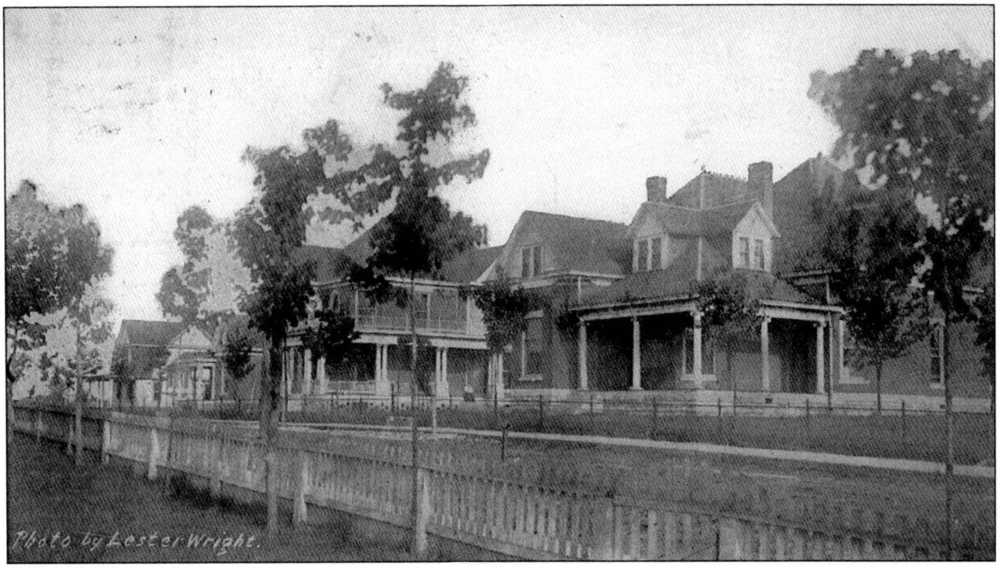

BROADWAY STREET IN SMITHS GROVE. This residential street in beautiful Smiths Grove boasted a number of substantial masonry homes for the town's wealthier citizens. George Wilcoxin (Wilcoxson), a talented local builder and mason, built several of the homes pictured here. Sitting on the L&N Railroad, Smiths Grove was a prosperous shipping point for the northeastern portion of Warren County and remains the county's second largest community.

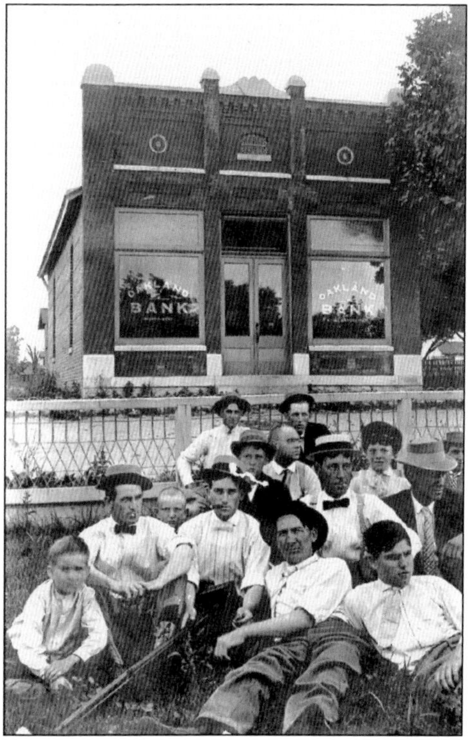

OAKLAND BANK. This group shot was taken in "Depot Park," the fenced lawn of the Oakland Depot. Looming in the background is the Oakland Bank which was organized in 1906 with a capital of $15,000. In December 1929, this was the location of an infamous bank robbery in which James Robert Kirby Jr., president of Smiths Grove Farmer's Bank, was killed. The bank closed in 1931.

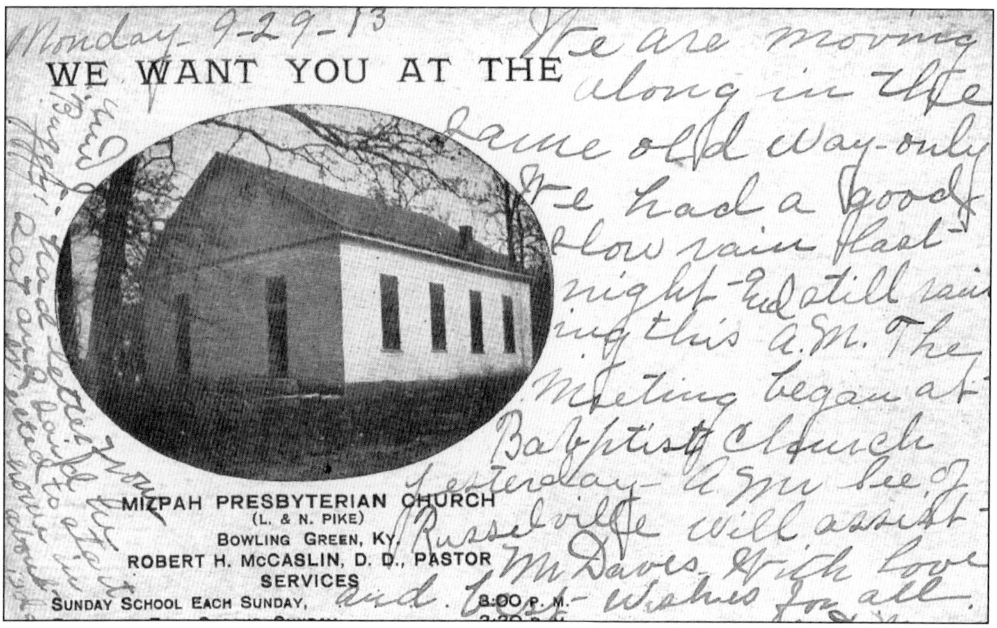

MIZPAH CHURCH. Although this card delineates this church as Presbyterian, it was actually a union church with several denominations meeting there. This building, which is no longer standing, was located approximately three miles northwest of Oakland. The building also served briefly as a school. The two front entrances were part of the vernacular architecture of most rural churches in the 19th century. One entrance was delineated for men and one for women.

WOODBURN METHODIST CHURCH. This lovely structure with its prominent centered bell tower was constructed on College Street in Woodburn in the late 1870s. The church remained active through the early 1970s when it merged with the nearby Rockfield Methodist Church. The structure was auctioned off in 1973, and it has been sad to see the building literally fall apart. The bell tower, although damaged, is still standing sentinel at the location.

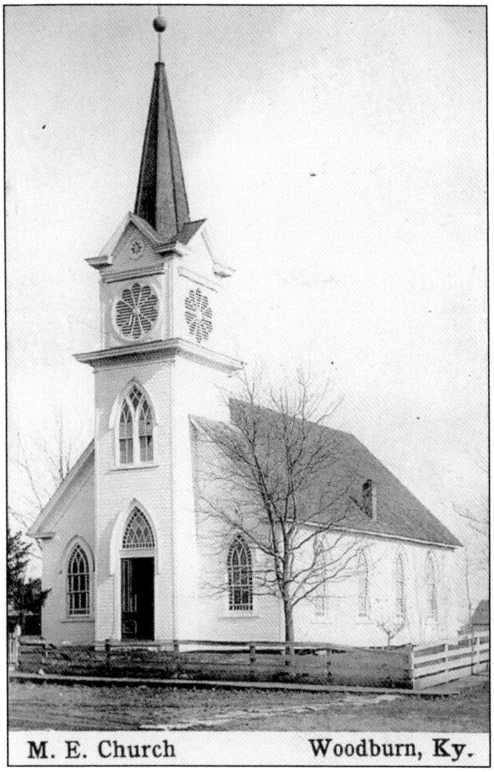

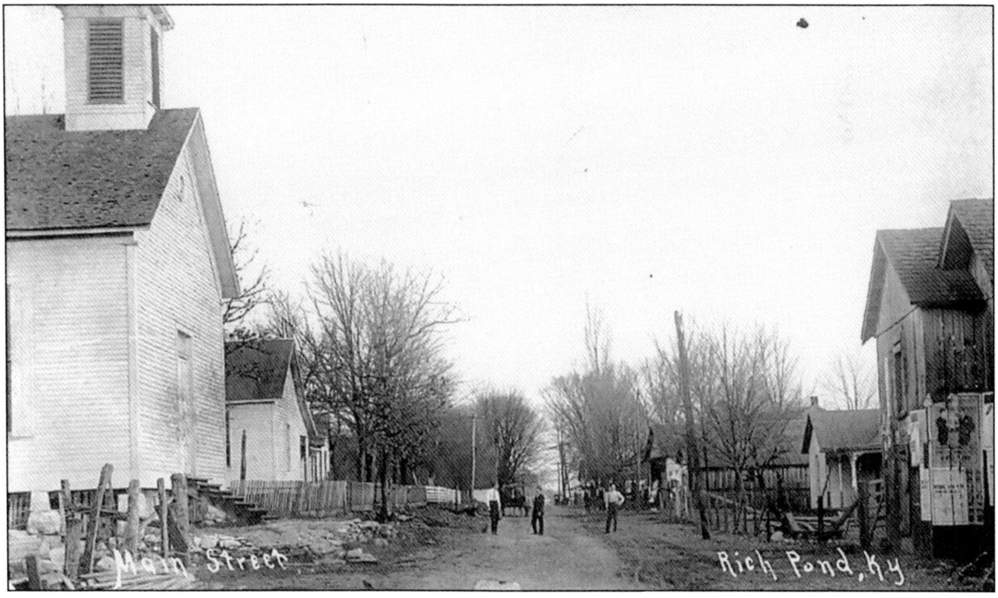

RICH POND, KENTUCKY. This is a rare real-photo view of Main Street in Rich Pond from 1910. No one seems to know the origination of the town's name. A number of natural ponds are located in the area. No families named Rich appear in extant census records. Rich Pond appears on early maps and is mentioned as early as 1811 in county land records. The large church in the foreground is the Church of Christ.

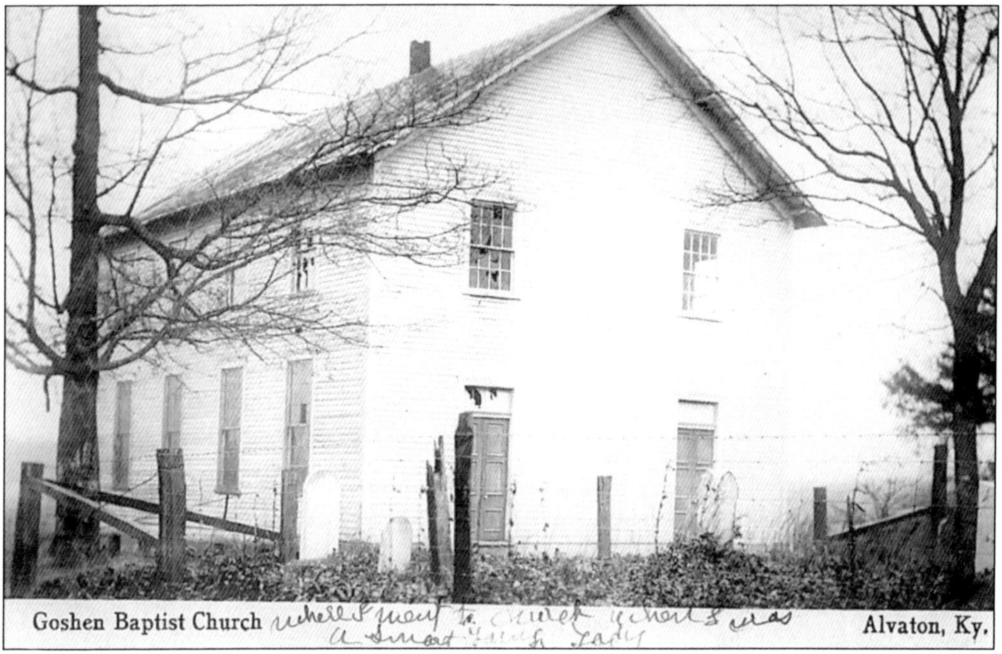

BETHANY BAPTIST CHURCH. Organized on February 26, 1848, Bethany is sometimes referred to as the Goshen Church because the congregation first worshipped in the nearby Goshen schoolhouse. The structure pictured here was built in 1868 at a cost of $1,818, a portion of which was paid by the local Masonic Lodge that met on the second floor. The building was substantially damaged during the April 1998 hailstorm and tornado.

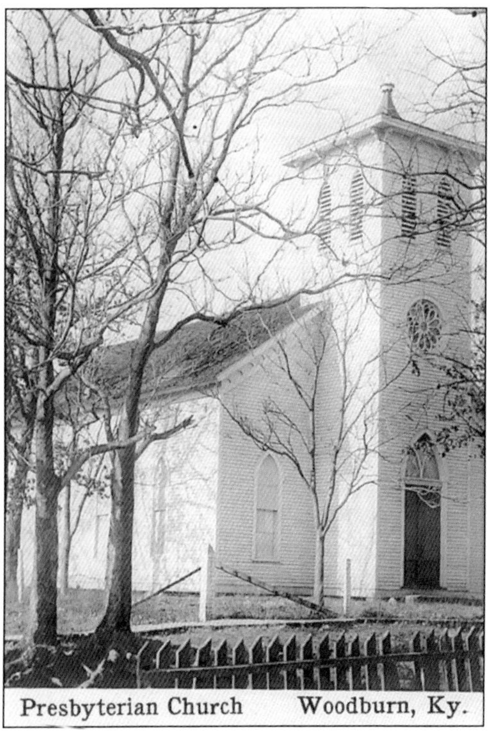

WOODBURN PRESBYTERIAN CHURCH. This Presbyterian Church still stands as a testament to the former prosperity of this railroad and farming community, although it is no longer a church. A master builder utilized the Gothic arch on the windows, doorway, and louvered vents of the bell tower. The tower was further accented with a stylized rose window, decorative brackets, and topped with an unusual finial.